The Good
Pirates of the
Forgotten
Bayous

Ken Wells

The Good Pirates of the Forgotten Bayous

Fighting to Save
a Way of Life
in the Wake of
Hurricane Katrina

Yale University Press

New Haven and London

Set in Berkeley type by Keystone Typesetting, Inc.,
Orwigsburg, Pennsylvania.
Printed in the United States of America by R. R.
Donnelley, Harrisonburg, Virginia.

Library of Congress Cataloging-in-Publication Data
Wells, Ken.
    The good pirates of the forgotten bayous : fighting
to save a way of life in the wake of Hurricane Katrina /
Ken Wells.
        p.   cm.
    Includes bibliographical references.
    ISBN 978-0-300-12152-0 (cloth : alk. paper)
    1. Hurricane Katrina, 2005—Social aspects—
Louisiana—Saint Bernard Parish. 2. Saint Bernard
Parish (La.)—Biography. 3. Working class—Louisiana
—Saint Bernard Parish—Biography. 4. Disaster
victims—Louisiana—Saint Bernard Parish—
Biography. 5. Bayous—Louisiana—Saint Bernard
Parish. 6. Community life—Louisiana—Saint Bernard
Parish. 7. Saint Bernard Parish (La.)—Social life and
customs. 8. Saint Bernard Parish (La.)—Social
conditions. I. Title.
    F377.S12W45   2008
    976.3'36044092—dc22
    [B]   2008017764

A catalogue record for this book is available from the
British Library.

This paper meets the requirements of ANSI/NISO
Z39.48-1992 (Permanence of Paper).

10 9 8 7 6 5 4 3 2 1

A Caravan book. For more information, visit
www.caravanbooks.org.

For the people of Da Parish
and all they have endured.

And for Kraz,
Cajun kindred spirit.
Rest you, my friend.

Contents

AFTERMATH

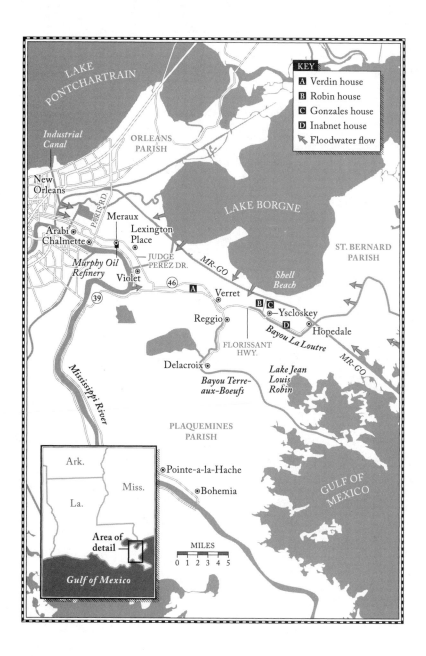

KEY
A Verdin house
B Robin house
C Gonzales house
D Inabnet house
↙ Floodwater flow

LAKE PONTCHARTRAIN

Industrial Canal

ORLEANS PARISH

New Orleans

PARIS RD.

LAKE BORGNE

Meraux

Arabi
Chalmette

Lexington Place

JUDGE PEREZ DR.

Murphy Oil Refinery

Violet

MR-GO

ST. BERNARD PARISH

Shell Beach

46

A

Verret

B C Yscloskey

39

Reggio

Bayou La Loutre

D

Hopedale

FLORISSANT HWY.

MR-GO

Delacroix

Bayou Terre- aux-Boeufs

Lake Jean Louis Robin

Mississippi River

PLAQUEMINES PARISH

Pointe-a-la-Hache

Bohemia

GULF OF MEXICO

Ark.

Miss.

La.

Area of detail

Gulf of Mexico

MILES
0 1 2 3 4 5

Prologue

On Monday, August 29, 2005, the day that Hurricane Katrina began its assault on the Louisiana and Mississippi Gulf Coast, I was thirteen hundred miles away, looking fitfully out my ninth-floor office window with an unfettered view of the hole in the ground that once was the World Trade Center. That chronically dispiriting sight notwithstanding, it was a pleasant enough morning in lower Manhattan, but it had gone by fidgety. I was a reporter with the *Wall Street Journal* and had spent some of the morning scanning the wire services on my PC for Katrina bulletins—and not only for journalistic reasons.

I'm a Louisiana native, having grown up in the bayou country near the town of Houma, about sixty miles southwest of New Orleans. Many friends and relatives lived in the region, including an older brother on the north shore of Lake Pontchartrain, just thirty miles above New Orleans, and two younger brothers who still resided in Houma. My brothers and their families had evacuated upon Katrina's approach, so I felt confident they would be safe. Still, their homes and lives were there, not to mention that the bayou country had remained my spiritual home, and New Orleans my favorite city in the world, though I'd moved away thirty years before.

Beyond that, I had a personal relationship with hurricanes, having seen up close their power to terrify and destroy. Growing up, I'd ridden out a number of them with my family, most memorably in 1965, when the roof-shaking winds of Hurricane Betsy forced us into a frantic last-ditch scramble out of our isolated farmhouse for a harrowing drive to safer quarters in town as the Category 4 storm aimed its eye at Houma. It was a wise move. Betsy chomped off part of our roof, broke windows, soaked several rooms with slashing rain, and blew away every outbuilding on our property (and our chickens with them). We probably would have survived—though our nerves might not have.

1

Four years later, as a junior reporter for my hometown paper, I'd followed a Red Cross relief caravan into Mississippi in the wake of killer Hurricane Camille, a Category 5 storm. I couldn't conceive how sea-going tugs had landed on houses hundreds of yards from the beach, or how entire stretches of four-lane highway could be rooted up and snapped apart like Lego blocks. I still recoil at the memory of that shocking and violent rearrangement of the landscape.

Thus when wire services first reported that New Orleans and the bayou region had dodged a giant bullet as Category 5 Katrina weakened to a Category 3 storm and made a last-hour lurch to the east, I'd gone to lunch much relieved (even as I grieved at the early bulletins that the storm had laid waste to the nearby Mississippi Gulf Coast). It was only after returning to my desk that the first shocking reports of flooding began to trickle in. I immediately emailed my friend and colleague Doug Blackmon, chief of the *Journal*'s Atlanta/Southern regional bureau, guessing that Doug, who had ably organized coverage of Hurricane Ivan and previous storms, would be in charge of any Katrina reporting. I offered my services as a guy who knew his way around the Louisiana hurricane belt. His reply: "Get your ass on a plane."

I managed to get a flight into Houston late Monday night and into Baton Rouge, the nearest operating airport, Tuesday morning, joining an extremely able team of *Journal* scribes covering the storm's aftermath. New Orleans was without power and 80 percent of it was under ruinous floodwaters, so accommodations were extremely scarce. For the first week or so we ran our reporting operations out of a single hotel room at a Hilton adjacent to the Baton Rouge airport. It was not exactly ideal to return, after a stress-filled fifteen-hour day, to sleep on a blanket laid on the cramped, thinly carpeted floor (by default, the first one back to the room each day got the sole king-sized bed). But reporters are used to making do. And as fate would have it, it was this arrangement that led me to write this book.

Like the rest of the press, the *Journal*'s reporting team focused its early attention on New Orleans, a city that had had decades to prepare for a killer hurricane but had transparently, or so it seemed, flunked its test. Soon it became obvious that the Katrina story, beyond the tallies of deaths and massive destruction, was a complicated one about failure, with a few notable exceptions, of government at all levels. As the story quickly moved in that direction, and away from reports of sniper fire, looting, anarchy at the Superdome, and horrific pictures of people trapped on rooftops, I found myself one evening with a rare spare moment in the lobby of the airport Hilton. There, I overheard the conversation of some evacuees who had booked two days in the hotel with the thought that Katrina—which, for much of its life appeared to be a storm that would wring itself out over Florida—would most likely swipe the Louisiana coast or slide by altogether. But it clearly had not worked out that way. Almost a week after landfall they were still here, prisoners of vast uncertainty.

The evacuees weren't New Orleanians. They were from the town of Chalmette in St. Bernard Parish (a parish being the equivalent of a county in other states). When they mentioned the place, I realized that my entire knowledge of Chalmette was that it sat just southeast of New Orleans, and that I had been there only once, as a high school student visiting the Chalmette Battlefield, where Andrew Jackson and Jean Lafitte had in 1815 fought the British in the Battle of New Orleans. As for the rest of St. Bernard, I vaguely recalled that the lower parish held a commercial fishing community famous for its production of oysters and shrimp.

As these evacuees continued to talk, in ever more desperate terms, I began to get a sense that Chalmette and the other towns that make up St. Bernard Parish had suffered some awful fate. The flooding there, they said, was at least equal to the most catastrophically flooded ramparts of New Orleans—in fact, it was perhaps worse because, unlike New Orleans, where the French Quarter, the Central Business District, and the Garden District had largely been spared, no place in St. Bernard had escaped unscathed. Thousands of people had been trapped there and some still were. But with the eyes of the world transfixed on New Orleans, these people had languished, deep in the city's shadow, virtually forgotten.

This was a compelling story if true, though Katrina had spun off a goodly number of unsettling rumors that turned out to be false. One egregious example that I heard over and over in the first few days after the storm was that hundreds of prisoners had drowned locked up in an Orleans Parish jail flooded by a tidal wave.

Not wanting to chase phantoms, I Googled St. Bernard Parish on my laptop. Besides learning that it was home to about sixty-seven thousand residents, I found a map with sufficient detail to show that northwestern St. Bernard lay just below the tsunami zones of the Lower Ninth Ward in New Orleans, a neighborhood that had suffered horrendous, killer flooding when levees along a man-made waterway called the Industrial Canal had been undermined by Katrina's surge. It made sense, looking at the map, that the St. Bernard areas abutting the Ninth Ward could have suffered a similar fate. But while the Lower Ninth Ward deluge had been all over the news, my hasty Internet searches turned up no first-hand accounts of what might have happened in St. Bernard next door.

As I studied the map more carefully, I saw that the parish's fishing community resided in a handful of hamlets nestled on a vast apron of marsh fronting Lake Borgne and the Gulf of Mexico. Some of these waysides stood a good thirty-five miles east and south of New Orleans— meaning they stuck far enough out into the hurricane's path that they could have taken a direct hit from Category 4 Katrina before it weakened into a Category 3 storm.

Journalists are always looking for the less well trodden story, and in these hotel lobby reports of St. Bernard Parish I sensed there might be just such a tale. And, besides, I'm a bayou guy and St. Bernard, at least the lower part of it, was bayou country. I felt a compelling urge to get down there.

The issue was access. As I interviewed the hotel evacuees, they were eventually joined by a St. Bernard firefighter who had stayed through the storm and had just made his way out by evacuation helicopter. His eyewitness accounts convinced me that a momentous disaster had occurred there. But he also said roads into the parish were still underwater and impassable.

To get there I would have to fly, but how?

Fate again intervened. Later that evening, I struck up a conversation with an amiable National Guard Blackhawk helicopter pilot who was also staying at the Hilton. He told me he had just begun to fly relief missions from the nearby airport into the heart of St. Bernard's darkness, to the very building where what remained of the parish's leadership was bunkered down still awaiting the arrival of officials from the Federal Emergency Management Agency (FEMA).

I told him I desperately wanted to get there.

"Be at the squadron at five in the morning," he said. "I can drop you off though I can't promise you a ride back. We'll probably be dropping back in there in the late afternoon, but it's all seat-of-the-pants now."

Getting there was crucial; getting back would just have to work itself out. So I jumped at the chance.

The chopper ride, in calm, azure skies, was an eye-opener. For the first time I could visually get my mind around the breadth of the catastrophe as we flew low over stricken communities and neighborhoods. New Orleans *was* a vast, rapidly putrefying, and darkening lake, a slick moat of silence where nothing seemed to stir save the occasional flocks of returning shore birds gliding low over the water, the wakes of occasional rescue boats still patrolling flooded residential streets for victims and survivors, and the drone of other helicopters all along our periphery. I began to make a mental calculation based on the reporting I'd done so far. The zone of devastation stretched from St. Charles Parish, on the western flank of New Orleans, south and east of the city to the tips of Plaquemines and St. Bernard parishes, and as far west and south as lower Lafourche Parish and Grand Isle, Louisiana, at the far end of Jefferson Parish, fifty miles away; it fanned out along the Interstate 10 corridor from the western boundary of New Orleans for thirty-five miles, through the sprawling suburbs of New Orleans East, where entire malls and car dealerships had gone underwater; it carved along the north shore of Lake Pontchartrain through the communities of Mandeville, Madisonville, and hard-hit Slidell. Including the city of New Orleans proper, and the tsunami-like wreckage of the Mississippi Gulf Coast, the area of devastation was mind-boggling.

Someone would later venture a startling analogy: that the sprawl of Katrina's disastrous footprint was bigger than the combined blast zones of Hiroshima and Nagasaki, the unfortunate targets of America's atomic bombs near the end of World War II. While it's hard to conjure up a horror greater than the explosion of an atomic bomb over civilian cities, the analogy was useful in explaining the breadth of the trauma the New Orleans region had suffered, and the rebuilding task it faced.

After a couple of stops that ate up much of the morning, the Black-hawk swooped low and noisy over the Mississippi River from the Belle Chase Naval Air Station on the west bank of the river. The pilot slowed and skillfully maneuvered the chopper through an intimidating corral of towering power lines and landed on a blistering hot concrete parking lot tucked just inside the river's levees. He pointed to a bunkerlike office complex next door that he said was on loan to parish officials as an emergency operating center. Such as St. Bernard had a command post, I would find it here.

I made my way inside, down generator-cooled, darkened corridors cluttered with boxes of files, foodstuffs, and water bottles, to learn that Henry ("Junior") Rodriguez, the parish president, and his cadre were, in fact, holed up with a recently arrived FEMA official. When I asked about an interview with Rodriguez, an aide with raccoon circles under his eyes brusquely told me to come back later. Junior was busy giving the FEMA guy hell. Since there was a lot of hell to be given, the aide said, it was going to take a while.

This was a disappointing pronouncement to a journalist who had hitchhiked in on a helicopter, but it turned out to be another stroke of luck. For outside in the parking lot I encountered a familiar sight: a guy with a grease-stained mesh-and-foam white ball cap, a blue T-shirt, and brown dungarees stuffed inside shin-high white rubber boots.

I didn't know this guy but I knew his boots. Down in the saltwater bayous where I'd grown up they were known as "shrimper boots," and almost everyone in the commercial fishing trade wore them. They told you this man was a shrimp-boat or oyster-boat captain, a deckhand, or a seafood factory worker as surely as a sharp twang gives away a Texan.

I went up and introduced myself, explaining my mission, and we hadn't exchanged more than five sentences before he declared, in his pleasing bayou accent, "If you lookin' for a story, podnah, I got a story for you."

His name was Ricky Robin. He was, in fact, a boat captain from the fishing village of Yscloskey (pronounced wye-closky) far to the south of here, and he wasn't lying: he did have a story for me. Propitiously, he also had a van—very likely the only operational civilian vehicle in all of St. Bernard Parish at that moment. Just as important, he had an official parish ID to get us past the National Guard checkpoints that had by this time sprung up throughout the parish. Over the course of that day, and then over weeks and finally months, I collected Ricky's story, a story at the core of a wider tale of uncommon heroism, ingenuity, and pluck by common folk who survived Katrina's onslaught in a forgotten backwater below New Orleans.

Many fine books have been published about the abject failure of government to fund and design an adequate hurricane protection system for the region, and about the fatal paralysis of government relief efforts in the first critical days after the storm. This book, though it deals tangentially with those issues, isn't such a work. Rather, this is a narrative of the human spirit, a story about a decidedly blue-collar, ruggedly independent people whose decisions to face down Katrina lay in deep cultural anchors. It is a story of people who—when they realize no one is coming to save them—rise up to save themselves and their neighbors in the face of raw peril and a disaster of unimaginable proportions. Finally, it is a story about the longing for home, and the determination of a proud bayou people to reclaim, against formidable obstacles, a sense of home in a place where the world has been forever rearranged.

PART ONE

The Storm

A Monster Cometh

Official Bulletins from the

National Weather Service

Saturday, August 27, 2005

4 P.M. CENTRAL DAYLIGHT TIME

A hurricane watch is extended westward to Intracoastal City, Louisiana, and eastward to the Florida-Alabama border. . . . There remains a chance that Katrina could become a Category 5 hurricane before landfall.

11 P.M.

A hurricane warning has been issued for the north central gulf coast . . . including the city of New Orleans and Lake Pontchartrain. . . . Coastal storm surge flooding of fifteen to twenty feet above normal tide levels . . . locally as high as twenty-five feet along with large and dangerous battering waves . . . can be expected near and to the east of where the center makes landfall.

Sunday, August 28

7 A.M.

Advisory Number 22: Katrina is now a potentially catastrophic Category 5 hurricane . . . headed for the northern gulf coast. . . . Maximum sustained winds are near 160 mph . . . with higher gusts. . . . Some fluctuations in strength are likely in the next twenty-four hours.

4 P.M.

Advisory Number 24: Katrina is moving toward the northwest near thirteen mph and a gradual turn to the north is expected over the next twenty-four hours. On this track the center of the hurricane will be near the northern gulf coast early Monday. However, conditions are already beginning to deteriorate along portions of the central and northeastern gulf coasts . . . and will continue to worsen through the night. . . . Katrina is expected to make landfall at Category 4 or 5 intensity.

1. Ricky at the Helm

"I feel it in me sometimes—the pirate blood in my veins."

RICKY ROBIN

Violet Canal, St. Bernard Parish, Louisiana, August 29, 2005

Ricky Robin suddenly has a bad feeling about things.

It's well beyond midnight, maybe three in the morning, who knows. Ricky's lost track of time.

It's incorrigibly dark beyond the glare of his generator-powered floodlights mounted above the fore and aft decks of the *Lil' Rick,* the sturdy fifty-six-foot steel trawler he built with his own hands three decades earlier. The wind has picked up and is bawling like a rabid cat; rain is machine-gunning his wheelhouse windows.

The *Lil' Rick* is beginning to shudder and rock and, worse, tilt.

It's not supposed to tilt. Ricky Robin, a seaman all his life, has tied down plenty of boats in plenty of storms. His boats, once tied down, just don't tilt.

Besides, the *Lil' Rick* is tied down with redundant ropes—ten in all—*and* under power, and Ricky, or so he believes, has history and lore on his side. He's hunkered down at Violet Canal, a man-made appendage to an ancient natural bayou named Dupre. It's been a trustworthy hurricane hole for the storm-wise local shrimping and oyster fleet going back to the days of Reconstruction.

Bounded by ten-foot-high levees north and south, the canal dead-ends at an abandoned lock just off a major thoroughfare called the St. Bernard Highway, less than two hundred yards from the towering levees

13

of the Mississippi River on the west. Lying to the east are two more
protective levee systems: two miles away, a ten-foot-tall inner ring of
levees along a historic colonial-era waterway known as the Forty Arpent
Canal; and about eight miles away, a seventeen-foot-high levee along the
western shore of a seventy-six-mile-long, man-dug shipping channel
called the Mississippi River–Gulf Outlet (or MR-GO), known hereabouts as the Mister Go. That's why sea captains like Ricky Robin con-
sider Violet, while nobody's version of a scenic harbor, an impenetrable
fortress against violent storms.

That the seventy-ton *Lil' Rick,* snugged in hard against Violet Canal's
north levee, is now being shoved around like a puny kid on the play-
ground is for Ricky a bad sign.

Ricky needs knowledge. He keys his VHF marine radio and broad-
casts out into the pummeling blackness. He raises another shrimp-boat
captain on his ship-to-shore radio at Empire, a fishing and oil-patch
marina across Breton Sound in Plaquemines Parish, about thirty miles
south-southeast. He can barely hear the guy yelling into his radio above
the din of the raging storm. "We're catching hell. Wind and water like
you wouldn't believe. The gulf's pouring in over the floodgates."

The captain is on his own oceangoing trawler wedged in a cluster
of commercial fishing and oil-field work vessels at a protected harbor sitting inside the Mississippi River levee. He's under power but almost every boat that isn't manned has been sunk—pulled under when
an astonishingly powerful and fast-moving storm surge overcame the
length of the tie-down ropes and flipped them. Those still afloat are
heading for other disasters.

The captain is probing the rain-slashed darkness with his spotlight.
He tells Ricky what he sees: a hulking ghost rips by—a ninety-foot-long
steel menhaden deep-gulf seining ship, torn from its moorings. It's running dark (meaning probably no one's aboard) and is propelled by
nothing more than seething tides and tornadic winds. Giant anchors
and ropes fat as pythons secured this boat. But it's been loosed, and the
captain watches it being tossed up, in a froth of whitecaps, on a nearby
levee—as if it were some toy boat. Others will end up in the middle of
highways and on the up-ramps to bridges.

"This wind and water—it's coming your way," the man tells Ricky. "Get ready."

Then, in a squall of static, he's gone.

Ricky Robin thought he was plenty ready, but now he's not so sure.

He leaves the Lil' Rick's wheel and makes his way unsteadily, the trawler leaning in the gale, back to his cluttered galley. The boat's pitch has worsened and Ricky realizes the problem. He'd raised his two forty-foot booms, the steel mechanical arms that hold his trawls, to forty-five-degree angles above his decks and secured them with chains to hold them in place. His worry: if he left the booms down and his trawler broke loose in the storm, they would carve, like giant steel wings, through any nearby boats in the narrow canal. Violet Canal is packed with vessels: maybe thirty other manned boats are hunkered down under power and another forty or fifty are tied hard to docks.

But in the shrieking, whipsawing east-southeast wind, the raised booms are acting as airplane wings and the trawler has swung sideways to the gale. With tornadoes about, Ricky's fear is that a rogue gust will whisk the windward boom skyward—and flip the Lil' Rick over.

Against the thrum of his generators and engine, and the din of the wind outside, he has a tense counsel with his co-captain and cousin, Dwight Alphonso—Tee-Tee, to his friends—who has volunteered to ride out the storm with him, along with Dwight's eighteen-year-old son, Dwight Jr.

"Look, Tee-Tee, if the boat rolls over this way," Ricky says, manning the trawler's wheel and pointing toward the port-side exit to the wheelhouse, "we'll try to get out this door."

It's a sobering moment—contemplating having to feel their way in confused blackness through the tight exits, the boat keeled over or capsized, water pouring in. Assuming they make it out, unpleasant things could await them at the storm-tossed surface.

Soon, another roaring gust tilts the Lil' Rick precariously. Ricky knows he has to do something. "Too much lean," he tells Tee-Tee. "I gotta lower the booms or we ain't gonna make it."

He pushes through the aft door, sucked shut in a thud behind him by the blasting wind. Outside, raging gusts pummel his head like a boxer. Rain blasts in horizontally in buzz-saw sheets. He feels his way to the first boom and begins to inch out toward the end of it, eyes shut. Opening them isn't an option. Imagine being strapped to the hood of a car and driven, face first, through a power wash: that's what it's like.

Luckily, Ricky knows his booms the way a blind person knows his route to the kitchen. He gains the end of his starboard-side boom and, in the glare of his floodlights, grapples with the chain, tied in double half-hitches—a mistake. This isn't a quick-release knot. As he struggles to untie it, he feels that he could be scraped off the boom at any second and spit into the dark, howling maw. He yells crude curses at the storm—he calls Katrina a mother_____—and yanks harder at the chain. The knot finally gives. The boom releases.

The *Lil' Rick* lurches, then rights itself.

Ricky edges his way down, then repeats the operation to the port-side boom, holding on to a long boom rope as he descends to the trawler's aft deck. But the wind kicks his legs out from under him and sends him skidding.

For a long moment, it's as if he's in a bad pirate movie—he's lifted up and suspended in air above his railing, his purchase on the rope doubtful. But a wind dervish slaps him back to the deck.

The battered ship captain lands with a thud. Still clutching the boom rope, he manages to secure the booms by lashing the rope to giant steel cleats welded to the outer wall of the *Lil' Rick*'s galley.

The wind makes standing impossible. Ricky crawls on his belly, squirming wet as an eel, toward the aft door. He wrangles it open and steps into the lighted galley. He shuts the door behind him and looks at Tee-Tee, shaking his head.

Katrina's a damned handful.

Given the violence of the wind, Ricky decides the trawler could use still more ballast to keep her on an even keel. He switches on electrical pumps, powered by his generator, to fill his trio of three-hundred-gallon water tanks, normally used as live-bait wells, on the windward side, and then he, Tee-Tee, and Dwight Jr. take up positions on that side as well.

At fifty-one, Ricky's still in good shape, save for a mild red-beans-

and-rice paunch that is a signature of middle-aged men in these parts. Still, at about five-foot-six, he's compact as a bulldog. But Tee-Tee and his son are hefty guys—six-footers weighing in at about 230 apiece. "It's a good thing we got your fat asses aboard," Ricky tells them.

Even Tee-Tee thinks this is pretty funny. It's about the only thing they have to laugh about.

Ricky moves forward again to the wheelhouse, guns the three-hundred-horsepower diesel engine, and turns the *Lil' Rick's* wheel to shore up the trawler's position into the wind. "Let her blow now," says Ricky.

He almost regrets saying it—eyewall winds will gust up to 150 miles per hour here, and hit-and-run tornadoes will throttle boats, buildings, houses, trees, and vehicles.

At some point, with a glimmer of light in the sky, Ricky sees a chilling sight: out of the east, a small shrimping skiff, maybe twenty feet long, is tumbling—through the air—on the howling wind toward the *Lil' Rick*. At fifty yards away, it touches down and skips on the bayou's surface like a skittering stone.

Ricky guns his engine again, hoping to goose the *Lil' Rick* harder up against the levee and out of the boat's way. The small trawler skitters by—just grazing the *Lil' Rick's* stern. There's a scraping sound, and the boat whirs off into the ether.

Ricky knows the connection between hurricanes and tornadoes. He's seen mini-tornadoes dip out of the clouds like jet-propelled Ferris wheels and scoop up everything in their path, tossing it all skyward. That could explain the flying boat.

This is one of Ricky's moments of near panic. Any boat hammered by one of these microbursts—even a seventy-ton trawler like his—is in trouble. "That's your ass," he says. "You're gone, even if you've done everything right."

Ricky looks grimly at Tee-Tee and his son and decides they all need to be lashed together on a rope with a life ring that Ricky will control. If they get blown over or washed out of the boat, they'll at least have a chance to stay together.

He orders Dwight Jr. into the shelter of the *Lil' Rick's* lower bunk off the galley (below the window line and thus out of the path of any penetrating flying objects), and he and Tee-Tee take up watch in the wheelhouse.

With daylight edging into the sky and the wind, though still formidable, slackening some, Ricky is thinking, *Well, damn, we made it through.*

Indeed, at around 8:30, he twists through the dials of a portable radio and hears a news report from New Orleans saying that the city seems to have been spared a direct blow; the storm has made a slight but propitious jog to the east and is grinding its way toward what forecasters predict will be its terrifying last act, on the Mississippi Gulf Coast about fifty miles northeast.

But for Ricky Robin and the knot of a few hundred others hunkered down on boats and in dwellings in and around the historical safe haven of Violet Canal, the slackening wind is Katrina's cruelest feint. The center of the eye of the most destructive storm in U.S. history—an eye thirty-two miles wide—is passing a mere twelve miles east of here.

On the back side of that eye, the wind will return with a vengeance, and far worse things are about to happen.

2. Ronald on the *Invincible Vance*

Ronald Robin, Ricky's older first cousin and best friend, is tethered a few boats west of Ricky's, on the *Invincible Vance*, a handsome, broad-keeled fifty-seven-foot boat known hereabout as an oyster lugger. The boat belongs to his eldest son, Van Robin. Ronald's own boat, the elegant, hand-hewn thirty-eight-foot *Evening Star*, is tied down to a dock on short ropes a few spots away on the south side of Violet Canal. The captains standing at Violet regard each other more or less as family—indeed, many are in fact related, even if only distantly. It's a small world down here.

Van, a successful oyster fisherman who learned sea craft at his father's knee, is away on business. With the approach of Hurricane Katrina, Ronald volunteered to look after the boat for him. And anyway the *Vance* is a more substantial boat than the *Star*; Ronald figures it doesn't hurt to have a little more boat under him should Katrina strike head on. His younger cousin Elwood Perez, also a commercial fishermen, is with him.

Ronald, mostly retired from a lifetime of dredging oysters, got to Violet Canal before Ricky did. He's secured an advantageous spot—tied to an imposing shrimp boat that itself is tightly lashed to a hulking hundred-foot-long steel barge near the canal's dead-end. If the *Vance* and its neighbors are dislodged, it will be a very bad omen for everyone else.

Ronald is a compact, intense man. He has piercing blue eyes, short-cropped hair, a pronounced though pleasing Creolized bayou accent similar to Ricky's. On the cusp of sixty-nine, he possesses the wiry, muscular build of a welterweight boxer, a build that served him well in the street-brawling years of his youth. With his finely weathered face and square jaw, he bears a rugged resemblance to Paul Newman—a likeness not overlooked by the ladies.

Like Ricky, Ronald grew up in the fishing village of Yscloskey, a speck of high ground sheltering maybe fifty families and built along and around the levees of the ancient Bayou La Loutre, about twenty miles below Violet Canal. Ronald went to sea the first time with his father at age four. And, like Ricky, by twelve he could run a boat better than most men. In this low country, among seasoned fishermen and boat wranglers, Ricky and Ronald are legendary for their boat-handling prowess.

Ronald, the fourth of seven children, has been through a few calamities. Excluding a half dozen other hurricanes, these include four wives and three divorces; the death five years ago from a lung mass of his fourth wife, whom he continues to call "my guardian angel." His temper, a decidedly jaded view of authority, and, for a while, a drinking problem led to a string of arrests for street fighting as a young man. (Fifty years ago, when St. Bernard's bayou communities supported several saloons—including one called the Bucket of Blood—street fighting was the semi-official Saturday night pastime. Ronald likes to say, half jokingly, that he retired from the sport at age thirty with a record of twenty-one and zero, knocked silly but never knocked down, a record Ricky vouches for.)

And then, starting in 1982, came a strangely nomadic four-and-a-half-year tour of federal prisons after Ronald was convicted for running a pot-smuggling ring out of his oyster boat. In his first week of prison, he tangled with a fellow inmate who turned out to be a convicted mobster. He had the bad form to win the scrape by picking the fellow up and squeezing the air out of him until he broke a couple of ribs. The mobster put a hit on Ronald. Prison authorities, to protect him, shuffled him through sixteen separate penitentiaries before he was finally released in 1987. (The hit was rescinded when a prison pal of Ronald's negotiated a truce with the hit man's mob boss near the end of Ronald's prison term.)

It's fair to say that it's hard to rattle Ronald Robin after what he's endured.

While the *Lil' Rick* is being knocked around and Ricky is fretting mightily, Ronald checks out the *Vance's* impressive ropes, tied fast to the neighboring boat. Assured that all is well, he bids goodnight to Elwood and goes to bed. He sleeps soundly through the night as Katrina roars like a freight train all around him. "Why fight the storm?" he says. "It'll only beat you up."

Well past dawn, he startles awake, roused by an alarming report from Elwood, who, though twenty-five years Ronald's junior, is a seasoned seaman as well.

"Ronald," he cries out. "I think it's a tidal wave."

"What?" says Ronald.

"A tidal wave, I'm pretty sure."

Ronald is at first skeptical. He rises and peers out the *Vance's* aft door and realizes the boat is suddenly engulfed in sheeting rain frothed by a radical wind. All he sees is seething dark gray.

Tornado, he's thinking.

The *Vance* is pointed west, its bow to the imposing Mississippi River levee. Ronald walks forward and manages to crack open the boat's port forward door, hoping for a better view. Looking left, through the slashing rain, he sees an odd sight: not a tidal wave, exactly, but a current ripping in on a swiftly rising tide.

The current is so fast that it's creating a jet of water as it begins to pour in, seemingly out of nowhere, and course around the corner of a nearby building, a well-known bayou-side saloon known as De Pope's Tavern and Boat Launch. (The bar's name derives from its owner, a local minor celebrity, who dresses in papal finery to cheer at New Orleans Saints football games, and hence is known as "de Pope.")

Ronald, who rode out Hurricane Betsy on a trawler at Yscloskey in September 1965 and used a long wooden pole to keep floating houses from crushing the boat he was on, is perplexed. "Damn, Elwood, that SOB is coming up like I've never seen."

So fast, in fact, that Ronald stares in amazement as the water begins to leap up the side of De Pope's Tavern and other nearby buildings, as well as vehicles parked in surrounding gravel lots.

Just fifty yards east of the saloon sits a machine shop in a nondescript white cinderblock building, with three eighteen-wheel trailer-trucks parked outside. Ronald peers at the trucks. Water starts lapping at the tires; then climbs to the hubcaps; then climbs to the trucks' floorboards. Soon it's up the hoods and next it's lapping at the windows.

All this in a matter of minutes. Ronald has a good view of the building and the trucks being swallowed up by the sea because the *Vance,* the boat next door, and the barge are all being lifted up by the surge.

The next thing Ronald sees: the trucks rise in unison and head briskly west—roughly in his direction. Ronald is temporarily confused. Have drivers leaped in, trying to drive the eighteen-wheelers out of the water's way?

No. The startling answer is that the trucks are now afloat on El-wood's "tidal wave" and are being pushed—at maybe five to ten miles per hour—on the fulminating currents.

Ronald watches, mesmerized and fearful for just a moment. If the trucks come his way, their weight, mass, and speed will easily torpedo the *Vance,* the boat next door; hell, maybe even the barge. "We're all sunk if we're hit," he thinks.

Instead, the trucks float rapidly past, between the protective barge and De Pope's saloon, and head off toward St. Bernard Highway about twenty-five yards away.

Within fifteen minutes, the water will be coursing over the ten-foot-high Violet Canal levees.

Ronald has parked his Chevy pickup truck atop the north levee, about seventy-five yards east of where the *Vance* is moored, figuring the vehicle will be plenty safe up there, even if the storm produces some localized flooding. In Hurricane Betsy—before St. Bernard Parish had a proper storm-protection levee system—the residential streets in and around Violet Canal got maybe a foot or two of water. No way, with levees, would the water be worse than that—he was sure.

But Ronald watches in dismay as the water sluices up the side of his truck until only the roof is above the water line. In a few minutes, his truck will float away as well.

The thirty or so boat captains at Violet Canal are in an advantageous position. They see the water coming and they are at least afloat. But Violet Canal is both harbor and settlement. Its north bank, from St. Bernard Highway to a blue-and-white "Violet"-stenciled water tower a third of a mile east, holds a four-by-five-block settlement typical of the loosely zoned blue-collar burghs that dot St. Bernard Parish.

About a hundred homes stand here: faded faux-brick shotgun shacks and weather-beaten double-wide trailers wedged in tight alongside prefab aluminum-sided houses and a few four-bedroom brick suburban ranch homes, all built along narrow, potholed macadamized streets paralleling the canal.

Although St. Bernard Parish officials strongly urged all residents to evacuate at Katrina's approach, the Violet boat captains aren't the only ones who have stayed. A few dozen people are camped in the Violet subdivision and hundreds more are riding out the storm in houses and mobile homes within a five-mile radius of the harbor.

The water is catching everyone by surprise.

With the stern of his boat providing a lee, Ronald moves aft and steps outside. It's not just the roar of the wind that stuns him. The air is suddenly filled with dangerous objects: sheets of tin from nearby roofs come helicoptering just overhead—*wap-wap-wap-wap*—and then explode like muted mortars when they crash into nearby buildings or scrape and skitter across rooftops.

A loosened board sails by, whistling like a missile. Ronald hears what sounds like a thunderclap or the loud report of a gun and involuntarily ducks for cover. Ronald will later discover a splintered two-by-six embedded deep in the shower wall of the shrimp boat next door. To get there it had to stab through the triple webbing of the boat's trawls, its fiberglass hull, and *two* three-eighths-inch plywood interior walls.

Just out of Ronald's vision, a man inside his mobile home on the street fronting the canal a block in from the St. Bernard Highway suddenly finds his place engulfed in water. He has a small fishing boat—a Carolina Skiff by brand—parked out front and he flees toward it from his trailer. The skiff makes it over the now engulfed Violet Canal levee but is suddenly picked up and flipped by the wind, leaving the man thrashing around in a seething current—think killer whitewater rapids on, say, the Colorado River.

Ronald is slightly hard of hearing, and out on the stern of the *Vance* the wind is still raising a racket. But above the din, an anguished word—"help!"—cuts through the gale.

"Elwood," Ronald exclaims, "someone's in the water!"

Ronald turns in the direction of the cry, hops from his boat to the boat next to him and then up on the barge. Elwood follows him. They are immediately flattened by the wind, forcing them to crawl across the barge to the other side.

Ronald peers down over the barge's edge. A man clings precariously to a rope—serendipitously sagging just above the water—tied from the barge to a tree on the bank. If he loses his grip, it's a death sentence. He'd be sucked under the barge and nearby boats.

Ronald, trying to be heard above the din, yells at Elwood to hold on to his feet. On his belly, he edges as far off the barge as he dares and reaches down, offering his right hand. The man grabs hold, then lets go of the rope.

There's a precarious moment as Ronald wonders if he'll be the victim of his own good deed—if Elwood isn't holding tight and he slips off the barge, he and the man will both be dead. But Ronald snatches the victim from the currents.

There is no time for civilities and Ronald won't officially meet Leo Perez (no relation to Elwood) until some weeks after the storm. All three men crawl back together along the deck of the barge, raked by wind, debris, and slashing rain until they reach the safety of the *Vance*'s cabin.

Leo Perez's rescue is one of the first of hundreds that Ronald, Ricky, and the other boat captains at Violet Canal will make that morning, when Katrina's powerful surge descended on hapless St. Bernard from three different sources. The deluge will plunge 95 percent of the parish under water up to twenty feet deep. As the world became fixated on the unfolding tragedy of New Orleans—where poorly designed U.S. Army Corps of Engineers levees catastrophically failed, stranding tens of thousands and killing hundreds—the fishermen and families of St. Bernard would remain largely forgotten, and abandoned by almost all formal authority, for the next three days.

At the moment, though, the Robins have far more immediate concerns. As Ricky first begins to see the encroaching water from the helm of the *Lil' Rick,* he is on his cell phone, which improbably still works, yelling frantically into the receiver. His wife, her two daughters, and three other members of his extended family are riding out Katrina in a single-story house in Violet just two long blocks away.

And he is telling them they need to get out, and get out fast.

3. Susan Robin Goes for a Drive

Susan Robin, Ricky's wife of thirteen years, has spent a jittery night in her brother's modest home on Violet Street just two blocks off the Violet Canal and three long blocks from the St. Bernard Highway. She had begun the day in her father's smaller house two streets away, where she, Ricky, and her two teenage daughters have been staying with her dad, an ailing widower, while they remodel their family home down in Ysclos-key. But everyone has gathered at her brother's now because his house is a bit closer to Violet Canal, where Ricky is standing by with the trawler. Indeed, Susan's only comfort on this unnerving night is that Ricky is not two hundred yards away, and that, despite the howling winds, their cell phones still work.

Ricky's been reporting in all evening, trying his best to speak in measured, reassuring tones. But a call at 4 a.m. is disturbing. "A tornado just passed between us," he tells Susan. "The house behind you just lost its roof. I saw it go."

Susan has barely hung up the phone when she hears a terrible roar and then a thudding sound.

The whole place shudders.

Susan—well, everyone—screams. She's there with her two daughters by her first marriage, Natasha Mullins, sixteen, and Brittney Mullins, fifteen, and her brother, Sidney E. Roberts, and his wife, Shizuka Roberts, both in their sixties. In their collective care is Susan's frail eighty-three-year-old father, Sidney T. Roberts, who has been diagnosed with early-stage Alzheimer's disease.

Susan and her brother go to investigate the noise. A giant pecan tree has crashed down—and cleaved off a back corner of the house. Luckily, they were all riding out the storm in the living room when the tree did its damage.

Ricky's next call, well after daybreak, seems to be bringing happier news. He delivers the report from the radio that Katrina has dodged eastward toward Mississippi and is being downgraded to a Category 3 storm. He's looking out from the wheelhouse of the *Lil' Rick,* surveying the Violet neighborhood. "We've got a lot of damage everywhere, but I think we'll be all right."

His next call, however, sometime around 9 a.m., is alarming—a fast-moving flood is beginning to pour into the canal from the direction of Lake Borgne to the east. The *Lil' Rick* is being shoved around, Ricky tells her, and a gush of water, as if someone had opened up numerous fire hydrants, has begun coursing down the center of the Packenham Road, the street fronting the canal, heading toward the St. Bernard Highway.

"I have a bad feeling that something's happened, Susan," Ricky tells her. "The way that wind's coming down the bayous—the waves have gotta be beating down those levees [on the MR-GO]. Those levees just can't hold. You need to get out of there."

What Ricky intuits—and what tens of thousands of people hunkered down in the region don't know—is that Katrina, though officially downgraded to a strong Category 3 storm, is still pushing a Category 5 tidal surge.

Susan's first reaction is "what water?" But then she goes to the front door and cracks it open, and what she sees shocks her. Water is indeed sheeting down Violet Street like a fast-flowing stream and beginning to lap at the tires of her six-year-old Chevy conversion van parked in the driveway hard up against the house.

"Get Daddy out of bed," she barks to her daughters. "Throw a change of clothes in some garbage bags. Ricky says we need to go."

But leaving Violet for higher ground, Susan knows, has the makings of an ordeal. Susan, in fact, might have preferred to evacuate upon Katrina's approach, but there were complications. She's recovering from recent back surgery and is under treatment for chronic pain. She's also been taking care of her father since her mother died just eight months before. Sidney T., in his day, had been something of a swamp lion—a carpenter by vocation but a man who, like many in these parts, supplemented the family larder as a gifted hunter and trapper. His progressive Alzheimer's has required him to be under constant medical care. All of his doctors (and hers) are in St. Bernard Parish. Evacuation, even for a few days, would have required her to find reliable backup care in whatever place they chose to dodge the storm. It seemed not just a hassle, but risky as well.

Part of the dynamic, too, is that a goodly number of residents in the parish and throughout the New Orleans metropolitan area are suffering from evacuation fatigue. In the past five years, a seeming plague of hurricanes has menaced the New Orleans region, but all have missed or caused only minor damage and disruptions if they hit. Many who have dutifully heeded past warnings and made the slow, expensive, frustrating, traffic-snarled evacuation to points north have grown weary of the voyage. A widespread skepticism of the accuracy of hurricane forecasting has set in.

And anyway, Ricky wasn't going to leave—he fervently believed that the *Lil' Rick* was the safest place to ride out the storm. In fact, he'd briefly thought about weathering Katrina in Yscloskey in their house under renovation there. The major improvement: they had hired a contractor to raise it up on twelve-foot-high steel-reinforced concrete pilings, bolted to the foundation, in preparation for redoing the interior. The last meaningful hurricane to strike Yscloskey, Hurricane Betsy in 1965, had pushed four- to six-foot tides across the place, and no one could imagine a storm delivering more water than that. The new elevation ought to provide plenty of freeboard; Ricky could tie down the *Lil' Rick* to a dock in the bayou seventy-five yards away, and keep an eye on the boat from the rear window of his house.

But Yscloskey, permanent home to about two hundred, sits outside St. Bernard Parish's flood protection levees, and Ricky, who had been out shrimping two days before the storm, began to feel uneasy as he listened to Katrina-tracking reports. He'd motored in from the gulf up the MR-GO en route to New Orleans to sell his shrimp and noticed that tides were already being pushed up well above normal by brisk, unrelenting southeasterly winds.

So he and Susan had settled on a plan. He'd bring the boat to Violet, and Susan and the rest of the family would hunker down in the house nearby. At worst—if a head-on strike by Katrina seemed likely—the house dwellers could simply evacuate to the boat.

It seemed like a good plan—until this moment.

Susan's peek out the door brings the disturbing realization that she's made a logistical mistake, parking her van so that its side-loading doors are facing away from the house, which will make it difficult to get Sidney T. aboard. She'll have to turn it around.

By the time she fetches her keys and makes her way out into the storm, the water is up to the van's hubcaps. She sloshes through the flood and the driving rain and finds out the hard way that even Category 3 winds are still dangerous—a gust almost rips off the driver's door when she opens it.

Susan bulls her way into the van, cranks it up, backs out, makes a U-turn, and steers it into position, with the loading doors as close to the front of the house as she can manage. She rushes back in to help secure her dad. Short of being physically carried out, her father simply can't be hurried. Her sixty-two-year-old brother, Sidney Eugene, might have lugged him—but he's just had knee surgery and can't bear any weight on it. So between them all they essentially drag Sidney T. to the van and get him cinched in with a seatbelt in the back seat. Everyone else piles in. The effort probably takes only five minutes, but it seems like an eternity.

In that time, the water has already risen about another foot—and is beginning to enter the house.

From his perch on the trawler two blocks away, Ricky sees Susan making a slow left turn from the driveway and nosing ahead in the direction of the nearby St. Bernard Highway. By this time, he realizes that any chance for the occupants of the van to gain the shelter of the *Lil' Rick* has been dashed—the rising water and still bullying wind would make a transfer extremely risky.

For a moment, Ricky thinks about abandoning the *Lil' Rick* and going with them—the cascading water, if he timed his jump off the boat just right, would carry him directly toward the van. He and Susan conduct a brisk debate over their cell phones, but she persuades him to stay with his boat and his passengers. And anyway, they know from earlier radio reports that Chalmette High School, a substantial two-story building, is open as a shelter only a few miles north and west up the

St. Bernard Highway. They both know, too, that the highway, tracking the banks of the Mississippi, is built on relatively high ground and, indeed, probably sits two to three feet higher than the back end of the Violet subdivision, which borders on a marsh. Even in Hurricane Betsy much of the road stayed above the flood. They're confident that if Susan can get to the highway, she can make it to the high school.

Susan's van is one of those old-fashioned kinds—a boxy vehicle with oversized sceni-cruise windows. Its one virtue will turn out to be that it sits slightly higher than a conventional sedan.

As Susan noses her way up the street, headlights on, wipers slapping frantically at the driving rain, harrowing sights greet her. Wind bursts have toppled trees, torn apart mobile homes, knocked some prefab houses off their foundations. Power poles are down. Severed electrical and phone lines are snapping like whips in the wind.

At an intersection a block away, Violet Street is blocked by a huge fallen tree. Susan turns right, onto a side street, seeking another way out. A downed telephone pole lies in her way. The wind is rocking the van. Her daughters are beginning to grow fearful.

"We should've left, Mama—we should've evacuated," Natasha says.

Susan is beginning to panic herself.

"Drive over it," her brother tells her of the telephone pole. "We got no choice—just drive over it."

Susan eases up to the pole, feels the front wheels engage, gooses the engine. Wheels spin, then the van darts forward, jolting unsteadily as it scrapes, grinds, and thumps over the obstacle. Something rips off her driver's-side mirror. For a moment, it seems the van might topple over.

The girls scream. "Momma, we're gonna die!"

But the van lurches forward, free of the tree.

Minutes later, they reach the intersection of the St. Bernard Highway. Susan begins a slow right turn—and the van is struck by a violent gust and rocked precipitously. Her speakerphone is still on and Ricky hears more shrieks from the van, but the phone's slipped from Susan's hands to the seat; with the noise, they can't hear his frantic attempts at coaching her driving.

Susan's brother is doing his best to talk her through this. "Hold it into the wind or she'll flip you over," he says.

"I'm doing my best," Susan replies.

In a strange bit of luck, Katrina's winds have begun to shift from the east to the north-northwest—meaning the back side of the storm is now buffeting them. This part of the highway angles mostly north, and Susan, when she completes her turn, is in fact heading more or less into the wind.

But a third of a mile up the highway, with gales continuing to knock the van around, she loses heart and wheels into the driveway of a large brick home, hoping to use the house as a lee. By this time, water has begun to sheet across the high ground of the highway.

Her maneuver provides no haven: about two minutes after they park, the house's roof begins to disintegrate—showering the top of the van with shingles, nails, and splintering wood. It sounds like they're under attack. Frightened, Susan pulls back onto the highway, making another right turn toward Chalmette.

Peering ahead, she feels guarded optimism. The highway, though covered in a deepening layer of water, seems at least passable, even if it is littered with small tree limbs and detritus blown from houses and buildings. But the wind actually seems to be picking up again. The high-topped van is proving almost impossible to control.

Sidney E., her brother, has an idea: "Drive to an open section of the road and stop. We'll just wait it out there."

Susan brakes perhaps fifty yards east of a grove of stately oaks that hem in the highway on both sides—the grove is a local landmark planted by a well-to-do landowner in the early 1900s. She leaves the engine running and they sit for a few minutes, peering ahead, wind gusts continuing to pummel the van.

Suddenly, something isn't right.

Something's coming slowly at them—something so improbable that they dismiss it at first.

But it soon becomes clear that this is no mirage.

It's a slow-moving wall of brown water, the leading edge of a wave that will soon help cover the world here in eight to seventeen feet of water.

"Oh, my God!" Susan exclaims.

She can't know that about ten miles west of her, levees on the

Industrial Canal, the channel connecting nearby New Orleans to Lake Pontchartrain, have suffered two massive breaches. The deluge she is seeing has already drowned people and flattened houses in the historic Lower Ninth Ward bordering St. Bernard Parish.

And if she can't get away, it may drown them, too.

4. Stormy Traditions

If you ask the Robins why they stayed to face Hurricane Katrina—a storm that turned out to be the most destructive and costly natural disaster in U.S. history—they give a lot of stock answers. They didn't think Katrina was really coming their way; by the time the storm changed tracks and grew dangerous, evacuation was no longer an option; they know and trust their boats and feared losing them if they left them tied unmanned to the docks.

But the bedrock answer lies in a kind of nonchalance born of long experience, and the power of stories.

Hurricanes run deep in Robin history and lore, and riding them out is a family tradition.

It was a fair Tuesday in late September, Indian summerish, a few wispy cirrus clouds high in an otherwise pristine sky. Nicholas Robin awoke to the serenity of Lake Borgne, the sprawling brackish bay that lay between his rough-hewn beachside shanty and the Gulf of Mexico, an easy half-day sail to the east. Nothing stirred, save for shore birds gliding along the lake's becalmed, sun-dappled, green-gray surface.

A seasoned fisherman who captained *The Five Brothers,* a handsome thirty-two-foot seine boat he'd built himself, Nicholas went about his daily chores, including scooping up a mess of soft-shelled blue crabs from the lake's shallow grass beds. They would make a nice meal for his wife and five young sons. As the Robins went to bed that night, the weather deteriorated slightly, with clouds forming on the southwestern horizon. A light breeze stirred from the northeast, making for a pleasant night. They retired with no sense of foreboding.

Sometime after midnight, however, the wind began to blow, more blustery than ominous. It blew unabated through sunrise, gradually switching to the southeast. Nicholas awakened to a much different scene than the previous morning: swells began to appear in the lake, lapping at the sandy, shell-lined shore. Still, the Robins, one of a handful of families living in the tiny fishing hamlet of Shell Beach about forty miles east-southeast of New Orleans, weren't alarmed.

They were in the middle of lunching on the soft-shell crabs harvested the day before when a midday squall forced them to shut their doors and windows to the rain and wind. An hour later, Lake Borgne was a froth of whitecaps atop growing swells. Low clouds began scudding across the sky.

The sea-wise Nicholas peered out and felt something was wrong. This clearly wasn't some ordinary late summer thunderstorm or low-pressure trough of the kind that often welled up out of the seas here. He told his wife Eleanor to begin gathering a few possessions as he went out to secure his boat.

By then, the swells had grown and the water began to rush up on the beach—a bad sign. Nicholas hastily gathered his family and announced they had to leave. The boat was the only choice. Rising tides had already rendered impassable a rutted road paralleling a railroad trestle that led to a more substantial road to New Orleans. A daily steam train that brought supplies, and hauled away the bounty of the area's fishermen to the New Orleans markets, had come and gone.

By the time the Robins had gotten to the boat—an open hull with no cabin—a fifty-mile-per-hour gale was blowing. Nicholas had fortuitously snatched up a tarp, a hammer, and some crude nails. Whipsawed by the wind, he still managed to nail the tarp so that it formed a canopy over about three-quarters of the boat, and sent his wife and five sons, all under the age of thirteen, scrambling under it.

He fired up the seine boat's rudimentary engine, a first-generation five-horsepower outboard, but it proved useless in the gale. Then—finding the boat being lifted on a strong tidal surge—Nicholas steered it with an oar through steadily increasing gale-force winds and blinding rain toward the one place that might save their lives.

The place of impromptu shelter was the Pull-Boat Canal, a narrow, cypress-shrouded waterway built by loggers in the tracks of an ancient bayou that snaked west and north to a point about six miles below Violet Canal. At least a dozen feet of water now covered the land, and Nicholas used this to his advantage, guiding the boat deep in among the wind-shielding cypress trees. There, with a rope and their hands, the Robins held fast to branches high up on the tree trunks, praying for survival.

The storm lashed them all afternoon and well into the night, hammering the coast with 120-mile-per-hour sustained winds and roaring tides, and tearing off roofs and blowing down buildings in New Orleans. Still, Nicholas, in an all-night vigil, kept the boat afloat and his family safe.

By dawn, the storm had wiped out Shell Beach, several other low-lying fishing hamlets in St. Bernard Parish, and numerous other fishing towns in two coastal parishes to the west. The hurricane had claimed more than 275 lives—including 21 people who drowned at a fishing camp at the Rigolets, a chain of barrier islands between Shell Beach and the gulf. The death toll might have been much higher had not some of those towns been wired to a telegraph system that provided a twelve-hour warning for residents lucky enough to learn of it.

The devastation was so great, and the land had been so rearranged, that it took Nicholas Robin and his family almost five years to return and rebuild. But they had survived one of the century's great natural calamities—the Hurricane of 1915. It was, by today's measurements, a Category 4 storm.

Nicholas and Eleanor Robin were Ricky's and Ronald's great-grandparents. Ricky's grandfather, Charles Robin I, and Ronald's grandfather, John, were boys aboard the seiner. Their great-uncle, Nicholas Robin Jr., was a toddler who survived the hurricane in diapers. Their harrowing escape is the most detailed of their ancestral storm narratives, but hardly the only one.

Depending on which history of Louisiana hurricanes you trust, generations of Robins, their roots about 250 years deep here, have stood in and survived about thirty hurricanes of various severity since Gils Robin Jr., their first Louisiana forebear, pitched up on this marshy coast sometime before 1776. To understand the Robins, the other captains who kept watch at Violet Canal, and the residents clustered in their nearby houses, it's helpful to know the wider, colorful history of St. Bernard Parish and the pioneering people who came to inhabit its lower coasts.

By many measurements, it has long been—and still remains—a place apart.

5. Cajun-Spanish Roots and Pirate Connections

Gils Robin Jr., Ricky and Ronald's first known ancestor in Louisiana, is enumerated as an adult in the 1776 Spanish census of this low country, but he almost certainly got here years before then. He wandered into a wild, pristine, and oddly populated paradise. Though of French Acadian stock—Cajun in modern parlance—Gils would soon enough find himself living among Spaniards from a world far flung even from Europe.

Gils Robin (in the old days, pronounced Roe-BEHN in the French) settled first in neighboring Plaquemines Parish but came to make his permanent home on lands that would become part of St. Bernard, an astonishingly fish-rich and fertile estuary forming New Orleans' eastern doorstep to the nearby Gulf of Mexico. The 1,830-square-mile parish, with the Mississippi River flanking part of its western border, is perhaps 90 percent water and wetlands. It is named for Bernardo de Gálvez, the Spanish adventurer and soldier who himself settled in nearby New Orleans in 1776—just ahead of the destructive hurricane of 1778. (Galveston, Texas, is named for him, too.) The Louisiana territories had a decade earlier been ceded by France to Spain, and Gálvez, though but twenty-nine years old, used family connections to get himself appointed governor.

The lad had his work cut out for him. Spain's age-old enemies, the British, ruled the territories of West Florida next door, a sprawling swath of the New World that carved a panhandle from the eastern bank of the Mississippi River through what is now coastal Mississippi and Alabama, and ran the length and breadth of modern-day Florida. Gálvez had good reason to believe that the British had designs on Spain's New World empire (big parts of which England had previously controlled) and might be causing more mischief than they already were, save for one small problem: their American colonies were rising up in full revolt. Spain, allied with France, threw its lot in with the American upstarts and used its control of the mouth of the Mississippi to help provision the rebels far upstream.

Gálvez realized he needed a lot more bodies to staff the river delta garrisons he had in mind. Starting in 1777, he reached deep into the fringes of Spain's military outposts, calling on soldiers stationed in the faraway Canary Islands, a thirteen-island archipelago a hundred miles off the coast of Morocco, to come to Louisiana. The Canaries (named for a huge, ferocious breed of indigenous dog, not the singing bird) had been claimed for Spain in 1402, prized as a convenient reprovisioning stop about a fifth of the way to the exploitable riches of the New World. Christopher Columbus himself dropped by in 1496 on one of his voyages to the Americas.

The majority of the Louisiana-bound Canary Islanders arrived in two groups, first a company of seven hundred, followed quickly by another thirteen hundred or so. They were essentially conscripts who, for the trouble of transferring from their arid, windswept post off the coast of Saharan Africa, got land, a little cash, a couple of horses, cattle or oxen, and a one-way ticket to their swampy, mosquito-plagued, hurricane-susceptible new home. Their women would follow a year or two later bearing trunks of heavy, ornate dresses, hats, and coats necessary for the Canaries' blustery, chilly winters, but mostly unsuitable for their lives in the sweltering, subtropical South Louisiana climate. They came bearing some books and their *decimas,* the elaborate, satirical folk tales that they kept alive in a mostly oral tradition, relying on their poets and singers to render them into performance pieces at festivals and celebrations. Gálvez was somewhat picky: his Louisiana-bound colonists had to be at least five-feet one-inch tall and without easily discernible vices. Gypsies and mulattoes, and men who had served as executioners on the seven inhabited Canary Islands, need not apply.

These are the people who eventually came to call themselves the *Isleños,* and many of them settled on land grants along the serpentine, oak-lined ridges of Bayou Terre-aux-Boeufs (Ox Bayou) in lower St. Bernard, an easy horse's gallop below the present site of the hurricane hole at Violet Canal. Until the end of World War II, when paved roads, telephones, television, and oil exploration more fully opened their isolated hideaways to the rest of the world, the Isleños hewed to their reputation as a ruggedly independent, hard-working, hard-fighting, clannish culture, keeping their archaic Spanish customs and language alive, and adapting spectacularly to their new maritime environment.

They clearly brought some farming and seafaring skills with them and applied them with alacrity to their new home. In the islands, they had become masters of domesticating cattle, and many started small-plot cattle-raising operations here (some, in fact, were so fond of their oxen that they brought them on the 3,850-nautical-mile voyage to Louisiana). The Isleños also became master boatbuilders, boat handlers, fishermen, and hunters. They tapped the surrounding wetlands— the eastern quadrant of a vast estuary stretching to the Texas border and easily rivaling the Florida Everglades—for muskrat and other fur-bearing animals. They seined and trawled the brackish bays, bayous, and nearby gulf for crab, shrimp, and oysters and a startling variety of marketable fish.

Until the crash of muskrat stocks in the late 1950s (because of habitat loss, overtrapping, and the invasion of a rival South American fur-bearing rodent called the nutria), Isleños trappers—the Robin family among them—accounted for a large part of the lucrative pelt trade that sent Louisiana muskrat hides all over the world. To this day, St. Bernard's Isleños fishermen, Ricky Robin in their number, continue to be among the chief suppliers of shrimp, oysters, and crabs to the New Orleans retail and restaurant market.

Although Gils Jr. was a Cajun, the Robin family would intertwine itself deeply into Isleño culture through generations of marriage. Gils Robin migrated here from the island of Trinidad sometime between the late 1750s and 1776. Family history is silent on exactly what brought Gils to Louisiana. Most likely he came with a contingent of Acadian exiles who had settled temporarily in the West Indies and who, in 1767, were boatlifted by the Spanish to join a contingent of Cajuns already living in South Louisiana's bayou country. Or he may have simply come on his own, seeking a less precarious home. Or, as Ricky Robin theorizes, Gils might well have been a pirate, a fairly common trade in those days. Trinidad then was a well-known redoubt of pirates and privateers (legalized pirates operating under commission to various European royal governments), not to mention rumrunners and slave traders of various persuasions. Pirate factions, including Black Beard's crew, plundered the island from time to time.

South Louisiana itself then was a notorious pirate haven, and no wonder. The St. Bernard estuary was an untrammeled, in parts uncharted wilderness, a labyrinth of unpopulated barrier islands, sinewy bayous, sprawling marshes, all ringed on the west and north by an almost impenetrable moss-draped cypress swamp full of alligators and poisonous snakes. It lay an easy day sail northeast of Barataria, itself a marshy, mysterious complex of islands, bayous, and bays that, shortly after the Louisiana Purchase in 1803, became the lair and fortress of the pirate Jean Lafitte. (A Frenchman in love with the works of Cervantes named Barataria after a mythical island in the Spanish author's classic novel *Don Quixote*.) Lafitte used Barataria as a staging ground for his raids on ships of various nationalities and as a sorting station for plundered booty before he smuggled those goods onto the black market in nearby New Orleans. His New Orleans front for a while was a French Quarter blacksmith shop that he owned with his brother, Pierre Lafitte. In fact, the building, at Bourbon and St. Philip streets, still stands today and is home to a bar called Lafitte's Blacksmith Shop.

Gils, by age, would have been an older contemporary of the pirate, and Lafitte certainly knew Gils Robin's stomping grounds in St. Bernard and nearby Plaquemines Parish quite well. In fact, a small Plaquemines town only twenty miles southwest of Violet Canal as the gull flies bears Lafitte's name. And St. Bernard lore has it that Lafitte sometimes used the St. Bernard estuary as a kind of extra back door to the nearby New Orleans black market.

Most famously, Lafitte provided invaluable intelligence—not to mention arms, men, knowledge of terrain, and military cunning—to Andrew Jackson and his American forces during the pivotal Battle of New Orleans in January of 1815. That clash, in which a battle-hardened British army of eight thousand men suffered two thousand casualties and lost most of its key officers to Jackson's much smaller force in a matter of hours, was fought almost entirely in St. Bernard at Chalmette Plantation, not five miles above Violet Canal. Three companies of Isleños volunteers from Bayou Terre-aux-Boeufs—upset with the British trespass into their backyard—fought alongside Jackson with the Third Regiment of Louisiana, though most were equipped with little more than the shotguns they used for hunting small game. (The battle marked the effective end of the War of 1812 and of British territorial ambitions in America.)

Historians also know that the St. Bernard estuary has its own long history of low-grade, homegrown piracy. Smuggling—of rum, whiskey, guns, and other contraband in the old days all the way through Prohibition and, in more contemporary times, illicit drugs—is an enterprise as old as the settlement itself. And few families knew the lay of this watery land better than the early Robins.

The most extravagant Robin family story, in fact, is that Lafitte's mother may have been a Robin, therefore Jean Lafitte and Gils and his successors would have been blood relatives. There is no proof of this, though claiming relationship to the famous pirate is a wildly popular preoccupation throughout South Louisiana. Neither can it be disproved; serious historians simply don't know for certain where Lafitte was born, or who his parents were. Informed conjecture believes him to be of French stock, though a book published some years ago purporting to be Lafitte's diary (which many dismiss as a hoax) says his mother was a European Sephardic Jew.

One intriguing clue of a possibly close Lafitte-Robin connection is contained in a genealogy of Pierre Lafitte that was published in 1930 in a book called *Lafitte the Pirate*. The text lists a Martin Robin as one of the sponsors at the christening in New Orleans in 1791 of Marie Louise Villars, the woman who would eventually become Pierre Lafitte's mistress and bear him seven children. (Her sister, Catherine Villars, became Jean Lafitte's mistress.) Robin was not then a common name in the region, and a Martin Robin emerges in Ricky and Ronald's direct family three generations after Gils. Given the propensity at the time for family names to travel down the family tree, the speculation of the contemporary Robins is that Martin Robin was perhaps Gils Robin's brother.

Surely, if he was that close to the Villars family, he could easily have come to know the Lafittes.

Another circumstantial clue is that the vast majority of Acadian immigrants like Gils arrived in Louisiana impoverished; they had been expelled by the British from their Canadian maritime homeland years earlier with little more than the clothes on their backs. But by the time Gils' great-grandson, Jean Louis Robin, came to adulthood around the Civil War, he had acquired enough status that two waterways in the south central St. Bernard estuary were named for him. Ricky's theory, based on foggy family stories, is that his great-great-grandfather— whether by conventional commerce or the methods of piracy—had amassed a fortune great enough that he owned all of the land in and around Bayou Jean Louis Robin and Lake Jean Louis Robin. The waterways continue to bear Jean Louis' name, though the land no longer is in the Robin family, perhaps having been confiscated for taxes after the Civil War.

Bill Marigny Hyland, St. Bernard Parish's official historian, says that in his ongoing research he comes across recurring though vague tales that "the Robins ran with Lafitte," but like a great deal of the famous pirate's mystery-shrouded life, proof is elusive. (Hyland is familiar with ancestral connections to locally famous figures: He is a descendant of Bernard Philippe de Marigny, who parceled out the original St. Bernard land grants to the Isleños on behalf of Governor Gálvez. The historic Faubourg-Marigny district bounding the French Quarter is named for him.)

Ricky Robin does know, however, through painstaking genealogy, that he is a grand-nephew through his maternal grandmother of one the greatest swashbucklers in New Orleans history, Don Jose ("Pepe") Llulla. He was a dueling swordsman of such skill that he is enshrined in a book from 2001 called *The Deadliest Men,* a kind of global all-star roster of history's most famous or notorious sword fighters, gunslingers, soldiers, and mercenaries. Because of their ages, Llulla and Lafitte couldn't have been confederates—though Llulla's wax image stands next to the pirate's in the Musee Conti in the French Quarter of New Orleans. Llulla would at best have been a child by the time Lafitte quit Louisiana for Galveston Island shortly after the Battle of New Orleans, when a series of raids and seizures of his properties by government forces embittered him toward the Americans he had helped.

But Llulla was almost as legendary in his day as the great pirate was in his. A fencing master, the Spaniard fought at least thirty duels with all manner of sharp weapons—including Bowie knives—and reportedly never got a scratch. Some of his victims, meanwhile, were said to be buried in a New Orleans cemetery he'd purchased (though most duels of that era ended in the swordplay humiliation of one's rival and seldom in death). Llulla had another oblique connection to Lafitte—he bought Grand Terre Island, the Barataria enclave once owned by Lafitte, and retired there in 1880, remaining until his death in 1886. One of Ricky Robin's prized possessions is a sword, owned by the grand master himself, passed down to him over the generations.

The Robin family history reflects the way that much of the New Orleans and South Louisiana region evolved over time into what Bill Hyland calls a "Creolized culture," with the state's founding French influence at its core. But it also was infused with the spicy mix of many other cultures—Spanish, German, Swiss, Alsatian, Afro-Caribbean, Italian, English, Irish, and Croatian—thrown into the gumbo pot.

Gils Robin's father, Gils Sr., was born in the Canadian maritime province of Nova Scotia and almost certainly ended up in Trinidad as part of a notorious act of eighteenth-century ethnic cleansing known as *le Grand Dérangement*. Until 1702, Nova Scotia had been a French colony called Acadia, or Acadie, and peopled mostly with French-speaking Celts who had settled it decades before from the northwestern French region of Britannia Minor (Brittany today). These settlers called themselves Acadiens, a term first shortened to *'cadiens* and eventually bastardized in the New World to Cajun. They were a peace-loving, enterprising folk, tending farms and fishing the seas for cod and lobster, but war and history caught up with them in 1755.

The British had recently gone to war again with the French in a long dust-up known as the French and Indian Wars. Canada's British overlords decided that the fifteen thousand or so Acadians in their midst ought to be shown the door, though they had done little to provoke the British, save hewing to their seventeenth-century country French language and declining to renounce their Catholicism. They were forced from their lands and homes and, midwinter, put on ships (some in deplorable condition) in a diaspora during which about half their number died of various calamities—shipwrecks, disease, and starvation.

Some Acadians stayed behind, fleeing into the Nova Scotia wilderness, where they hid out until the British occupation ended. Still others returned to Europe, while many settled up and down the East Coast of America. A large group—Gils Robin Sr. most likely among them—was sent to work camps in the West Indies, from where they would eventually relocate to South Louisiana. Estimates vary as to the number of Acadians who eventually made it to Louisiana; two thousand is a commonly used figure. Yet, of all the bayou ethnic groups, it is the Cajuns who have left the most indelible mark on Louisiana and American culture. Beginning in the 1960s, after about two hundred years in relative isolation, the Cajuns' simple though savory French country cooking and their exuberant, rough-hewn music (sung in their antique country French) began to surge from the lowlands and onto a national stage.

Gils of the 1776 census married a woman of French descent, but his son, and most Robin males for generations to follow, married Isleños women, and Isleño names ubiquitous to St. Bernard's bayou country—Alphonso, Campo, Fernandez, Gonzales, Gallardo, Rodriguez—entered the Robin family tree. In fact, the Robin family became so Isleñosized that Ricky's mother, Celie Robin, is these days considered St. Bernard's foremost amateur ethnographer, having been the coauthor of a book a few years back on early Isleño folk remedies painstakingly collected over the years from Isleño elders. Ricky's father, Charles ("Charlito") Robin, a retired fisherman known for his intricate carved models of indigenous fishing boats, has held high office in the St. Bernard Isleños Society, a preservation group that operates a local Isleño museum and puts on an annual St. Bernard Parish Isleños Festival. Once a year for this cultural celebration some of the musty, ornate Canary Island outfits borne to Louisiana by the original Isleños are dusted off and put on display, and occasionally the old decimas, or folk tales, are recited.

Although the Isleños came to dominate St. Bernard's lower bayous, they were not the only early settlers there. A small cadre of French gentry, awarded vast land grants from the monarchy as far back as the founding of New Orleans by Jean-Baptiste Le Moyne, sieur de Bienville, in 1718, already operated large plantations on St. Bernard's high ground by the time of the Isleños migration. These are what most historians call the "ancien population," the original Creoles—a term that gradually became complicated through its association with people of color.

Back then, though, "Creole" essentially meant "homegrown," or, more clearly, it was used by the progeny of the founding French gentry, with roots recently in the old country, to distinguish themselves from more newly arrived French speakers: the Cajuns, Haitians and other Afro-Caribbeans, and former African slaves who spoke a simplified form of French that they learned on the Creole plantations on which they toiled.

Thus, Creole French and Creole cooking today are largely synonymous with people of African-American descent. One difference between Cajun music and its bluesier black derivative, zydeco, is that zydeco is usually sung in Creole French patois.

By the approach of Hurricane Katrina, modern-day St. Bernard Parish had evolved into a bustling New Orleans suburb of about sixty-seven thousand people, though it remained a place, culturally at least, that had surprisingly little to do with its famous next-door neighbor. Most of its population, relative to the Creoles, Isleños, and Cajuns, were johnny-come-latelys who began arriving in the late 1960s on successive waves of white flight from New Orleans. That exodus began with the integration of New Orleans public schools but continued as the city's politics came to be dominated by its growing African-American majority. (The city's soaring violent crime rates of the 1970s and 1980s were unquestionably another factor.)

One of the first waves into St. Bernard, in fact, was from the storied Ninth Ward, a reclaimed cypress swamp on the flood-prone southeastern fringes of New Orleans abutting St. Bernard. Beginning in the late nineteenth century, poor Irish and German immigrants, seeking cheap land and housing, settled in among poor African-Americans on these marginal lands, bounded in their early days by a natural bayou to the east and the Mississippi River to the south. In the 1920s, the Ninth Ward was sliced in two by the dredging of the Industrial Canal connecting the river to Lake Pontchartrain; everything on the east side of the canal became known as the Lower Ninth.

And much as the impoverished Mississippi Delta gave birth to the melancholy vibrancy of the blues, the Ninth Ward over the decades pawned or nurtured numerous notable African-American artists and musicians—the self-taught painter Sister Gertrude Morgan lived there; New Orleans R&B mainstay Kermit Ruffin grew up there; and Fats Domino, though he hailed from Vacherie, a Mississippi River sugar-farming town upriver from New Orleans, honed his world-famous Swamp Pop sound at his home and studio in the Lower Ninth. But well before Katrina smacked the region, the Lower Ninth (an actual political ward of New Orleans) had become a dispiriting and ever declining neighborhood, its population 98 percent black, its housing stock crumbling, its streets in decay, poverty, drug abuse, and crime its hallmark.

To be sure, not everyone who moved to modern-day St. Bernard came to avoid racial integration. Many came to take advantage of plentiful jobs, cheap land, and low taxes. The parish, with its laissez-faire attitude toward planning and zoning, had welcomed the kind of heavy industries—oil and gas refineries, oil-field-equipment fabrication plants and shipyards, for example—that fancier places spurned. By the 1990s, in fact, upper St. Bernard, notably the cities of Arabi and Chalmette, the parish seat, had undergone a radical economic and esthetic transformation. Gone were sleepy little towns with potholed blacktop roads and a mostly mom-and-pop retail establishment. In their place cropped up sprawling burghs with traffic-choked four-lane thoroughfares lined chockablock with strip malls, fast-food joints, big-box retailers (including Wal-Mart), and cookie-cutter subdivisions full of look-alike brick ranch houses. Much of the place, in fact, seemed indistinguishable from the homogenized sprawl-mall clutter of a great deal of Wal-Martized America.

But this facade was deceiving. The old ways, though sorely tested by growth and development, still hung on in the lower bayou country, and in some ways St. Bernard lived down, not up. Or, put another way, bayou rhythms still captured the local spirit and imagination more than urban or suburban preoccupations. For all its in-migration, St. Bernard remained a strangely insular place—85 percent white and content with its sprawl and its laissez-faire attitudes; it was friendly, family-centered but somewhat wary of outsiders, and fairly uninterested in matters much beyond its borders.

No survey exists to prove it, but pre-Katrina you'd likely find more people from Chalmette (who call themselves Chalmations) spending a summer Sunday afternoon crabbing down at Delacroix Island or Ysclos-key, the Robins' hometown, than at brunch in the New Orleans French Quarter not ten miles away. (One explanation is that home cooking is generally so good throughout Creolized South Louisiana that the locals simply prefer to eat at home.) It's common to meet St. Bernard residents who, as almost a matter of pride, brag that they seldom set foot in New Orleans except perhaps for Mardi Gras, or on trips through the city to the airport, which lies west in the suburb of Kenner.

St. Bernard's underdog mentality explains some of this. As old and colorful as the parish's bayou settlements are, their residents have always been looked upon—at least by some in the New Orleans upper crust—as provincials, a bit too loud, uncouth, and undereducated for the city's sophisticates. The era of white flight didn't help this reputation, although in fairness New Orleans whites also fled to many other surrounding communities. And St. Bernard—at least before Katrina ripped through—supported a robust and civically active upper middle class of doctors, lawyers, engineers, and business executives, even minting its share of home-grown millionaires.

But fair or not, St. Bernard over time had become to New Orleans what New Jersey is to Manhattan—slightly déclassé, an object of low-level derision. If New Orleans was the birthplace of jazz and Creole cooking, St. Bernard, New Orleanians would joke, was the birthplace of mosquitoes, trailer parks, and oil refineries. Though its bayou hamlets and pastoral countrysides still retained a rustic charm, St. Bernard also harbored neighborhoods so esthetically unappealing that they proved the jaded aphorism that there is no place so ugly that somebody won't proudly call it home. The accented speech of many parish residents earned them the label "Yats"—as in the colloquial interrogative, "Where y'at?" Thus, New Orleanians found it acceptable to dine now and then at Rocky and Carlo's, an old and unpretentious Chalmette eatery with an almost cult following, or to drive the roads down the St. Bernard bayous to buy fresh shrimp, crabs, and oysters from the bayou-side stands. But no right-thinking person should ever want to *live* there.

When Katrina roared in, it was perhaps unsurprising that the wider world transfixed itself on the plight of storied New Orleans, and the horrifying pictures of people trapped there, and few in officialdom seemed to notice or care that six thousand people were stranded in extremely perilous conditions in St. Bernard next door. When, on the first day after the storm, Walter Boasso, a St. Bernard resident and a state senator whose district includes the parish, tried to round up National Guard troops to venture with him down into his stricken homeland, he could only muster two volunteers, and they were quickly siphoned off into the wrecked Lower Ninth Ward. Indeed, the parish president, Junior Rodriguez, and a cadre of staff members who had stayed through the storm were marooned on the roof of the parish government complex for almost forty-eight hours before state or federal officials took note of their plight, and then only because Junior was able to dictate a short note by cell phone that was posted on an Internet forum. The first relief group of any kind that found its way to Junior's perch of exile was neither the Louisiana National Guard nor FEMA: it was a small contingent of Royal Canadian Mounted Police that arrived near the end of the second day after the storm.

In fact, Ricky and Ronald Robin and the other boat captains at Violet Canal would spend three full days rescuing and shepherding refugees, using only their wits and whatever resources they had on hand or could scrounge, before *they* would see anyone with a badge or a uniform.

"We were totally forgotten," says Boasso.

And yet no contiguous place outside of the savaged Mississippi Gulf Coast took a bigger beating from Katrina than did St. Bernard Parish.

6. Charlo's Dawn

Charles Inabnet—"Charlo" to his friends—is another man not given much to worrying. But he's a bit worried now. Dark has long come, the wind is raising an awful racket outside, and he's alone in his compact three-bedroom wood-frame cottage on the Hopedale Highway. It sits about three miles south of Yscloskey, where Ricky and Ronald Robin grew up, and about twenty miles below Violet Canal, where the Robins are now riding out the storm. Charlo's power went out three hours before, at 7:50 p.m. He has made a brief excursion outside since then, worried about rising tides from Katrina's vicious and increasing easterly winds. But to his relief, his yard and the nearby road, though slicked by wind-whipped rain, show no signs of flooding.

He's lit candles and broken out a flashlight, but it can't penetrate the black-hole darkness outside his rain-slashed windows. Clearly, bad stuff is happening. He can hear the thud and snap of things that sound as if they're being torn apart. A few unnerving gusts have set his house to swaying. It's as if he can feel the foundation shift, as if the very bones of the place are being rearranged. He decides to pry open a back door for a peek but he can't see a thing. He hears plenty, though: the wind bawls and growls as if modulating electric hairdryers have been stuck into each of his ears.

Charlo has a contingency plan if his house seems it isn't going to stand up to Katrina. Now he's thinking it might be time to put that plan into action. In fact, Charlo wouldn't be here at all, if fate and timing hadn't trapped him.

His house, jacked up on five-foot stilts, sits perched on a skinny 50-by-250-foot lot separated from Bayou La Loutre by the narrow, black-topped Hopedale Highway. Neighbors live on both sides in stilt houses bigger and higher than his. But they've evacuated—as has almost everyone else at this latitude. On this night, Charlo is alone at the edge of a suddenly uninhabited world. His boat, an aging fifty-foot oyster lugger called *The Captain John J.,* is tied down with multiple ropes to his wood-planked dock in the bayou across the road. This is deep Isleños country, implacably open and flat, most of it at or below sea level, and all of it miles outside the St. Bernard Parish flood protection levees. Much of Charlo's backyard wanders into what is in reality a prairie of alligator grass and spartina that fans out into an endless marshy plain inscribed here and there with bayous, bays, and lagoons. Lake Jean Louis Robin sits only about five miles due south.

There are maybe fifty other dwellings, some grander, some even more modest than Charlo's, on the ten-mile stretch of road between Yscloskey and Hopedale. There, past a cluster of mostly weekend fishing camps and a sportfishing marina, the highway fizzles out into a narrow dirt track that dead-ends on the banks of MR-GO, the gaping deepwater navigation channel dredged (against fierce local opposition) more than forty years ago. From there, the Gulf of Mexico lies less than fifteen miles down the MR-GO. Locals not only blame the salt-bearing waterway for decimating protective freshwater marshes hereabouts, they have also long feared what might happen if a hurricane roared directly up the channel, dragging a killer surge with it.

Charlo moved here with his wife Terry eleven years ago from Plaquemines Parish next door. Lower Plaquemines, where he lived, has its own pastoral charms. But it's a place dominated by the busy shipping lanes of the mighty Mississippi; a place subject to the constant hubbub of the comings and goings of thousands of workers servicing oil and gas wells and processing facilities in the deepwater canyons of the Gulf of Mexico. A commercial fisherman most of his recent life, Charlo acquired some oyster leases in the nearby Lake Borgne area and decided he liked the lay of the land here. He found the marsh, bays, and bayous less crowded and polluted, liked the slower ebb and flow of the place. Hopedale, Yscloskey, Delacroix Island, the nearby settlements of Reggio and Florissant, the lower ramparts of Bayou Road along historic Bayou Terre-aux-Boeufs—these are waysides still observant of the seasons of the sea; places where self-reliance ranks high as a virtue, where the ability to handle a boat, weave and set a trawl, use a castnet, cook a

gumbo or an Isleños version of oyster spaghetti, handle yourself in a
fight or in a squall at sea, are not trivial skills.

The presence of the odd double-wide trailer or metal-skinned modular home aside, these are also scenic places, settlements of eclectic
hand-hewn houses and camps designed and built by blue-collar archi-
tects and carpenters, and set along brooding bayous lined with hackberry and dwarf oaks. The fishing fleet that operates from here is both
functional and decorative, for it is almost entirely indigenously crafted,
from gallant, handsome trawlers like the *Lil' Rick* to swift, welded aluminum crabbing skiffs, to sublimely graceful cypress-planked oyster luggers, including one hilariously named the *Cajun Viagra* (in honor of the
lowly oyster's reputed aphrodisiacal powers).

Uplanders might find the greater landscape monotonous, the way a
driver across Kansas might finally declare the endless canvas of golden
wheat fields monochromatic. But bayou folk never tire of it, for they
divine, in observations steeped in time, how these landscapes shift with
the light and the tides and the seasons; how routinely they give up their
wonders and their mysteries. Round the right bend in the summer
twilight on the road to Delacroix Island and you might catch a bull
alligator nosing out to feed, carving a V-shaped ripple on still waters
painted by a dying sun. Or you can watch pelicans clowning above
schools of cavorting porpoises not a half mile down from Ricky Robin's
house, where the MR-GO meets sleepy Bayou La Loutre. Or you might
drive the back road into Yscloskey in the fall and be startled by the
sudden appearance of a marauding school of redfish in a placid lagoon
that looks like it's been there for ten thousand years.

Post-Katrina, many folks far from here asked the sensible question
of why people would choose to live in a floodplain set in one of the
world's busiest hurricane alleys. But for bayou people like the Robins,
Charlo Inabnet, and thousands of others up and down the Louisiana
Gulf Coast, the question becomes, "How could I live anyplace else?" Life
is inseparable from their work, and much of the work is inseparable
from this land.

Though a relative newcomer, Charlo, born in New Orleans to a
French-Yugoslav mother and an Arkansas father, temperamentally fits

in here. A shy, almost reclusive man, his politics, such as he has any, run to the blue-collar libertarian side. You can learn this after a few Miller Lites, of which he is fond, coax out his deep-set gregarious nature. He often splits his time between oyster dredging and shrimp trawling, depending on the season and the appetite of the New Orleans area seafood markets. Sometimes he'll hire out to friends—"podnahs," as he puts it in his bayou accent—who run a profusion of crab traps in the sprawling Lake Borgne estuary.

Nearing sixty, Charlo is a certified old salt and adventurer, big boned and rangy, with a tanned, finely lined face that gives away a life lived mostly outdoors. He speaks with the earthy eloquence of the self-taught man that he is. He left home at sixteen, joined the Merchant Marine soon thereafter by lying about his age, and in his salad days wandered the far corners of the world, with stops in Egypt, Pakistan, Israel, and the Far East. He witnessed Hindu-Muslim riots in 1971 and was in a port at risk during at the outbreak of the Yom Kippur War between the Arabs and Israelis in 1973. For extra adventure, and a double bonus, he signed on to U.S. munitions ships delivering bombs and other weaponry to Saigon harbor during the Vietnam War.

Charlo is also hurricane hardened and hurricane wary. In September 2004, he guided his oyster lugger, the *Captain John J.*, through the dangerous chop of Lake Borgne as powerful Hurricane Ivan bullied the Louisiana coast while sweeping eastward toward the beaches of Alabama and Florida. In a safe harbor in New Orleans, when the harbor police tried to run him off, he told the cops they'd have to arrest him—no way was he going back out in the open water. The police retreated, and Charlo spent a restful night in the lee of the locks in the Industrial Canal.

At the moment, he would far rather be hunkered down there, or at least in the cloistered harbor at Violet Canal, which were among his possible destinations before fate intervened and caused him to wait out Katrina here in his house on the Hopedale Highway. At the approach of the storm, Terry, his wife, had gone ahead to stay with her sister in north Louisiana. Charlo's plan had been to take his boat to some sheltered point toward the west and north and ride out the blow there. But by the time he finished his preparations, his most direct way out, up through

Bayou La Loutre and the MR-GO, got blocked when operators of the bridge over the bayou at Yscloskey abruptly evacuated their posts and left the bridge in a closed position. His alternate route would have been a long, roundabout loop to the south and east, *toward* the approaching storm—and a dangerous gambit should the *Captain John J.* break down. Not wanting to abandon his boat, he was stuck.

Sometime around 11:30 p.m., Charlo begins to feel anxious. From the groaning and shuddering of his house, it's clear that the wind has kicked up appreciably. Loud, grating sounds in the rafters make him fear parts of the roof are being ripped away.

This house is not going to make it, he thinks. So he gathers up the bare necessities—his flashlight, a candle, a life jacket, and a life ring, tethered to a twelve-foot rope that he'd secured from his boat earlier in the day as a precaution—and leaves.

He steps outside into the howling maw and heads down his porch steps to his front yard. He has two possibilities. Does he head for his boat in the bayou across the road, or make for the neighbor's house not fifty feet west of his?

Before evacuating on the weekend, his neighbors had invited him to stay there, leaving him the key. It's a substantial house, ostensibly hurricane-proofed, a towering camp perched on and anchored to fourteen-foot-high creosote-soaked pilings driven into a deep foundation. Six eighteen-inch-diameter interior pilings, placed and bolted strategically to joists and load-bearing walls, run vertically up to the attic to give the dwelling more strength. The windows are crafted from hardened Plexiglas to withstand violent winds and blowing objects. In theory, it's as Katrina-ready a house as you might find. Its availability was so reassuring that earlier in the afternoon Charlo had moved some clothing, miscellaneous valuables, and foodstuffs into the camp. Even if his modest house got slapped around by Katrina, surely things stowed there would be safe.

Charlo makes his decision—whether to head for his boat or the big camp—near the bottom of his porch steps, when he finds his stoop flooded up to the second step and probes the dark around him with his flashlight. What he sees and hears—horizontal rain, caterwauling wind, the scudding, rising water—makes him think he'll be better off in the house next door than in the rickety *Captain John J.* He loves the boat, but if Lil' Abner owned an oyster lugger, the *John J.* might be it. Charlo increases his grip on his life ring in the crook of his left arm, turns right and sloshes toward the big camp. In the thirty seconds it takes him, the water rises from his ankles to his knees.

Charlo mounts the exterior stairs and is relieved, when he steps inside and wrestles the door shut, that the camp offers something of a reprieve from the storm's debilitating din outside. He glances up and sees a battery-operated clock on the wall. It's fifteen minutes before midnight.

Exhausted, Charlo would like to sleep but can't—he fears closing his eyes because he feels the need to stay vigilant at every moment. But the time creeps by fidgety. He tries to sit quietly, but every time he settles in, a gust of wind rattles the house or some flying object thuds against it. Charlo is a smoker. Around 1 a.m. his nicotine cravings drive him out on to the camp's rambling front porch. But once outside, he has misgivings. The wind seems stronger than ever, having already ripped away the camp's screen door and the screens from nearby windows. He peers into the blackness trying to divine the fate of his own house but he can't see a thing. As he tries to muscle his way back into the camp, the wind snaps the door from his hands. It takes all of his strength to shut it behind him.

An hour later, an unsettling thought has crept into Charlo's mind—*this house isn't going to make it, either.* He tries to brush it away, but too many unnerving things are happening. Bigger and bigger objects are crashing into the house; the roof and exterior walls in some places sound as if they're being gnawed away, as if the storm is inexorably eating its way inside. The windows are bowing in and out.

He puts on his life jacket and fetches his life ring, goes into a guest bedroom, away from all the windows, sits in a chair and rolls up his pants legs. To one leg, he duct tapes his driver's license; to the other, a Sam's Club discount store ID with his picture on it. If something bad happens, recovery crews won't have to worry about identifying him.

By 4 a.m., his prospects are beginning to look grim. One by one, the camp's fortified windows are being blown out and fierce winds are now ravaging through the house like so many poltergeists, stripping objects off the walls and hurling them violently around. He's thinking his last refuge is the windowless attic, so he makes his way down a center hall to a spot where a pull-down ladder lies tucked into the ceiling. He reaches up for the ladder cord, pulls down the steps and, clutching his life ring and flashlight, heads up.

The climb isn't that easy. The camp is now swaying demonstrably, as might a boat in a swell. At the top of the staircase, Charlo pushes aside some storage objects and grabs on to a sturdy brace that attaches the roof to the rafters. Suddenly, the house lurches—and the brace breaks free.

The attic now seems like a bad idea. Charlo's thinking: *If this gets any worse, I'm going to die.*

He's nominally a Catholic but not a particularly observant one. Still, he begins to recite a Hail Mary aloud. He prays his way down the ladder and contemplates his diminishing options.

A surreal arc of time floats by; the house is being stripped away as he watches. He decides his only chance to prevent being blown into the ether is to try to lash himself, using the rope attached to his life ring, to the centermost of the interior pilings that strut from the foundation to the roof. But the whipsawing wind howling through the hallways makes this difficult.

He is still struggling with this task when the matter is settled for him.

Charlo sees a glimmer of light, perhaps the first muted strains of dawn, then something shimmering and green. He hears a loud crashing sound and he is suddenly off of his feet, clutching his life ring with all of his might, and thrashing violently to avoid being sucked under.

A wall of water, head high, has crashed through the windows and walls of the camp and washed him into the churning void.

He's got his arm in his life ring and is being pulled down and he's thinking, "Well, that's it, I'm dead." But for some reason this doesn't bother him. He doesn't fight the water, he just goes with it, because he realizes there's simply nothing else he can do.

7. Matine's Dilemma

Armantine Marie Verdin, ninety, lives seven miles below Violet Canal with her disabled son Xavier, seventy-one, in a cozy peach-colored house on Bayou Road, just down from the lovely eighteenth-century Bayou Terre-aux-Boeufs Cemetery. Hers is a countrified neighborhood and a countrified existence.

Her yard holds a garden bearing tomatoes, cucumbers, green beans, and squash that she plants and tends each spring. Wisteria and bougain-villea paint their way up posts and trellises. Hackberry, live oak, magnolia, and even an imported palm tree grace the yard. An old-timey cistern catches rainwater, which Matine, as she is called, still prefers to drink over the "city water" that comes piped into her house. Her front porch faces a vestigial bayou, lined with young cypresses and clogged with bull tongue and elephant ear, that separates the yard from the road. Frogs, turtles, herons, and egrets (and now and then a baby alligator) wander through.

Long widowed, Matine defies her age; she could easily pass for seventy. Spry does not adequately describe her. Besides gardening, she still does the household chores and cooks dishes—gumbos, red beans and rice, etouffees and snap beans with salt meat—for herself and her son. Xavier—Neg to his family and friends—does simple chores in the nearby cemetery. His job around the house is to fetch the cistern water. Eldest of Matine's seven children, Neg was hit by a car at age twenty-one, spent three weeks in a coma, and suffered brain damage. His functional intelligence is that of about a nine-year-old, and he has lived with his mother ever since the accident. He's a short, quiet man with thinning hair and an upright posture. He's able, when inclined, to exchange pleasantries, and given now and then to bursting out into the odd soliloquy. Matine dotes over him.

Matine seems like a spirit from another time, and in a way she is. Diminutive and determined, soft-spoken and stoic, she grew up in an extended French-speaking Native American family in the marshy wilds near Pointe-aux-Chenes in Terrebonne Parish, about fifty miles to the southwest. Well after the twentieth century had come, her clan held on to nineteenth-century ways, in part because their poverty gave them little choice. Radios, telephones, electricity, running water, plumbing, schools—Matine knew nothing of these things as a child. She can neither read nor write. Yet she remains the matriarch of her clan, revered and respected as a storehouse of knowledge and lore. Her first language is French, as is her surname, both owing to the intermarriage of her clan's women in the nineteenth century to French fur traders and trappers. Her English is halting (as is Neg's) but passable as long as the conversations aren't too complicated. Ask her what she is and she will reply: "Je suis un Indien Français."

Matine's people lived on bayou banks and *cheniers*—natural alluvial mounds rising from the marsh—in clusters of planked cabins on stilts with thatched palmetto roofs and baked mud fireplaces. They were proud, independent hunter-gatherers and small-lot farmers scratching out a subsistence living in the marshy, isolated oasis of scenic poverty they called La Pointe. Though they lacked in material goods, the land proved bountiful. A seed put in the ground grew readily; the marshes, swamps, and bayous teemed with fish and game. A few hardy Cajuns lived in their midst, but for generations, until the coming of oil exploration brought a wave of new settlement, the French Indians had the Pointe-aux-Chenes wilds pretty much to themselves.

La Pointe also had its dangers. Matine vividly remembers when the 1926 hurricane howled through their finger of land, blowing down huts and swamping the village in raging tides. She was eleven years old and recalls spending a terrified night on the veranda of a neighbor's cabin, sitting with her siblings in a pirogue, a low-slung version of the canoe, while her stepfather, chest deep in water, held the small boat so it wouldn't blow away. She remembers cows, bawling with terror, floating past the house during the peak of the flood. The Verdins survived, but their house didn't, and they went hungry for days before relief teams reached them.

The history of the French Indians is somewhat murky, save that they are the remnants of once mighty tribes—most likely the Chitimacha, Biloxi, or Choctaw—that lived on and roamed the uplands of Louisiana and Mississippi, only to be slowly and eradicably washed down to the ridge ends of the bayous of Terrebonne and Lafourche parishes by the relentless incursions of the white man. Matine's father, Lovency Billiot, was a muskrat trapper, fisherman, and jack-of-all-trades, as was her husband, Toussaint Verdin.

Matine and Toussaint left Pointe-aux-Chenes in the 1940s with a knot of other La Pointe Indians, invited by an entrepreneur to form a colony of muskrat trappers in St. Bernard Parish. They came at the apex of the muskrat trade. The Indians were experienced and hardy trappers; they got leases of muskrat lands and a cut of the profits from the sale of the furs they trapped. For many years, it was a good living and a good life. Where they came from, white people sometimes called them "sauvages," and stole communal lands to which the unschooled Indians could produce little formal proof of ownership. But here no one much messed with them, even as their pastoral landscape slowly filled in and began to feel slightly suburbanized.

The Verdins and their French Indian friends, the Dardars and Billiots among them, settled on property that forms part of the ridgeline of old Bayou Terre-aux-Boeufs where the early Isleños put down their first roots. Eventually, the Verdins and others were able to buy the land and build their own houses. In the topography of St. Bernard, the French Indian settlement sits on relatively high ground.

Which is why, in part, Matine, with the approach of Hurricane Katrina, resolved not to leave. Fierce Hurricane Betsy in 1965 had dumped tons of rain and high tides on St. Bernard, yet her house, elevated on two-foot wooden and concrete piers, got only a few inches of water in it (and again, the parish at that time was unprotected by hurricane levees, which were built in response to Betsy). A bigger reason, however, was Neg.

Neg, though perfectly ambulatory, isn't very portable. Change disturbs him. He has his routines, which include sitting on the covered front porch and watching the world go by, and his obsessions, including an unexplained fear of the police. The cemetery, where he goes sometimes to pull weeds and gaze over the whitewashed aboveground tombs and grandiose religious statuary, mesmerizes him. Graves date back to 1787, and many early Isleños pioneers are buried there. Neg has his own crypt with his name on it, birth date in granite. He often seems mystically attached to both his home and the cemetery, and Matine understands that evacuation would be traumatic. Still, she would have preferred to go; when cajolery failed, she told Neg, in exasperation, "If we don't leave, the police will come." It didn't faze him. As stubborn as he is gentle, Neg dug in his heels.

This doesn't stop Matine's family from urging her to go anyway. On Saturday, two days before the storm's landfall, Matine's twenty-five-year-old granddaughter, Monique Michelle Verdin, the only child of her youngest son Herbert, visits her grandmother to strongly suggest that she evacuate. Monique, a photographer, lives in New Orleans with her boyfriend, Mark Krasnoff, an actor and documentary filmmaker with an interest in South Louisiana ethnography, and their plan is to wait out Katrina in Baton Rouge about a hundred miles west. She invites Matine and Neg to come with them. The radio and television are abuzz with Katrina warnings—indeed, Junior Rodriguez, the parish president, is strongly suggesting that all residents get out, and George W. Bush, at the urging of Governor Kathleen Blanco, has declared a federal state of emergency in South Louisiana. But Monique finds there's no alarm at her grandmother's house. The laundry is flapping in a light breeze on a clothesline out back and Matine is at the stove in her tidy kitchen, frying up a batch of fish and putting the finishing touches on a shrimp etouffee for supper. It's clear, after a few minutes of discussion, that Matine isn't going anywhere.

Matine says not to worry. Herbert, Monique's dad, is planning to stay and has been joined by Matine's grandson Mike Vetra, who does odd jobs with Herbert and has driven over from his home in the nearby New Orleans suburb of Harvey. Matine assures Monique that she and Neg will be in good hands should something go awry.

Everybody likes Herbert Verdin, who has lived on and off with Matine and Neg for the past couple of years. Medium tall, dark, ruggedly built with a mild gumbo paunch, his Native American heritage is transparent: he has the dignified yet fiercely feral features of those Plains

Indians in some nineteenth-century daguerreotype. He's a gifted raconteur, hilarious and profane, spinning out stories in a deep, slip-sliding voice with an accent as thick as a cane syrup. Herbert's idea of a perfect evening is sitting around with his podnahs, drinking a few beers and swapping tales.

Like many skilled but undereducated men from deep bayou country, Herbert does whatever he can to make a living. At the moment, it's air-conditioner repair and installation with Mike, a strapping thirty-something who is the son of Herbert's older sister, Imelda Verdin Vetra, Matine's middle daughter. Mike has an extravagant story of his own: a few years back, he was ambushed by a drunk who, angered that he had been tossed out of a bar, shot Mike at close range in the face with a sawed-off shotgun. The drunk's quarrel was with others, not Mike. He simply happened to be the first person to leave the bar as the drunk lay in wait outside the door, determined to shoot whoever walked through it. Incredibly, Mike survived, though disfigured and with slurred speech.

Herbert, though for now content to wrangle air conditioners with Mike, is agile at many crafts not particularly practiced or valued elsewhere, but worthy here. He can trap, hunt, and skin fur-bearing animals; he can fish, set a trawl, build a crab trap. He can operate all manner of boats, including the tippy pirogue. The boat is prized hereabouts for its ability to float a paddler in extremely shallow water, making it easier to hunt frogs and alligators or fish tidal flats for redfish. No official census exists, but probably every other household along Bayou Road has a pirogue stashed in the garage or tilted up on its side against the house. This cultural idiosyncrasy will prove providential in the wake of Katrina.

On Sunday, the Verdin household carries on as it might otherwise on a late summer afternoon. Herbert and Mike buy a mess of fresh blue crabs from a seafood vendor happy to get rid of them cheap—he's evacuating in advance of Katrina's approach. Matine and Herbert boil them up spicy in Zatarain's, the local seasoning mix, and they feast on the succulent crustaceans. Matine has also cooked a pot roast. She is edgy and Neg is fidgety, but Herbert's and Mike's presence is reassuring.

Nothing much rattles Herbert anyway. Besides, he has plotted a couple of escape scenarios, having dragged up onto the front porch one of two pirogues he keeps at Matine's house. The other sits strategically on the back porch. And a neighbor just down the road, before evacuating, also has come over to say he's leaving his outboard-powered flatboat on its trailer in his yard, keys in the ignition. "If you need it," he tells Herbert, "take it." Herbert thanks him profusely.

By 11:30 p.m., Katrina is delivering some blustery winds and driving rain but not much more. Matine and Neg retire to their rooms and go to sleep.

Their rest ends at 4 a.m. when the house is shaken by a roaring gust. Mike rouses them, calling from the hall, "You better get out of there, just in case we've got to leave." The storm is blasting away at the trees outside; the house is moaning and groaning. Slashing rain on its tin roof sounds like a herd of stampeding animals. Matine peers through a window at the raging storm and thinks, "We can't leave now, even if we want to. We've come to the dance, and I guess we're gonna dance now."

Neg pads into the living room and sits silently on the couch while Matine goes to the kitchen. She hits a light switch, realizes the power is out, but still manages to light the gas stove and oven. She makes a pot of coffee and puts on a batch of biscuits. Their cheery aroma soon fills the small house and everyone has breakfast. Herbert has been in and out of the house, occasionally wandering onto the covered front porch to watch the storm. He reports that, despite the raging wind, all seems well.

The wind, though, isn't giving any quarter and Matine begins to have a premonition—something bad is coming. Neither she nor Neg can swim, so she tells Mike to drag one of Herbert's pirogues into the house. Mike's a big guy—maybe 280 pounds. He goes out on the back porch and returns, bearing the light fourteen-foot wooden boat under his arm. He plunks it down with a thud on the wooden kitchen floor.

Daylight comes and around 8:30 the phone rings. It's Monique calling her father. She's watching the storm on TV from Baton Rouge and sees the eye passing over the eastern edge of St. Bernard Parish.

"Are you OK?" she wants to know.

"The weather's real bad," Herbert replies, "but we'll be all right. That old dead cherry tree in the yard—it's still standing."

Monique, somewhat relived, hangs up. Neither realizes how prematurely Herbert has spoken.

He walks back out on the porch. He sniffs. Something is in the air—something different. Matine and Mike smell it, too, and they know it well. It's the warm-muck methane aroma that boggy marsh releases when you walk on it. It's almost overpowering.

Matine, in the kitchen, looks out and suddenly sees water coursing down their driveway. Herbert sees it, too. The velocity startles everyone. Matine, alarmed, calls out: "Mike, I think we're gonna need a bigger boat, cher! Tell Herbie!"

Mike relays the message but Herbert already knows something is terribly awry. He looks out of an eastward-facing window and sees a startling sight: a pickup truck wandering along the narrow track, called Billiot Lane, that runs parallel to the Verdin driveway. Herbert knows the truck belongs to a neighbor—and he also knows the neighbor is gone.

No one's in the truck—it's floating, on a brisk current.

With water already coursing up to the top of the concrete porch steps, Herbert dashes onto the front porch, unties the second pirogue, and pushes off to fetch the neighbor's boat. He's suddenly in the wildest ride he's ever taken in a pirogue.

In a matter of minutes, the water has formed itself into rapids frothed by howling winds. Herbert finds himself literally sailing down the driveway and out across the highway, paddling like mad to keep the small boat on track. The reason for the marsh smell becomes obvious: Katrina's surge has run through the wetlands like a huge plow, scooping up vast marsh mats into her turbulent maw. The rapidly rising water is full of these hazardous chunks.

Pirogues are made for flat water, not for navigating the windswept whitewater river that Katrina has suddenly created here. But Herbert at least has the wind and current more or less at his back. Still, it's raining, he's taking some wave froth over the side, and it requires all of his paddling skills to keep the boat from flipping over. He goes flying in toward a chain-link fence where the powerboat is tethered. The wind drives him hard up against the fence, where he's able to grab on to the bigger boat and hop in. He scrambles to the steering console, sees the keys in the ignition and tries to start the boat.

Chooga-chooga-choo, chooga-chooga-choo.

The engine sputters and coughs but won't start.

He tries the manual gasoline choke, hits the ignition again. Same result.

Panicked, Herbert looks back toward Matine's house.

The water by now is at least four feet high and pouring in.

Damn, Herbert says to himself. *I better get my ass back over there.*

Indeed, inside the house, events have taken a surreal and dangerous turn.

Matine, returning from the kitchen to join Neg in the living room, suddenly finds herself in moving knee-deep water. She watches as a pair of shoes from her bedroom float by. She turns back to look toward the kitchen and hears a loud noise. Peering in, she's startled.

"Mike," she yells, "the refrigerator just went over!"

A river is suddenly running through the house. Objects are rising, tumbling, floating past. Mike sloshes into the kitchen and beckons Neg and Matine to get into the pirogue. They manage, with some difficulty, to do so. Mike decides he'll climb in, too—a mistake.

His weight is too great and the pirogue tilts—and dumps its occupants into ripping currents.

They all come up sputtering, working desperately to regain their footing. "Y'all have got to get on the couch, Grandma," Mike yells.

They wade with the rising water to the living room, Matine and Neg clambering onto the couch. By this time, water is up to Matine's chest. The couch, though, proves surprisingly buoyant. Mike has followed them, towing the pirogue. He watches in amazement as the couch begins to rise toward the ceiling—with Matine and Neg on it.

Matine suddenly fears being trapped inside the house.

"We've got to get out of here," she says. "We've got to get to the porch."

Mike agrees. The water is now up to *his* chest.

The front door has been knocked open by the current. Mike maneuvers the boat alongside the couch and Matine and Neg get in. He begins to tow them out and realizes that, at the velocity the water is rising, soon he won't be able to float the boat under the eaves of the front door.

"Duck down," he says.

Mike scrambles forward, pulling the boat, dog-paddling furiously to gain traction. Matine and Neg bend forward as far as they can—and they barely clear the opening. Another few minutes and they would have been sharing space with a ceiling fan.

They're scarcely outside when there's a sudden lurch: the porch has separated from the house, but its concrete footings keep it from floating away. Matine looks behind her and realizes she's within reaching distance of a bracket that supports a large room air conditioner slotted high up into the exterior wall. She grabs the bracket and holds on to help Mike keep the pirogue from being blown into the open. She could be a kid again in that hut in Pointe-aux-Chenes in the 1926 hurricane. In fact, the effect is like being on a ship in steep swells as the disconnected porch rolls from side to side.

Herbert, meanwhile, finds both the wind and currents in his face as he fights his way back toward the house in his pirogue. He uses partially submerged cars and fences as temporary lees, lying up behind them during strong gusts and paddling like crazy during the relative lulls. Arriving, he peers up under the eaves of the porch.

"How ya doin', Ma?" he asks.

"I'm OK. How you makin' out, Herbie?"

"I'm fine. Now, listen, you need to come out of there—you and Neg need to lie down so you don't hit your head. Mike will push and I'll pull."

"You need a bigger boat, Herbie," Matine replies.

"OK," he says. "But let's get you out first."

Neg lies back; Matine does, too, but straightens up as the pirogue floats out from under the porch eaves. She bumps her head on an exposed nail.

Matine groans in pain. "You do that one more time, Herbie, and that's it!" she snaps.

Herbert laughs. "Oh, Ma. C'mon, we gonna make it."

"OK, Herbie. But let's stop talkin' about makin' it and go."

Matine is serious about another boat. She's surveyed her suddenly drowned and calamitous world and doesn't think much of their chances of crossing any distance to safety in the pirogues. She tells Herbert she knows of one more or less across the highway, at a neighbor's house just down from the graceful old Spanish-Isleños style St. Bernard Catholic Church where she and Neg attend mass. He makes the arduous crossing again as Mike manages to hold the pirogue in place. He comes back, having swapped his pirogue for an aluminum flatboat—it has no engine and isn't much longer than the pirogues, but it's far wider and thus much more stable.

"Will this work, Ma?"

Matine manages a smile. "Oh, yeah, this will work."

After some difficulty, all four of them find themselves in the flatboat.

Herbert surveys their situation and decides they have two shelter choices within reach. The nearby church has a bell tower they might be able to climb into. Behind and south of them about fifty yards, a neighbor has a compact tin-clad red barn with a second-story hayloft.

By now, though, the wind has shifted from the west-northwest, meaning it's blowing directly down the highway. Crossing the road with this load in the boat might prove impossible—they'd simply be flushed south to points uncertain. If they struck an object in open water—a submerged car or a fence—they could easily capsize. Nobody has life preservers.

Herbert decides on the barn and they shove off, towing the pirogue behind them on a short rope. It soon becomes clear they're going to have to triangulate—the wind and currents are taking them smack toward the barn owner's house about fifty yards away. But suddenly they're stuck; the pirogue, trailing on a rope, curls around a tree trunk and gets hung up.

"Cut the rope!" Herbert yells, handing Matine a knife he's carrying. She makes surprisingly swift work of the rope—the pirogue floats free.

They're down to one boat.

The flatboat picks up speed on the wind and goes in so hard that they smack the side of the house, watching in amazement as about half the bricks covering that side of the building fall off like an avalanche into the water. Herbert and Mike then use their hands to pull their way along the house in the direction of the barn behind them and, during a lull in the wind, paddle fiercely to make the final twenty-five yards.

The deluge has done them one small favor. When they arrive at the barn, the water is now about seven to eight feet high—about three feet below the sill of the barn's second-story window. Herbert stands and finds the window locked, so he breaks the glass with the board he's been using for a paddle and scrambles in. With Mike holding the boat steady, Herbert beckons Matine forward. He kneels in the window, reaches down and grabs her hand.

At that moment, the wind shifts and blows the boat out from under her. Herbert doesn't have the best purchase or angle to pull her up and suddenly she's dangling, her legs swinging back and forth, as Herbert groans to get leverage.

"Ma, what you got, some junk in your trunk?" says Herbert.

"You doin' this on purpose, huh, Herbie?" she says.

"No, no, Ma. C'mon, Mike, give me a hand."

Mike by this time has pulled the boat back into position. He puts his hands on Matine's rump and pushes. Hebert pulls. Matine rises, gets her foot on the windowsill, and makes it into the barn, ruffled but unhurt. Soon, Neg is safe inside, too.

Mike—all 280 pounds of him—is not so easy. When he grabs on to Herbert's hand, Herbert almost comes out of the barn. The boat goes out from under Mike and he's dangling, too, yelling at Hebert not to let go. Matine and Neg grab onto Hebert and all three of them pull. Slowly but surely Big Mike rises.

The water, meanwhile, continues to rise, too.

All four of them stand, looking out the barn window at the sprawling lake around them. Drowned cars and trucks float by; furniture washed out of houses bobs up and down. Water covers Matine's house almost up to the rain gutters. This has taken less than fifteen minutes. They are all mute with shock.

Soon, though, the Katrina tide slackens, as does the wind. It appears that the loft is high enough to keep them safe from the flood. But they have nothing—no food, no water, no flashlights, no candles, and no immediate way to get any of those things. They have one distraction:

slapping at the vicious swarms of fleas rising from the loft floor and attacking their ankles, arms, and faces.

Almost three hours go by. An eerie calm and silence set in—as if they might be the only living creatures about. The sun peeks through clouds. But the silence is soon cut by a familiar sound—an approaching boat. A small outboard appears, puttering down the middle of the Katrina-made bayou that was a few hours ago Bayou Road.

"Here, we're over here!" yells Herbert.

The man at the helm waves and comes over; he's a guy named Frankie Asevado whom Herbert knows, another survivor washed out of a house nearby. He surveys the Verdins and decides the boat he's in is too small to take them.

"I'll be back quick with a bigger one," Frankie says. "I've got to pick up my dogs, anyway."

Frankie returns in a matter of minutes in a broad aluminum outboard, a nineteen- or twenty-footer, and he wasn't lying about the dogs. Four of them—all pit bulls—are anxiously pacing the deck.

Matine doesn't like dogs.

"I gotta go in there, Herbert?"

"Up to you, Ma."

Matine looks things over.

"I'm goin'," she says.

Getting in Frankie's boat from the barn window poses the same problem they faced getting out of the flatboat: a gap. But Herbert and Mike solve this by battering out two of the barn's tin wall panels so that Frankie can slide his outboard right up alongside the barn.

With Herbert's help, Matine and Neg board the boat.

After settling in, Matine looks at Herbert and then her drowned house. An anxious look washes over her. "Ma boîte, cher. J'ai oublié ma boîte. Je ne peux pas aller sans ma boîte."

Many bayou elderly of Matine's generation eschew banks and stash their money and valuables in mattresses or small boxes. Matine's un-adorned metal box—her "boîte"—Herbert knows, is hidden in the freezer compartment of the toppled refrigerator in the flooded house. It contains about three hundred dollars and some personal papers. Matine is obsessed with her box.

Herbert points to the house. "Ma, you can't go in there. It's wrecked. But, look, don't worry. I'll catch up with you. Me and Mike will get your box."

Herbert has no idea how he'll retrieve his mother's box with eight feet of water in the house, but he knows he has to try.

"And watch the house, too?" says Matine, plaintively.

Herbert realizes Matine is in denial about what's just happened to her house. The water will have to go down precipitously before even Herbert can enter it.

"Where do you think you'll go?" he says to Frankie. "These two, they might not do too good in a shelter."

Frankie says he isn't sure but has one idea. He's heard there's a clutch of fishermen at Violet Canal who have big boats and ample provisions and may be taking in survivors. They will head that way and hope for the best.

8. Ricky's Ark

Back near Violet Canal, the scene outside Susan Robin's rain-streaked van windshield, looking northwest up the St. Bernard Highway, is disturbing to say the least.

The half-mile-long canopy of stately oaks up ahead is rapidly becoming a tunnel filling with a gathering tidal surge. Giant branches are bending and swaying. Water is also beginning to sheet in higher from the roadside off to her right. The wind continues to buffet the van. Power and phone lines are crackling, snapping, and whipping overhead.

Any thoughts of getting to shelter in Chalmette have been crushed. But returning to Violet—where clearly a major flood is also rising from the east—seems like folly, too.

Panic begins to set in. The turquoise Chevy Express van, parked on the open highway between two converging, wind-whipped tidal surges, now seems like awfully flimsy cover.

Susan and her brother Sidney talk it over and, folly or not, feel they have no choice. The surge bearing down on them in a slow, mounding wave will easily overwhelm the van.

Susan puts the van in reverse, backs onto the shoulder, and steers for the center of the highway back in the direction of Violet Canal. One thought is to simply try to get as close to Ricky as possible and pray for rescue. She has great faith in both Ricky and his boat.

As she begins to drive the short distance, she's suddenly confronted with a nightmarish obstacle course: the water is now so high on the road that she can no longer see the center line, nor the growing number of submerged obstacles in her way. She needs to drive fast but can't, fearing the van could stall if the wheels splash too much water up into the engine block. She can feel her tires crunch and bump over logs, boards, fence posts, and other detritus. She cringes each time. A flat tire could be a fatal disaster.

Floating and flying objects—including bricks and roof debris blown from nearby houses—continue to bombard them, putting sizable dents and nicks in the side of the van, miraculously missing the windows. The utility poles ahead are bowing so precipitously in the raging wind that the van barely has clearance.

Suddenly, just ahead of her, Susan sees a pole sag and sway like a giant slow-moving wiper blade. She brakes, grips the wheel, and prepares for the pole to smash through the windshield.

The van just squeaks under it.

Susan can't understand how they're still under power. She's pushing a wake ahead of her like a boat, and the water coursing across the road is splashing up on her windshield. They're running out of time.

Rising up on her left, Susan spots the Violet water tower. She is only a couple of blocks from the canal and—if a way could be found to get aboard—the safety of the *Lil' Rick* or one of the other boats in the harbor. But to her right, she sees something even more heartening—a short, narrow lane that cuts up to the top of the twenty-foot-high Mississippi River levee, by far the highest ground around. The lane previously served a ferry terminal. These days it's used mostly by locals wanting a view of the river and fishermen who utilize a small-boat launch on the other side.

In a flash, Susan realizes this is her only chance to survive; the upper slopes of the levee are still high and dry. With the road entrance already covered by swirling floodwaters, she has to make an educated guess where the turnoff is. She slows and makes a wide right and then, feeling the roadway beneath her, urges the sputtering van onward. As she begins to gain elevation, she guns the Chevy out of the rising water and scoots up to the top of the levee.

Her relief is immense—and fleeting.

Two or three other vehicles, also bearing fugitives from the flood, have made it up to the top of the levee. From their collective perch they witness a calamitous sight. People are being swept from their houses in the Violet subdivision and are clamoring to get to any place—roofs, trees, small boats—where they can escape the rising water. Meanwhile, the Industrial Canal surge that chased them up the levee is colliding with the Lake Borgne surge swamping Violet Canal, creating malicious currents and threatening to do the unthinkable—spill over the levee and into the Mississippi River, from the *land* side.

Susan thinks their situation can't be worse—till she glances at the river. The Mississippi itself has begun to flow rapidly *upstream,* threatening to leap from its banks—brown, turbulent, debris-clogged waters are scouring their way up the *other* side of the levee. Their safe perch no longer looks safe at all.

If the river keeps rising, they'll be caught between the colliding floods and washed from the top of the levee to God knows where.

Ricky Robin has temporarily lost track of Susan and the crew in the van. He would be more frantic than he is save that his own safety—and that of many others now scrambling out of harm's way at Violet Canal— seems in no way guaranteed. From his perch in the wheelhouse of the *Lil' Rick,* he is seeing close up the chaos that Susan is witnessing from high on the levee a quarter mile away.

Merely watching isn't an option. The *Lil' Rick,* though its booms are down, has been bullied sideways again to the Katrina wind. Between the wind and the ferocious currents, Ricky is having to use every bit of his seaman's skills to hold the trawler steady in its position hard up against the Violet Canal north levee. Though the boat is under power and throttled up, the trawler's redundant high-strength nylon tie-down ropes are stretched to the breaking point—and singing in high octaves on the gale. Ricky isn't at all sure they will hold. If his boat breaks loose, engine power alone won't save him. The seventy-ton *Lil' Rick* would be a pawn in the maw of the storm, and a battering ram that could sink any boat smaller than it in the tight quarters of Violet Canal. Caught in the wrong position, the trawler could easily capsize.

Ricky also has a feeling he'll soon have company besides his cousin Dwight Alphonso and his son Dwight Jr. The escalating surge has over-run the lower-lying ramparts of the Violet subdivision down by the water tower; houses have water up to their windows and the flood is rising rapidly. More and more people are being flushed from their homes. Those who don't have powerboats, or at least pirogues, are stumbling through the water, some clutching meager possessions, most with nothing at all, heading for the levees on both sides of the canal—or, at any rate, those parts of the levees that haven't already been topped. Some have started to swim. Others, on slightly higher ground nearer the St. Bernard Highway, are desperately trying to make it across the road to the Mississippi River levee. But the water is beginning to trap them. Others are scrambling out of windows or clawing their way on to roof-tops. Pandemonium is setting in.

Ricky has experienced some bad blows before: he's been caught in numerous squalls at sea, when steeply pitched waves quickly mounded to fifteen feet in blinding rain. And once, as he entered the MR-GO from the gulf, his cargo hold laden with shrimp, the *Lil' Rick* was struck head-on by the dancing funnel of a huge waterspout. The trawler heeled over to port about sixty degrees—like a catamaran sailing precariously on its gunwales—and only a "Hail Mary" rotation of the wheel by Ricky kept the boat from capsizing.

But this is different. This is a treacherous, unpredictable storm play-ing havoc with scores of people suddenly cast into peril in a tight radius around his boat. Ricky now knows there's a great deal riding on his captain's skills, and on the *Lil' Rick* itself.

There's a funny aphorism that floats around down here: that bayou men are more faithful to their boats than to their wives. Ricky laughs that one off but it perhaps holds a kernel of truth. For Ricky and the trawler are not just man and boat. If a great deal is riding on the *Lil' Rick,* a great deal of Ricky's life, love, and skills have gone into it.

Ricky Robin designed the *Lil' Rick* in 1974 in an empty parking lot at St. Bernard High's vocational school with a piece of chalk, some string, and a stick after having envisioned the boat for some time in his head. He sketched out its contours, full scale, on the rough gray concrete surface, then set about laying the keel. His workshop was his high school shop class, where he'd excelled at welding. Ricky never both-ered to render his parking-lot sketch into drawings. The design simply stayed in his head. It was an ambitious project for a kid barely nineteen years old.

Then, realizing he didn't have the means to get the heavy steel keel for a fifty-six-foot trawler home in one piece, Ricky cut it into sections with a blowtorch, loaded them on a school bus (with the permission of a friendly school bus driver), and hauled them home to Yscloskey. There, they sat for a while in his parents' backyard, amid the trawls, fuel tanks, rigging, and other functional ornaments of a commercial fisherman's home, as he pondered how to raise the cash to build his dream boat.

Ricky had always been a bright but fitful student, clearly more enamored of crafts than art, and prone to skip classes. He'd even tried to drop out of school once, with intentions of commercial fishing full-time. Celie, however, his diminutive but feisty mother, put her foot down. Ricky, however long it took, was *going* to graduate from high school.

Impish, Ricky was a guy you couldn't overlook. He was good-natured and boisterous, with a disarming smile and a sharp working-class wit. Even as a young teenager, he was prone to sneak away from home to hitchhike up the road to a party where there was music and beer. Such shenanigans kept him in constant low-grade trouble with his parents. Once, when a spray-painted message appeared overnight across the face of the soaring Yscloskey water tower, Celie Robin instantly recognized her son's mischief. The message read: "This is God's Contry"—country being a word Ricky often misspelled. But a ready smile and an irrepressible sense of humor usually won him a quick pardon.

He also possessed a fondness for the girls and dancing—he even enrolled in dance lessons. Celie recalls him practicing his steps with the same ardor and determination that he approached his other favorite pastime in those days: muskrat trapping. Ricky favored ballroom styles with an Isleño cultural anchor, dances on the Latin side like the tango and rumba, though disco was in the mix. He still has in the far back of his closet a ruffled sequined shirt—now a few sizes too small—and high-heeled disco boots that look like they came right out of *Saturday Night Fever.* Somewhere along the way, Ricky also picked up the trumpet and learned to play it on his own. He can still blow a respectable rendition of the New Orleans jazz standard "When the Saints Go Marching In."

Ricky, second of the Robins' four children and firstborn son, never thought much about college. Yscloskey boys just didn't. He'd grown up fishing with his father, Charlito, an old-school Isleño taskmaster, and his cousin Ronald, and Ronald's father, John Robin, and he couldn't imagine any other life. He recalls being three or four years old and lying atop the warm and thrumming wooden housing of the flathead Chrysler engine that powered his dad's twenty-six-foot hand-hewn trawler, the *Theresa R.,* as they idled in and out of Yscloskey on early mornings on their way to nearby fishing grounds. Often cousin Ronald and Uncle John fished nearby in their boat, the *St. Phillip.*

By the time he was seven or eight, Ricky had mastered the pirogue and would rig tiny trawls that he would pull behind the small boat as he paddled up and down a slough near his home, sometimes catching a handful of shrimp or some unlucky minnows that he'd throw back. At fourteen, he'd graduated to an outboard-powered flatboat kitted out with a sixteen-foot-diameter trawl and rigging he'd designed himself. Yscloskey kids had great freedom to roam the surrounding woodlands, bayous, lakes, and marshes—indeed, before the ravages of saltwater intrusion wrought partly by the construction of the MR-GO, vast oak-clad cheniers ran deep into the marshes in and around Yscloskey and served as havens for upland wildlife like deer and wild boar, not to mention playgrounds for rambunctious kids. It was, as Ronald Robin describes it, "like the Wild West down there back then"—and Charlito's only admonition to his son was that he get home by dark.

But once, as Ricky trawled for shrimp without success in an out-lying bayou where an old family friend had a camp, the friend convinced him to stay and try his luck at the change of the tide. Ricky made his last set about an hour before sunset and soon found his trawl too heavy to pull in. He thought he'd snagged a stump or filled up the trawl with bottom muck—both common hazards of dragging nets in these relatively shallow bayous. He faced a difficult choice: to cut the trawl free, an expensive loss that most certainly would displease his father, although it would allow him to get home before dark. Or, he could putter home at a snail's pace, dragging the net behind him, knowing he would run afoul of Charlito's strictly enforced curfew.

He puttered until he encountered another family friend heading to the Yscloskey docks in his own substantial trawler. Ricky explained his problem and the man offered to lift Ricky's trawl with his winch and load it on his boat, freeing Ricky to scurry home before dark closed in. When he did, however, Ricky's heavy net had a gratifying explanation:

he hadn't caught the bottom. His trawl held what a scale would later verify as nine hundred pounds of shrimp.

Ricky hitched his flatboat to the trawler and they motored in on the slow-moving shrimp boat. They arrived at a darkening dock, Ricky greatly alarmed to see his father and a group of neighbors pacing anxiously. Charlito was a disciplinarian with a flash of temper. He was on the verge of thinking Ricky was spinning a tall tale when he stepped aboard the boat and examined the shrimp-filled trawl for himself. It had been a season when shrimp were scarce, and even seasoned veterans were coming back empty-handed. Charles Robin, a man spare in his praise, declared to all within earshot, "My son, he's quite the fisherman."

Boatbuilding for Ricky was almost a matter of osmosis; there always seemed to be a boat in progress up on blocks in the Robins' Yscloskey backyard. Charlito had absorbed the skill from his father and his father from his. Bill Hyland, the parish historian, says there's no official census on the number of backyard boatbuilders in lower St. Bernard Parish, but a significant percentage of the male population still practices the craft. "You see this in certain isolated cultures," he says. "Since they have no one else to turn to for the skills and products fundamental to their lives and livelihoods, they learn to do it themselves."

By nine or ten Ricky was learning how to swing a hammer and use a saw, a level, and a sander, and when Charlito wanted to trade up from the *Theresa R.*, he started building a second wooden shrimp boat, a forty-two-foot flat-bottomed trawler they would christen the *St. Raymond*. Ricky recalls being mesmerized as the boat came together under his dad's painstaking backyard craftsmanship, though he wasn't skilled enough yet to be of much help with the carpentry. But he loved the boat. "It was a lucky boat," he recalls, "and my father always told me I brought him luck on that boat. 'Eres buena suerte,' he would say to me in Spanish. It was like that all my life with him. Every time I went with my father on the *St. Raymond*, it was shrimp, shrimp, shrimp—piles of shrimp."

Ricky was in high school when his father laid the keel for his third and most ambitious project, the fifty-two-foot *Ellie Margaret*, and by this time he was a good carpenter and welder both. He helped on the boat at home, and in shop class at school he designed and welded some steel into an ornate oversized steering wheel that was so big that, when mounted on the *Ellie Margaret's* console, it took up too much room in the tight cabin. It had to be replaced with a wheel of more orthodox size. Ricky also roped his entire shop class into a somewhat clandestine project to build the complex metal double booms for the *Ellie Margaret's* trawls. This involved raiding the pipe yard of a local oil-field equipment fabrication company for raw materials, and using a misappropriated school bus to haul the booty back to shop class, where the outriggers were welded together by Ricky and his pals.

"We should have stayed together," he says of his shop class friends. "We would have our own shipyard by now." The booms, too, got delivered by school bus to the Robin backyard. Ricky never told his dad where the materials came from.

Ricky had his own boat-building ambitions, based in part on pragmatic considerations, in part on his dream to fish in waters far beyond those his father had ever imagined. For one thing, the hot, humid, corrosive South Louisiana climate took its toll on wooden boats. "I didn't want a wooden boat," he says. "Too much caulking, too much sanding, too many nails, too much paint. And anyway, a wooden boat wouldn't have done me any good. The way I fished it would never have held up in the seas." Ricky also wanted to sail far beyond the St. Bernard estuary. "I wanted the open gulf; I wanted to get out of the marsh, out of the heat, out of the mosquitoes and the gnats."

To fulfill these ambitions, Ricky needed money. He hired on as his father's full-time deckhand aboard the *Ellie Margaret,* saving his pennies by living at home and "messing with the keel in my spare time," gradually welding it back together. In between, he enrolled in a vocational school welding course to further sharpen his skills for the ambitious project ahead. Yet even friends who knew of Ricky's energy and determination were skeptical that a seaworthy seventy-ton steel trawler—what would be the first homemade *steel* shrimp boat in all of St. Bernard Parish—was going to emerge in the Robin family backyard from the welding torch and rivet gun of a kid.

His project was going slowly—not yet twenty-one, Ricky married his first wife, Denise, his longtime high-school sweetheart, and moved into a house next to his parents. The distraction of being a newlywed and Charlito's demands on his time seemed to leave little room for boatbuilding. Then fate intervened.

Father and son were coming in one Friday from a long, taxing trip. It had been a blustery day, the seas were rough, the shrimp were scarce, and Charlito had snagged and torn up a couple of trawls. They were headed home pretty much empty-handed; Ricky had promised to take his new wife out dancing and they were running late. "I was aggravated and my father was in a bit of a mood, and when he got like that he could be a rough man to work with—like Captain Bligh. Actually, worse than Captain Bligh. He was particular how things got done on his boat. He would show you once, but that was it and you had better be paying attention."

As they motored in to their dock, wind at their back, Charlito slowed the boat and instructed Ricky to lasso a piling with the *Ellie Margaret's* bow line. Ricky kept tossing the rope but the wind kept blowing it off course.

Irritated, Charlito snapped, "Catch the piling, dammit!"

Ricky's retort: "I would catch the piling if you knew how to run this boat. Use your power, Pop!"

Charlito goosed the engine and the trawler almost rammed the dock before he roughly popped it into reverse to back it off—a development Ricky should have taken as a bad sign. Charlito was a proud boat handler who could ease a trawler into a dock blindfolded if he had to. And the *Ellie Margaret* was still new and his father was careful with it.

Ricky had just managed to loop the rope over the piling when he heard his father's rapid footsteps behind him, then *pow!*—a jolt.

His father had whacked him across the back with a broomstick. "He was pissed—I just didn't know it," Ricky says.

The dock was across the bayou from Ricky's house. Stunned, he dove off the boat and swam the short distance to the other bank. Muddy and wet, "I went to my wife crying like a baby," he recalls. "I told her, 'I can't work with my daddy anymore. That's it. I've got to finish my own boat.'"

Charlito wordlessly sailed away the next day without Ricky. Ricky got busy. He phoned up a New Orleans sheet-metal company and ordered forty-six hundred dollars worth of steel plate—the money representing almost all of his savings and enough, he hoped, to build the hull. The steel arrived before Charlito returned from his weeklong trip, and by then the skeleton of Ricky's boat was already emerging.

For the next several months, Ricky worked like a man possessed, barely sleeping, putting in twenty-hour days. He and his father never talked. But each time Charlito returned from a shrimping expedition, he would stand silently for a while, surveying his son's work. The *Lil' Rick* was rising inexorably from their altercation. "Every time Daddy would come in from a trip," says Ricky, "I'd have something else done on the boat. The second month I had it framed. The third month I had the deck on it. The fourth I had the sides on her and I was starting to work on the bottom."

Word quickly spread up and down the bayous—the crazy kid was doing it. A Yscloskey neighbor named Snake, who happened to have a winch truck, showed up unannounced. Did Ricky needed help moving the heavy steel plate around? He did; hanging steel solo is a Herculean task and Ricky was trying to do the job with a small block and tackle, and a ratchetlike pulling device called a comealong. Other winch trucks seemed to show up as if on some unseen schedule whenever Ricky needed some heavy lifting done. He would try to pay the operators but no one would take his money. "I didn't understand it then," he says. "I was doing this crazy thing at such a young age and people wanted to help."

But as the hull of the *Lil' Rick* was nearing completion, Ricky one day found himself basically broke. He and his wife lived frugally on forty-two dollars a week for groceries, but he'd run through his boat-building cash. "The next thing I know, Daddy's at my door one morning. It was the first time he'd talked to me since that awful day," Ricky recalls.

"Well, you ready to go to work?" Charlito said. "You need money to finish your boat?"

"Yes, sir, Daddy. I need money. I'm ready."

"Well, be on the boat at 1:30 to untie the rope. If you're late I'm leaving without you."

"Daddy, did you ever leave me before?" Ricky replied.

Charlito managed a smile at his son's sardonic joke. It was as close to an apology as Ricky would get. "My father could be tough," Ricky says, "but this was his way of pushing me to finish the boat. He would raise hell, but it had a purpose."

It took Ricky more than another year to complete the *Lil' Rick,* having to divide his time between trips on the *Ellie Margaret* and ship-building. He saved sixteen thousand dollars from fishing with his dad and fur trapping in the winter, spending it on materials for the cabin and to finish the remaining ironwork and rigging. He borrowed twenty thousand dollars from the bank to buy his diesel engine, clutch, shaft, and propeller, going heavy-duty on everything. His life was a blur of work, but also immensely pleasurable. "In the winter, I'd come in from running my traps and fool with my fur, then I'd go to work on my boat. Sometimes I worked all night. I was too excited to sleep. And I woke one day and looked at my boat and said, 'Boy, she's coming out good.'"

Then one astonishing day in April 1977, Ricky stood before his dream—his gleaming, jaunty trawler, painted tooth-enamel white with a black bottom, rigged with bright ropes, graceful nets, and colorful pennants. With the help of a bulldozer supplied by a friendly local politician and Snake's winch truck, the *Lil' Rick* was pushed and pulled off its building blocks near the water's edge and its stern nudged into the brackish waters of Bayou La Loutre. As the bulldozer strained to shove the bow off the bank, Ricky cranked up his diesel engine and gunned the trawler into reverse, and the *Lil' Rick* spun out into the center of the canal. He nudged it into forward, cut a tight circle in the center of the bayou, and then skillfully eased it into a nearby dock.

Around two hundred people—about half of them Ricky's extended family—cheered from the bank. The *Lil' Rick* had been launched. "I landed my boat and then we had the biggest party in the history of Yscloskey. My grandfather guarded the beer to make sure nobody had any till the boat was in the water. It was a hilarious day." Among the well-wishers: Joe "Mr. Joesie" Gonzales, considered by all the master of the Yscloskey boat-building class in this small, talent-rich place. Mr. Joesie, being the perfectionist that he is, couldn't help but notice that the arc of the *Lil' Rick*'s keel was a little on the sharp side, giving the bow the jaunty impression of Popeye with his chest stuck out. Still, he was impressed and said so. All these years, Ricky has held on to that praise like a gemstone.

After a suitable series of shakedown cruises on nearby Lake Borgne, with Charlito helping to fine tune the *Lil' Rick's* mechanical systems and giving Ricky lessons in trawl mending, Ricky took her down to the mouth of the Mississippi River. There, one sunny morning in June, he struck out due west into the Gulf of Mexico seeking shrimping fame and fortune. "That first year, all I had was a fathometer with charts the old man had given me, and a radio with three channels. No radar or plotter. No autopilot. I just watched the bottom to figure out where I was and I went wherever I wanted to go."

Like some Creolized Odysseus, Ricky essentially stayed at sea for seven years, working the fishing grounds and ports clear to Texas and occasionally crossing the wide gulf to Mexico itself. He'd come home about every fifty days to reprovision the *Lil' Rick* and reacquaint himself with his wife. These sociability sessions were fruitful at first. Their three children, Ricky Jr., Tiffany, and Ryan, were each born a year apart during these early years at sea. After about a week at home, Ricky would set sail again. Three of those years, after adding a stove, a plotter, radar, and an autopilot to the *Lil' Rick,* he worked the wide gulf solo.

Ricky also lived up to his father's earlier praise of his fishing prowess. There were many spectacular years when he returned to port with his hatches bulging full of jumbo shrimp that would fetch six dollars a pound at the dock. Through about the mid-1990s—a period of mostly low and stable fuel prices and a brisk market for wild-caught gulf shrimp—Ricky and other talented shrimpers with a big enough boat could earn ten thousand dollars in profit on a single trip.

With his long absences beginning to put a strain on his family life, Ricky eventually settled down into a less nomadic existence, with Yscloskey as his anchorage, fishing as Charlito had in inside waters close to home. He hoped for a while to coax his own son, Ricky Jr., to follow in his footsteps; Ricky Jr., though, had other inclinations. He worked briefly with his dad aboard the *Lil' Rick* as a teenager, but the sea simply never called to him, and he didn't like the strenuous, often hot and grimy routine that is part of life on a shrimp boat. Ricky also admits that, like Charlito before him, he was a stern and demanding captain—another thing his easygoing son couldn't abide. Today, at twenty-nine, Ricky Jr. is a drummer who plays on and off for local rock bands while working at odd jobs. His dream is to be a professional musician.

Another factor was that Ricky and Denise divorced in 1992. The Robins' teenage kids spent most of their time after that with their mother, who lived well above the bayous in Chalmette and did not, by then, think much of the fisherman's life. Perhaps all divorces are complicated, but even Ricky admits one catalyst was when Denise discovered that he had taken on as his deckhand Susan Roberts—the woman he ended up marrying after the divorce was final. The altercation that followed was spectacular.

Throughout these ups and downs, there were two constants in Ricky Robin's life: one was his faithful boat, the *Lil' Rick,* which not only proved seaworthy but rewarded his early investment in a top-quality engine, clutch, and shaft by practically never breaking down. As he stood in the face of Katrina at Violet Canal more than twenty-eight years after launching his trawler, the only major part on the *Lil' Rick* that he had ever replaced was the prop.

The other constant was his life on the water: to be *out there,* afloat on the singing tide, with the sky, the gulls, the sun or the moon, and the salt breeze for company, reading the subtle signs of current, wind, temperature, the interplay of sunlight and daylight, the fetch and position of the moon, that told him when and where to drop his nets—this was what Ricky knew and craved.

In truth, this romance has faded of late for many independent shrimpers up and down the Gulf Coast. The past decade has been particularly unkind: coastal habitat decimation and competition for native shrimp stocks, some of it by giant corporate-owned trawlers, have taken a toll. Add increased regulation of seasons and catches, and many small fishermen have simply found it uneconomical to continue. Those holding on more recently have been beset by the twin and equally corrosive forces of soaring fuel prices and a tsunami of cheap imported shrimp—most of them farmed in Asia. Thus, the price for native shrimp has plummeted while costs have soared. Ricky was paying about fifty cents a gallon for diesel in the early 1990s when his jumbo shrimp were fetching six dollars a pound. Yet, in the run-up to Katrina, Yscloskey shrimpers were having to pay three dollars a gallon for diesel—and getting under two dollars a pound at the dock for jumbo shrimp that often show up in fancy East Coast fish counters at seventeen dollars a pound. Someone was making money, but it wasn't the independent gulf fisherman.

Ricky wasn't among the discouraged, perhaps because as a man now past fifty he simply couldn't envision another life or another livelihood. But the reason lies perhaps deeper still—in Ricky's preternatural understanding of his quarry and its environment. He once offered this discourse on fishing the equinox.

"Look," he says, "it's been the same routine all my life. When the days get as long as the nights, the shrimp come back out of the gulf. It's an easy thing to remember. I check the time: twelve hours of sunshine and twelve hours of darkness. When it gets there, you've got two weeks of big money. And you better get there because after the east wind starts to kick in, you'll be too late. All I do is catch shrimp passing through. Me and this boat here catch shrimp on the move. . . . Sometimes they're there, sometimes they're not, sometimes they'll bury themselves deep. But if you're patient and know what to do, you'll get them. Maybe the key will be the wind, maybe it's the tide, maybe it's the moon, but I'll find them. I tell Ronald, 'You know why I catch so many shrimp? Because I think like a shrimp.'"

It's little wonder, then, that Ricky stuck with his boat at Katrina's approach—no place feels safer to him, and he would never abandon the *Lil' Rick* to the uncertainty of tie-down ropes, no matter how secure the location might seem to be. And in the chaos enveloping Violet Canal, Ricky realizes he can't think like a shrimp right now. He has to think like the calm, collected, seasoned captain that he is. Lives are in the balance.

9. Charlo Adrift

It takes a while to surface from the dark, briny, tumultuous surge that sucked him under, yet Charles Inabnet finds himself strangely calm. For the moment, he can divine little of his circumstances save the lightening sky, the warm water, the fierce currents dragging him onward. He knows three things: his shoes and shirt have been stripped away, he's lost his dentures, and he isn't going to die—at least not immediately.

The beast that dragged him down has surrendered him back to the surface.

He starts to pray again, but not for himself. "I knew people were hurting," he says. "I knew other people were possibly dying. So I started praying for them."

Charlo is floating on his back, clutching his life ring to his chest, the twelve-foot rope tied to the ring running ahead on the current like a snake leading the way. The water is choppy.

Charlo seeks his bearings, glancing back against the current in the direction from where he came. There is no towering camp—just the dim gray outline of a few posts jutting from the water. He looks for his house. It's gone, or maybe he's just not looking in the right place. Nothing seems particularly recognizable; the world that he knew appears to have been utterly rearranged. He scans the periphery—water, water everywhere, moving in brisk circular eddies, frothed here and there by the still brutal winds.

Charlo floats on, trying to stay calm. Lying on his back, clutching his life ring, has its virtues—he has a nice view of Katrina clouds scudding low in the sky. But the water is full of peril, too. Debris is everywhere and a lot of it has sharp edges—splintered wood, posts with jagged nails, ragged pieces of tin torn from gutters and roofs. Charlo examines his arms and abdomen and sees trickles of blood oozing from cuts everywhere; it's as if he's been crawling through razor wire.

He has an idea: if he can get inside his life ring, the outer part of the tube should give him a buffer against the sharp flotsam. He tries a maneuver—to slip the ring over his head and down around his chest, but it's a tricky thing. He leans too far forward and finds himself suddenly upended, like a duck diving for food with his fanny out of the water. He panics and writhes out of the life ring, sputtering for breath as he reaches the surface. "I should have practiced this at some point," he says to himself.

He loops an arm back in the ring and floats on with the racing current. Bigger objects present themselves. Floating pilings and utility poles, roof remains, gasoline jugs, sodden furniture washed from camps, rafts of floating marsh. He and his part of the world are washing slowly west northwestward.

Up ahead, Charlo spies the first thing that gives him hope—a line of treetops. They poke up like huge apparitional spider webs on the gloomy near horizon. The trees at least provide a bearing, for he knows that trees, mostly hackberry, scrub oak, and an occasional cypress, line the marshy, uninhabited far bank of Bayou La Loutre across from his house. The trick will be to maneuver close to a branch substantial enough to grab on to. If he misses, he's in trouble: beyond the trees lie miles and miles and miles of what once was marsh, and now is open water, clear to the Mississippi River.

Still clutching the ring, Charlo kicks and paddles with his free hand in steering motions as a treetop looms ahead. It's a hackberry, a species known by bayou kids as a tree hard to climb because of its dense foliage and thorny bark that claw at exposed skin. But the tree is also known for its deep roots—good for surviving a hurricane, and anyway, Charlo isn't picky. At this point, any tree still upright would do.

He floats in, pushing the ring ahead of him, then grabs hold to a branch. He feels it bow slightly as it brakes his flow in the current. He comes to a stop, the current racing around him as though he's some stone in the middle of a stream. He loops his rope around the branch to secure his spot and looks about.

He figures he's about halfway up the tree trunk. He estimates seventeen to twenty feet of water now covers the land.

The time goes by fidgety until the wind suddenly drops and the current ebbs, then stops. The sun comes out, dappling the water. It grows eerily calm and still—the surface is slick, save for three-foot-high rollers that come cascading in, spaced perhaps every hundred yards, like those scenic glassy waves in some Hawaiian surfing movie. It's an odd experience, to be tethered high up in a tree to a life buoy, timing the waves, riding up and down their steep sides as might some recreational beachgoer on a sunny weekend day.

But Charlo well knows his predicament.

The calm center of Katrina's eye has descended on Hopedale, and the wind, clouds, and rain will soon return, but from the opposite direction.

He's far from out of danger.

He takes closer stock of his surroundings and notices for the first time he's got company, and the company is growing. Muskrats, nutrias, and snakes—though no poisonous ones, thank God—seem drawn to the cluster of trees and are swarming in tight circles. His worry: alligators might be next. Dozens of birds—warblers, herons, egrets, gulls, redwing blackbirds—are flocking into the branches all around him. Some are almost close enough to touch. He glances up and is startled at what he sees—about ten raccoons, sprawled in the branches above, staring down at him with their dark, implacable eyes.

There's hazy lore in Charlo's Louisiana family that his ancestors more than once lashed themselves to trees when they could not run from hurricanes. Charlo had somewhat doubted those stories, until now. He somehow finds his predicament—up a tree, surrounded by raccoons—suddenly hilarious.

There's a pejorative bayou slang term sometimes applied to people of Cajun origin: coonass. Its roots are murky, but it came to prominence during Louisiana's postwar oil boom, used mostly by transient Texas oil-field workers who, despite their own accents, often took pleasure in mocking the Cajuns for their rustic ways and French-tinted speech. "Coonass" is still a fighting word in some precincts, though certain kinds of Cajuns have come to use it, among likeminded friends, as a kind of defiant badge of honor.

Charlo, having heard the term uttered in bigotry, doesn't much like it. But from his circumstances, he manages to fashion a self-deprecating joke about getting trapped by Katrina in the first place. "There I am, up in that tree. And I'm thinking, all those coons—and I'm the ass."

A sobering reality has settled in: it's still morning, he has no shirt, no shoes, no water, no food, and no way to get any. He's hungry, thirsty, groggy, and bone-tired from his ordeal. His cuts are beginning to sting and burn. There's nary a sign of another living person about; no one calling out, no planes buzzing the sky above, no drones from the motors of approaching rescue boats. Katrina is still having her way with the world, and this tree, with its growing number of furry, feathery, and scaly inhabitants, will be his home for a while.

Charlo pulls his life ring closer, one hand clutching a tree branch, and settles in for the other side of the storm.

10. The Human Tide

"C'mon, get him in here."

Back at Violet Canal, Ricky Robin offers his hand to a man named Mellerine, who had been plucked a few minutes before from the roof of his house in the Violet subdivision. He's now in a small boat, one of several under power and operated by an impromptu navy of volunteers picking their way around the neighborhood. Having saved themselves from the flood, they are now trying to save others.

Peril awaits the rescuers. Katrina's gales still whip viciously, the currents are treacherous, and the water is jammed with flotsam. Boats getting hung up in moving logjams are in danger of being trapped and even crushed. As the man plucked from the water earlier by Ronald Robin can attest, a boat caught broadside to the wind in the wrong kind of chop can easily flip. Submerged objects are keeping any boats from moving very fast.

By this time Ricky knows that Susan and the family are safe—temporarily, at least—atop the Mississippi River levee. He can see the van in the distance. But when he glances in that direction, he realizes there are so many Katrina obstacles between him and the levee—sunken boats, floating cars and trucks, and downed utility poles—he doubts he'll be able to reach the occupants of the van today.

Ricky turns to the business at hand and helps Mellerine aboard the *Lil' Rick*. The man had spent the day before the storm boarding up his house and then, like many others, a sleepless night as Katrina raged around him. What energy he had left he spent scrambling onto his roof as water engulfed his house. He's exhausted to the point of dropping, and Ricky sends him into a bunk below.

Ronald Robin, meanwhile, has temporarily lost track of Ricky as he watches in mesmerized dismay the continuing havoc the water is creating. A family of four—a man, his wife, and two young daughters—go floating by on the swift currents on a raft of driftwood, yelling for someone to rescue them. But they are far out of reach of the *Invincible Vance* and so caught up in a thick mat of debris that not even people in small boats can get close. They float with the current for perhaps a quarter mile before they are able to grab hold of the top of a tractor trailer poking up from the flood and haul themselves out of the water. Ronald can tell by their body expressions—the waving of arms, cupping of their hands to their mouths—that they are still calling for help. But no one can hear them; they will be trapped there all night. Helpless to do anything for them, Ronald turns his attention to more immediate matters.

Glancing eastward, he finally spots Ricky. He realizes that the rising water has played tricks with his vision and perspective. He'd been looking for the *Lil' Rick* up Violet Canal, and the trawler is there, all right. But it's risen so far up on the surge, and Ricky has nudged it so far in toward the canal's north levee, that it's now essentially holding a position *atop* the levee. "So that's where you went," Ronald says to himself with considerable relief.

His relief doesn't last long. He glances back at his own boat, the *Evening Star*, tethered in a scrum of other unoccupied vessels about fifty yards away, and sees that the surge is trifling with the best tie-down efforts of the captains who left the boats behind. Ropes are stretching, groaning, popping. The *Star*, Ronald can plainly see, is caught in a tightening vice between bigger vessels and in danger of being pulled down, crushed, or both. Suddenly, her ropes pop and, pressed between two other vessels in a strange, noisy ballet, the *Star* rises between the boats and stands, for a bizarre moment, straight up on her fantail. Ronald is certain the boat is headed for the murky depths until she pitches up out of the water—the bow landing with a thud on the gunwales of another boat. There is screeching and scraping as some of the rigging is torn away. But she settles down, still afloat.

Many of the captains who stayed here are looking after multiple boats, and saving them has become as urgent as saving lives—for their owners, the boats may be the only possession to survive the storm. The captains have their work cut out for them. Most of the boats left behind are tied hard to docks on short lines designed to keep them as immobile as possible. But in the swift and enveloping surge these ropes are death traps—any boat that can't be loosed quickly will simply be dragged under or flipped. So the captains can be seen frantically hopping from boat to boat, loosening ropes to accommodate the flood, then retying the boats on longer lines so they don't blow away. But this creates other problems. As the water begins to overtop the Violet Canal levees, wind and currents are pushing vessels landward; the boats will have to be spooled back in quickly when the water starts to recede, or they will be left high and dry.

Ricky can't worry about other boats for the moment, for his view from the *Lil' Rick*'s pilothouse turns suddenly surreal. He sees a man floundering in the water, trying to swim toward the *Lil' Rick*. He eventually makes it. He spies maybe a half dozen other small boats approaching at various distances, all filled with exhausted, traumatized people lifted from houses, trees, car tops, the water. Other refugees have run up on the rapidly disappearing high land that was the Violet Canal levee top, and are yelling for Ricky to take them in.

Soon, Ricky has about forty-five people on the *Lil' Rick*, and more are clamoring to get aboard. Ricky and Dwight Sr. do quick triage. With space tight and getting tighter and Katrina still blowing a gale, he marshals kids into the trawler's hole, women into the galley-bunk area, and men who are able-bodied onto the aft deck. Dangerous objects are still flying around outside, but there isn't much choice. Other shrimp and oyster boats up and down Violet Canal are filling up with survivors as well.

His worry for the moment is that the water won't ever stop, and that the *Lil' Rick* will be snapped from its moorings by the wind and tides and set adrift with only the power of its diesel engine to save it. The backside of the storm is clearly now on them—the wind has radically shifted from the east to the north, then west-northwest, a shift accompanied by a brief window of calm and a strange and sudden change of atmospheric pressure. "It was like letting the air of a balloon," Ricky recalls. "Everybody's ears were popping like crazy."

But the wind shift makes an eastward jaunt possible, and Ricky

quickly formulates a plan: if the water continues to surge, he'll bull the
Lil' Rick over the Violet Canal's north levee and make a run for the Violet
water tower, the one object that he thinks is Katrina proof. He'll lash the
trawler to one of the massive steel pilings of the tower and try to ride out
the rest of the storm there.

Surely, nothing can dislodge the tower?

"Get a bow rope ready," he tells Tee-Tee as the increasingly nervous
passengers huddle around him. "If we break loose, that's what we're
gonna do. And don't be scared. You're safe on this boat. If we bump up
against anything, we'll knock it down. If we run into a house, we'll
knock that down, too." Ricky is now happier than ever that he built the
Lil' Rick from steel.

In truth, Ricky isn't quite as optimistic about this plan as he lets on—
the debris-clogged waters, the shifty wind, the currents, and the human
load he's taken on will actually make such a trip quite treacherous. But a
more immediate problem presents itself when west-northwesterly gusts
start to worsen the *Lil' Rick's* sideways drift.

He puts the trawler in neutral, trying to coax it to swing around into
the wind—a tricky move since it relies on his multiple restraining ropes
to break the *Lil' Rick's* momentum once it comes around. But as the
trawler slides off the levee and begins to strain against its ropes, Ricky
watches horrified as one by one the lines grow tauter—and then start
to snap.

Each rope, as it breaks, crackles like rifle fire, the frayed lengths
sizzling through the air.

Damn, what to do now? The trawler, if loosed, could easily capsize.

Ricky suddenly realizes he has one chance left to keep the boat from
its anarchic slide backward. As the last line breaks, he hits a lever that
controls the winch to his 150-pound bow anchor.

There's the metallic grumble of the release of heavy chain, the deep
chug of the anchor plunging into the water, the strange motion of
the trawler skidding backward, then a loud *clank* as the anchor chain
snaps taut.

The *Lil' Rick* is suddenly yanked perpendicular to the levee—but it
continues to lose ground to the current.

Ricky crosses himself, his mind whirring with what last-ditch maneuver he might try if the trawler breaks free—when the anchor grabs bottom.

Another violent lurch and then a deep *twuck*.

The trawler stops—the *Lil' Rick* has held fast.

Ricky throttles down his engine, puts it in neutral, and makes the rounds of his passengers, offering assurances that—at last—the worst really does seem to be over.

Many of them are still jittery so Ricky, being Ricky, decides some extraordinary measure is in order. He goes below, fetches his trumpet from the galley where he stashes it, and comes out on the deck and blows a few bars of "When the Saints Go Marching In." The notes ring sharply out across the slackening winds. Even shell-shocked Katrina survivors get a kick out of that, and the tense mood is broken.

Soon enough, the wind begins to drop, though it will not lie flat here until a little before dark. Boats bearing refugees continue to approach, and Ricky hears a shout—"Ricky, Ricky Robin! You got room for somebody?"

A boat idles up alongside the trawler and Ricky recognizes some of the occupants. One of them is an acquaintance, Vivian Nunnery, the girlfriend of Frankie Asevado, the man who plucked Matine and Neg Verdin from the loft of the barn off Bayou Road seven miles away. Ricky is a friend of Frankie's, too. The others are the Verdins themselves, who have been transferred from Frankie's boat to this one, operated by Frankie's friend Darryl Caruso, so that Frankie could continue his freelance rescue operations.

Vivian—B.B. to family and friends—and Frankie were staying with her grandfather when they were washed out of his house off Bayou Road at a place called Kenilworth, only a half mile or so below the Verdins' house. They fled in a boat to temporary shelter on the elevated porch of a multistory house across the way. Darryl, who also lives more or less in the Verdins' neighborhood, suffered an identical fate, escaping the rising water in his own boat with his elderly grandmother. They all ended up in a pod of boats working their way up and out of the drowned and broken ramparts of lower St. Bernard, taking in survivors such as they could find.

B.B. brings Ricky the grim news of the wider world. Based on patchy cell phone reports, marine-radio traffic, and eyewitness accounts all of St. Bernard seems to be underwater. The trip up from lower Bayou Road was both harrowing and tedious. A long stretch of the four-lane Highway 46, the major road connecting the lower bayous to Chalmette, was covered in eight-plus feet of water, but so clogged with driftwood that they were forced to dodge off the highway and navigate through the wooded shoulders of the road, picking their way through gaps in the trees.

The Verdins, overjoyed to be rescued, have nonetheless reached Violet Canal in a diminished state. Matine is calm but exhausted; Neg is wan and dazed. He seems incapable of speaking.

"If you have room," B.B. tells Ricky, "I think these two would be better off with you. The shelters are already overcrowded."

Word of the conditions at the two main shelters—St. Bernard High School below them and Chalmette High School above—has already filtered in. Both have been flooded and damaged and both now overflow with far more refugees than they are equipped to handle. In both places, Katrina's vicious surge has knocked out windows and battered open doors on the ground floor and filled the schools up with eight to ten feet of water, sending panicked shelter dwellers up to the increasingly crowded second floor. As citizen rescue boats bring in more survivors, the overflow is pushing people up onto the schools' roofs. B.B. is right: the schools are probably not the ideal situation for Matine with her poor English and Neg with his traumas.

Besides, Ricky has known Herbie Verdin since both were kids, and he recalls having now and then dropped in on Matine and Neg, in the casual way that bayou people still visit. "Of course," Ricky replies. "Y'all come on up here. We got plenty of room."

Matine and Neg are helped aboard the _Lil' Rick_. Ricky, owing to his Cajun roots, speaks a little French, and he and Matine exchange pleasantries. But then Matine looks at him with an imploring expression. "When do you think I can go home?" she says in halting English.

"Home?" says Ricky. "I don't know. I don't think any of us are going home soon, cher." He then ushers the Verdins below. He offers Matine a bunk but she insists that Neg take it. Ricky gets them bottled water—fortuitously, he'd laid in a six-week supply of water and food for at least a dozen people at Katrina's approach—and then returns to his command post at the trawler's wheel.

Before the afternoon is over, about ninety-five people will pass through the *Lil' Rick* and at least forty of them will spend the night. Ronald will take in about thirty-five people and keep a half dozen survivors—all of them old family friends rescued from the roofs of their houses—overnight on the *Vance*. Fortunately, Ronald had stocked his boat with a surplus of food and water just as Ricky had—in fact, both had cooked up giant pots of gumbo and red beans and rice as Katrina approached. Supplies are stretched given the number of people now aboard, but everyone gets *something* to eat.

The comings and goings from their boats reflect an odd diaspora, a steady stream of small boats manned by refugees looking for relatives and friends: people calling out names, people calling back. A dozen often tearful reunions take place alongside the *Lil' Rick* as survivors decamp to be with relatives or friends come to claim them.

Some will resettle on larger boats here in the harbor; some lucky enough to live in two-story houses have decided to ride out the night on the dry upper floors of the very places they were washed out of. In the lulls between these comings and goings, the faraway voices of people still stranded on roofs and in attics can be heard wafting across the water. Small craft manned by people like Frankie Asevado continue to search for them.

Improbably, cell phone service is still sporadically working. Ricky at least has one less thing to worry about: Susan and the family are safe.

Up on the Mississippi River levee, the scene in the dying wind with the sun beginning to poke through parting clouds is one of cautious relief. Susan and company, and a growing number of stragglers, had watched in fearful awe as the river clawed its way up to the top of the levee—cascading over by a foot or so in several places. Almost all of them thought they were going to have to swim for it, until the same radical wind shift that almost knocked the *Lil' Rick* off the levee acted as a siphon on the river.

As Susan and the family watched, the mighty Mississippi, which by official accounts had surged to twelve feet above normal, plunged like a rapidly draining bathtub to its normal stage in less than two hours.

This bit of serendipity is leavened by sobering realities. Susan, too, can see the logjam that stands between Ricky and her. She knows that she, her brother, her sister-in-law, her daughters, and her ailing father are all going to spend the night in the van.

There is a house nearby—a camp, actually, a place built long ago and perhaps the only dwelling in all of St. Bernard Parish on the *outside* of the Mississippi River levee. Katrina has cleaved off the back two bedrooms, but the front of the structure is intact, and perhaps a dozen people will make it their home for the night. Even after night falls, survivors continue to find their way here, drawn to an arc of light. For though the power is out for about three hundred square miles around, the generators on the shrimp and oyster boats at Violet Canal are running spotlights—beckoning beacons in an overwhelming moat of darkness.

Susan looks out across the water wistfully, wishing she and her family were with Ricky on the boat. They arrived with a couple of garbage bags full of extra clothes but nothing to eat—and no one else here has anything, either. Some scavengers come in, but their only contribution is a couple of cases of beer. For some refugees, this proves something of a palliative for the day they've endured. But Susan is unhappy when a couple of the beer drinkers get rowdy. There's enough stress already.

Stragglers continue to wander in after dark, bearing raw Katrina wounds—most of them psychological, though many people have suffered cuts, abrasions, bruises, and even broken bones. Everyone has a harrowing story, but Susan is most moved by the seemingly unstoppable tears of a girl, eight or nine years old, who has appeared atop the levee with her parents.

"Why are you crying, baby?" Susan asks solicitously. "You're safe now. You'll be fine up here."

The girl looks at her and swipes at her tears with her hands. She says, "I know. But it's the horse—the poor horse." She begins to cry again.

It takes a while to unwind the story of the horse. The family had been riding out the storm in a house near the grove of oaks where Susan encountered the Industrial Canal surge. Open pastures lie on both sides of the road there. In a seeming lull in the storm, the family had gone out to the back porch, only to be slammed by the surge.

The porch cleaved away from the house and began to drift on the swift, deepening currents. It floated over fences into a pasture, where they encountered the horse, confused and swimming desperately. The horse spied the floating porch and began to swim frantically toward it, perhaps instinctively realizing that the giant impromptu raft was its only chance of saving itself.

The horse caught up to the porch and tried to mount it, hooves flailing. But the porch was barely keeping the family afloat and the girl's father realized that if horse climbed aboard, not only might the spooked animal injure them but the porch could sink and they would all be thrown into the treacherous currents. He had no choice but to fight the frightened animal off.

He did, and the horse eventually gave up.

Exhausted, it sank under the water and drowned.

Susan realizes she has no adequate words of comfort for the girl; she's simply too young to realize that far sadder stories have likely unfolded in Katrina's onslaught.

Indeed, sometime during the night, a body floats into the area of the Violet Canal flotilla, although it will not be discovered for another day. He's a man whom eyewitnesses will later say was trying to make his way through flooding woods northeast of the Violet subdivision with a friend when he was apparently trapped by the water and drowned. The friend didn't make it, either, but his body won't be found for another two weeks, having floated into a marshy area a mile away. Still, news of the first body won't filter out through the Violet refugee encampment for a day or two.

Susan and her family climb into their darkened van, settle in, and try to sleep. Exhaustion eventually overcomes hunger and they drift in and out of fitful slumber. The levee dwellers aren't the only ones to go hungry. Bob Turner, a Violet resident who runs the Lake Borgne Levee District, a state-created agency that oversees St. Bernard's flood protection system, had been on duty when Katrina's water trapped him and others in the parish government building off Judge Perez Drive. He came here with two co-workers in a motorized flatboat to check on his house—only to find water almost up to the roof. They spent the night in the boat outside the house dining on a shared package of Skittles.

Still, full belly or empty stomach, survivors here are beginning to realize their luck at being alive, but also the trials they still face. For by now, thanks to transistor radios, a battery-operated TV or two, and a diminishing number of cell phone reports, everyone knows the breadth of the disaster. Eighty percent of New Orleans is also under water; thousands of people are trapped and some are dying, and rescue efforts are at best fitful.

Down here in Violet Canal no one has any illusions. If the authorities can't help fabled New Orleans, nobody will be rushing into the bayou lands of St. Bernard Parish. People here will have to save themselves, or they will not be saved at all.

11. Charlo in Limbo

Monday afternoon has grown late and Charlo, tethered to his tree, dozes in and out of consciousness. The backside of the storm has come and gone. The winds have dropped and an eerie calm descends. Birds chirp, squawk, and flutter. The sun comes out to dapple the water.

It would be an otherwise pleasant late afternoon on the bayou—a time of day, with the heat and humidity dropping, that you might boil up a bunch of shrimp or crabs on your butane burner out in the backyard and knock back a few beers—were not the land covered in a flood of biblical proportions.

At least the water's warm.

Charlo can't believe how wrinkled his hands and feet are.

After the eye passed and the wind and currents switched dramatically to the northwest, a frothy chop riled the waters. Charlo endured one precarious moment: he was forced to hastily retie the rope keeping in him place, to avoid being dragged into the tree branches, where he might become hopelessly entangled.

He still can't quite tell the water's depth, but he has a clue. As the calm of the eye descended, a ten-foot-long two-by-four floated by and Charlo grabbed it. More than once he's plunged it arm's length toward the bottom and there still was no bottom. But it seems to him, based on waterlines on the tree trunk, that the flood is now in fact beginning to fall.

In this he divines perhaps the single advantage of being in Hopedale: The place sits outside the St. Bernard Parish levee system—meaning there are no levees to bar this water from flowing back into the gulf from which it ultimately came. These are Katrina's highest tides and sooner or later, with the storm having moved northeastward and wrung itself out, these tides will have to drop.

Other than the feathered and furry company around him, there are no other signs of life: still no planes overhead, still no droning of engines from possible rescue boats, no one paddling about in a pirogue calling out for survivors. Charlo is hungry and extremely thirsty, but he's enough of an old seadog to know that there's no way he can drink the briny Katrina stew he is floating in.

As the day wears on, the water continues to drop, for Charlo notices that he's riding much lower in the tree. He also has come to the conclusion that it will be most uncomfortable to spend the night in these branches. While his hunger is gnawing at him, his deeper worry is that thirst and dehydration will sap what energy he has left if he doesn't find drinking water soon. He wonders: Is there anyplace but this brambly hackberry that offers shelter?

Glancing in the direction of where he's sure his house once stood, Charlo decides to swim for it, hoping to spot *something* familiar. There's only a slight current now. But the water is still clogged with debris. Snuggling deeper into his life jacket, he hooks his elbows into his life ring and strikes out, pushing the ring ahead of him, scanning the water as he kicks. Long minutes go by, he grows tired and disoriented, and he thinks about heading back to his tree. Then he spots a landmark, maybe a quarter mile away.

It's the bedraggled branches of a modest palm tree that grew in his backyard. He spies something else, what looks to be a rust-brown platform barely sticking up out of the water a short distance from the tree. He is momentarily confused as to what this object might be, then realizes it's the top of a large metal container—the kind they pack aboard cargo ships—that he'd installed in his front yard some years back to stow his fishing gear.

The container top, though not exactly a mattress, has the virtue of being flat and, having been under the warm sun for part of the day, most likely dry. It seems a far superior roost than the tree—at least it's a place where he can stretch out and dry off—so Charlo heads that way.

The swim takes what seems like an eternity, Charlo having to fight his own fatigue while kicking his way through debris. He reaches his destination and hauls himself out, winded but happy to be out of the water. The container is about seven feet high, so Charlo estimates that six feet of water still covers the land.

He looks around, examining his homestead up close for the first time. There's nothing left of his house, unless some remnant of the foundation lies below the water. The camp south of his is gone, too.

The view from the container also reinforces the memory of the violence that tore apart the substantial camp he was washed from. Nothing remains but the buttresses of the foundation, and the three towering pilings that ran up through the attic to gird the structure against hurricanes. Unrecognizable rafts of splintered, twisted wood and broken house parts lie floating in the foreground.

For the first time, he thinks about his boat, the *Captain John J.* He gazes toward the bayou, seeing the pilings to which the oyster lugger was tethered. But it's not there. He scans farther afield and spots a sad sight: the boat, canted over on its side, in a grove of trees way up on the far bank. It's in one piece, but even from this vantage point he can tell it's been badly battered. Retrieving it from that far up on the bank— assuming it's worth retrieving—will require costly heavy equipment.

Charlo dries out and places his two objects of comfort, his life jacket and ring, in positions that will give him some cushioning from the hard metal container. His platform is at least roomy: the container is perhaps six feet wide and twenty feet long. He can walk around some and stretch his legs. But this simply reminds him of how weary and battered he is. He examines his cuts, bruises, and deep scratches and realizes many are candidates for infection.

There's nothing he can do about that now.

Around dark, he sits down, preparing to settle in for the night, hoping at least that Katrina's scouring winds have blown away the hordes of twilight mosquitoes that Hopedale is famous for this time of year. Otherwise he could be in deep trouble. Anecdotes abound of fishermen, stranded overnight when their open boats broke down, being hospitalized from insect bites. One grim story tells of a commercial fishermen who had to be institutionalized after mosquito and gnat bites drove him mad.

As night falls, he glances south and suddenly sees something startling: a light. It's moving in an erratic arc like some lantern being swung in the hand of a person beckoning. It's a dim light, low on the horizon, impossible to say how far away. But Charlo is sure it's not some apparition.

Someone signaling? Someone in distress? Perhaps he is not alone in this suddenly drowned world?

Charlo calls out to the light, time and again, but there is no response. As quickly as the beam appeared, it vanishes.

He now wishes he had never seen the light. Charlo feels terribly alone. He wearily settles in to his roost, praying that morning will bring with it a way out of here.

Darkness settles in. The sky is ablaze with stars.

Enveloped in the warm embryonic night, Charlo sleeps fitfully. Dreams startle him awake. He struggles to recall what happened and where he is. The night floats by as if some long dark hallucination.

At least there are no mosquitoes.

The day breaks cloudless and clear. He glances up, groggy, at the pale blue sky. It portends to be a windless, scorching South Louisiana day. He thinks of his wife Terry, safe with relatives in northern Louisiana, and his married daughter, Charity, whom he and Terry proudly put through college. Now thirty-three, she lives with her husband in Dallas. Surely by now word of the deluge has reached the outer world. It pains him that they will probably think he's dead.

He rises and looks about. What he sees buoys his spirits. The water has dropped precipitously, perhaps enough that he can think about walking toward safety—if, in fact, a place of safety exists.

12. Herbie and Mike's Strange Adventure

The gray floating coffin is an unpleasant surprise. It is riding low, bob-bing in the light winds and current, moving slowly across the path of the boat in which Herbie Verdin and his nephew Mike Vetra are easing along. It's not the only shocking thing they have seen in the short recon-naissance of their stricken neighborhood. There are the dogs curled up in tree branches, too traumatized and afraid to come down.

Herbie, when he encountered the coffin, had come looking for two specific dogs—black-and-tan coonhounds that he feared had been left behind in a pen by their owners who live near the end of Billiot Lane, the narrow street running past the Verdin house. He's fond of animals, and he was hoping he might be able to coax the dogs into the boat and shelter them in the barn until he could scavenge for food. But those dogs are nowhere to be found, and the treed dogs, like many fearful, cornered animals, snarl when Herbie and Mike come too close. These dogs will have to save themselves.

After Matine and Neg boarded Frankie Asevado's rescue boat, Her-bie and Mike had slipped from the barn loft back into their borrowed boat and made a serious effort to find a powerboat that worked. After roaming around a bit, they succeeded, spying a partially submerged eighteen-foot aluminum outboard at a house across flooded Bayou Road. They bailed the skiff and were able to get it started. They managed to recover the pirogue that had drifted off and, just for good measure, pulled it into the boat as a backup.

Although Herbie wants to rescue dogs, and any human survivors too, his more pressing issue is his and Mike's physical state. Swept from the house with no provisions, they have no idea if rescue boats will wander back their way. It's late afternoon, the day has grown hot, and they are hungry, thirsty, and nearing exhaustion. Moreover, the thought of spending a night in the stuffy, flea-infested barn loft is extremely unappealing.

Hungry and thirsty or not, Herbie and Mike have a dilemma: what to do with the bobbing coffin?

Its origin is no real mystery—it no doubt washed out of the historic Bayou Terre-aux-Boeufs Cemetery just up the road. Herbie realizes that many of the aboveground tombs there, some more than two centuries old, might well have been vulnerable to Katrina's violent surge. He wonders if there are more coffins floating about.

He and Mike talk it over and decide it would be sacrilegious just to let the coffin bob around in the open. They spy a rope in the boat with a hook on it. They pull up alongside the coffin, affix the hook to one of its handles, determined to tow it to the church across the highway where they had briefly considered taking shelter from the flood. But when Herbie takes a closer look, he's shocked. There's a nameplate on the coffin and he makes the sign of the cross.

"I know this lady, Mike," he says. "She was my second-grade teacher."

There's a mild art to towing anything behind a boat. But the rectangular, low-riding coffin proves to be quite a challenge. It dips and bobs and weaves. Herbie has to steer a hilariously crooked course trying keep it in line. Moreover, he is constantly banging into submerged objects or running aground atop them.

"What, Herbie, you forgot how to drive a boat?" Mike chides him playfully.

Herbie's not in a mood for kidding around. Several times the coffin threatens to get hung up in trees, shrubs, or debris sticking up out of the water. His real fear is damaging the thing in any sort of collision that could cause it to sink—or worse, pop open. He's happy to be securing his former teacher's eternal dignity, but he doesn't want to see her again. So a trip of a quarter mile turns into a nerve-racking half-hour ordeal.

At the church door, Herbie and Mike discover that they made the right decision in not fleeing here. Its belfry might have provided a haven, but the church is locked up tight. Herbie puzzles over this for a moment, then sees opportunity in a railing that frames the steps leading to the door. It forms a kind of corral. Their best hope is to nudge the coffin up against the railing and hope that it stays put till the water recedes.

Beyond securing the coffin, Herbie realizes he doesn't have a plan, other than trying to stick around long enough for the water to drop so he can recover, as promised, Matine's metal money box from the toppled freezer. By this time, though, he and Mike are consumed with thirst.

Herbie suddenly has an idea: a nearby neighbor who evacuated had told Herbie that he was leaving his refrigerator-freezer stocked with water, food, and, even better from Herbie's viewpoint, beer. Should there be an emergency, he told Herbie to feel free to raid it. Herbie's been in the house before and knows his way to the kitchen where the appliance is.

"I got an idea, Mike," he says, "though it might take some work."

They motor over to the house, which sits up a little higher than the Verdin house. Floodwaters still lap high up near the gutters. "We'll have to get in through the roof," says Herbie. But how?

Herbie rummages around in the boat, finds a claw hammer, and mounts the roof. He begins ripping away at shingles, then boards, and after a half hour of sweaty work he's managed to pummel a decent-sized hole in the roof. He then drops down through the hole into the attic and begins to rip up floorboards above the kitchen. This operation goes reasonably quickly, though it's already stifling hot in the attic. Finally, he peers down and spies his prize: the refrigerator. It's still standing upright, but in water that is at least neck deep.

Drinking water is vital. But given what he's endured today, Herbie is actually salivating about the prospect of a cold beer.

Herbie calls to Mike, who clamors out of the boat onto the roof and peers down at Herbie.

"Drop on down," Herbie says. "I see the refrigerator."

Mike squeezes with some difficulty through the hole Herbie has made and walks over to the second hole.

"You goin' down there," Herbie tells him. "I'll lower you down, you'll get stuff out of the fridge, hand it up, then I'll pull you back up."

Mike looks at Herbie, incredulous.

"You crazy, Herbie. You might be able to lower me down but you ain't never gonna be able to pull my fat ass back up. I'll be stuck down there."

"No, you won't," says Herbie. "I'm sure I can pull you up."

"I'm sure you cain't," Mike replies. He shakes his head, then says, "How 'bout this? How 'bout if I lower *you* down there?"

Herbie peers down into the flooded kitchen and judges the chances that Mike might actually be able to extract him from the hole.

"Aw, man," he concludes, "I ain't goin' down there, neither."

For Herbie, this has been not just a disappointing detour but a physically taxing one. "C'mon, Mike," he says, "we gotta get out of here."

Now, clearly, the nearest possibility of getting provisions lies up the road toward Violet Canal and Chalmette, where there are a few convenience stores along the highway, or St. Bernard High School, about five miles away, where they know there's an official storm shelter. If they have to break into those stores, they are prepared to so do—whatever it takes to get food and water.

Herbie steers the boat out of the yard on to Bayou Road, which sprawls like a broad flat brown bayou before them, its contours marked only by the utility poles sticking up out of the water and the rooftops of flooded houses on each side. He figures his best route is to try to imagine the centerline of the actual narrow bayou that hugs the west bank of the road; the water will be deeper there and he's less likely to encounter submerged objects.

Herbie throttles the boat up until it planes and they go speeding west-northwest, but they don't get far. There's a loud bang and a jolt—and the boat suddenly veers hard right. Herbert yanks back the throttle, struggling to keep control. It takes him a moment to realize he's struck a submerged object—most likely the back window and roof of a car or truck, given the scraping, crackling sound—putting a big dent in the boat's bottom and badly damaging the prop. Their craft now can only limp along at about ten miles per hour, probably a wiser choice of speeds anyway. And it's sprung a leak. They go putt-putting along, hoping the boat won't conk out on them altogether, or sink, before they can find provisions.

With water in the boat now lapping over their shoes, they finally reach St. Bernard High School about a half hour before dark, but not before rescuing a man and his pregnant girlfriend from the roof of a house. Outside the school, they run into a small scrum of boats bearing other survivors who have already raided the contents of one flooded food store. They were unable to get food, but they did secure beer, whiskey, and bottled water, which they freely share with Herbie and Mike. Herbie knows one of the men, who also gives him some news. He'd detoured to the boat encampment at Violet Canal and seen Matine and Neg aboard the *Lil' Rick* in the company of Ricky Robin.

Herbie, Matine's obsession with her box aside, has secretly been fretting about the decision not to accompany his mother and brother. He is immensely relieved at the news.

Mike is tired to the point of exhaustion. He wants to find a place to sleep, not to mention investigate the possibility that the people running the shelter are serving food. Herbie doesn't like crowds so he tells Mike to go inside without him. He'll tend to the boat, try to keep it bailed out, and come in later.

The school is a dark, brown-bricked, bunkerlike facility. The bottom story is flooded. Mike wades through the water, finds some stairs, and makes his way up to the second floor. Hundreds of people are milling about. He passes ranks of bedraggled survivors, many of them elderly and infirm, most with nothing but the clothes on their backs, clustered in the halls randomly alight with the eerie glow of flashlights. People are speaking in hushed tones. No one in particular seems to be in charge. With the halls stuffy and crowded, Mike makes his way to the roof, where he carves out an isolated space on the tar-and-gravel surface and falls asleep. At some point he's awakened by someone passing out dinner—a single granola bar and a bottle of water. He gratefully accepts it, eats it quickly, and goes back to sleep.

Herbie prefers the solitude of the boat. Dinner becomes a couple of beers, a sip of whiskey, and a bottle of water. He falls asleep on the boat's cramped but dry deck.

Tuesday morning arrives clear, hot, and chaotic: the coming and going of boats with more survivors and vague rumors that efforts are being made to attempt a boatlift of St. Bernard Parish refugees by tug-boats and barges across the Mississippi River to the west bank towns of Harvey or Algiers, with Violet Canal as one of the staging points.

Mike awakens, stretches, and goes to the edge of the roof to survey the flooded land. He spies their boat. It's a sad sight: the water has gone down a little, enough so that the boat is now resting high and dry atop the roof of a submerged car that they couldn't see when they arrived the evening before. The skiff also appears to be about half full of water. Their pirogue is still in place in the boat, but Herbie is nowhere to be seen.

Mike makes his way down, searching the halls of the school for Herbie amid the swelling crowds. Herbie, meanwhile, has come into the school searching for Mike. Somehow, in the throngs, they miss each other. Herbie hears the chatter about a possible boatlift being organized to points across the river and concludes that Mike has gone to join it. Mike concludes the same thing about Herbie.

Herbie, still determined to honor his promise to Matine, decides to head back to the Verdin house. The skiff turns out to be immovable from the top of the car, so the trip won't be nearly as easy or as fast, since he'll have to paddle back the entire way in the pirogue. Before he leaves, the acquaintance who provisioned him last evening has returned, this time with some canned goods and a few other meager foodstuffs, plus some bottled water. Herbie at least has lunch and dinner, and enough water, if he's careful, for another day or two. He'll need the water, for by the time he eases away from the school, the temperature is already nearing the upper eighties and there's not a breath of wind.

Herbie travels slowly through a broken, flooded, surreal landscape, devoid of almost any sound save the slap of his paddle on the water. There aren't even birds about—it's as if they've all been blown away. Along the way, he's jolted by a realization: his former girlfriend, who evacuated, had mentioned to him that she planned to leave her dogs, chihuahuas named Julio and Selina, behind with enough food for a day or two. It's clear to Herbie that this ordeal is going to last more than a day or two, and that pets are likely to be at the bottom of the rescue priority list. So he makes a diversion to the house and breaks in, finding the dogs frightened and trembling on an upper floor. The dogs know him, so he's able to pick them up and get them into his boat. He grabs their remaining dog food. He strikes out again, strangely happy to have company, even if it's only two yappy chihuahuas, one of them, Selina, being pregnant.

Herbie is in no hurry. The trip back takes about half the day. He arrives at Matine's in the late afternoon to find that the water has dropped there only a little. Any effort to get to his mother's money box in the freezer will have to wait at least another day. He considers his lodging options and again decides against the flea-ridden barn. With the fair weather and the day promising to cool off, he thinks he'll be better off roosting on the flat roof of Matine's back porch. So he unloads the dogs, their food, and his provisions on to the roof. He'll search for another powerboat tomorrow.

Before dark, Herbie accumulates some more odd company. A piglet —no doubt from a litter of feral pigs that inhabit the woodlands around here—swims up onto the roof as well. The dogs are unsettled at first but calm down when the little pig keeps a respectable distance. Next a goose shows up, and then another. Pretty soon a small flock of geese has nested on the roof. Herbie feels bad that he doesn't have food to share, but the critters are welcome to his space.

Exhausted, he falls asleep under a star-struck sky, Julio and Selina snuggled up against him, wondering what morning will bring.

13. The Long March

Just after dawn on Tuesday, Charlo Inabnet decides: it's time to go. If he spends another hour or two atop the container, shirtless and shoeless with no protection from the sun on a morning already growing cruelly hot, he'll be broiled alive.

He lets himself down slowly, realizing how much his strength has ebbed, gingerly testing the bottom with his bare feet. His toes find spongy ground; the water comes to about six inches above his knees. It won't be an easy walk. He intends to head up through Yscloskey, just a couple of miles away, and from there in the general direction of Chalmette, hoping that a boat or a plane might come along and rescue him, or that he'll stumble on to other survivors who have what he desperately needs: water and food.

Charlo wades through the wreckage of his flooded front yard and in a minute or two feels the firm, smooth surface of the highway under his feet. He peers one more time across the bayou, spotting his battered boat wedged in among the trees. He nods, as if saying goodbye.

Charlo doesn't take ten steps, however, when searing pain scorches through his foot and up his leg. He cries out in agony, unsure at first what's happened to him.

Balancing on his left leg, he raises his right foot. He sees a bloody puncture wound in his big toe—from a nail, no doubt.

The throbbing pain is almost unbearable.

What to do now?

He gingerly lowers his wounded foot back in the water and shuffles forward, sliding his feet instead of raising them, fearful that he'll step on another nail. This is so slow and painful that he realizes he needs another plan or he simply won't make it.

He stops, gazes around, and sees in the flotsam two longish slender poles, an inch or two in diameter. He shuffles forward and retrieves them, deciding they will have to serve as makeshift walking sticks. With a pole in each hand, he plods forward, tapping the poles on the sub-merged highway ahead of him, testing for foreign objects in his path. When he finds none, he places his feet as he precisely as he can in the place where the poles have been.

Tapping and walking, tapping and walking, tapping and walking, Charlo, still reeling in pain, trudges up the flooded Hopedale Highway.

Perhaps a mile into his journey, Charlo hears a sound—unmis-takably the far-off staccato thumping of an approaching helicopter. He gazes up, shading his eyes from the sun, and sees a speck on the western horizon. The noise grows louder as the chopper comes into clearer view. It begins to circle at low altitudes, clearly above Yscloskey now, and no doubt surveying the storm wreckage. Charlo is about to begin to wave at it when he catches sight of unmistakable lettering on the helicopter's side: it's a news chopper of some fashion from a TV station in either New Orleans or Baton Rouge. "They've got a job to do and they won't be picking up survivors," Charlo thinks. Besides, there's no place for a helicopter to set down in the flooded landscape. At best, he can only hope they see him and report his whereabouts.

In a few minutes, the chopper makes another tight turn and flies off toward the northwest, a diminishing throb in a cloudless sky.

The trip to the bridge at Yscloskey—the very bridge that barred his escapes—takes what seems an eternity. Even at his achingly slow pace, Charlo is forced to stop and rest often. He grows disoriented under the hot sun. So many of the houses and camps that lined the road have been eradicated that he loses his bearings. "All the landmarks were gone," he recalls. "There were times when I just didn't recognize where I was."

At the bridge, Charlo sees firsthand what Katrina has wrought on the tiny fishing village. It's too awful to get his mind around. He knows that if he stands and contemplates this for too long, he might not have the determination to take another step.

He mounts the bridge and looks ahead. The bridge's concrete and iron span has been knocked out of line; the bridge tender's hut battered open and ruined. Just across the bridge, some three-wheeled all-terrain vehicles are hanging from sagging power lines some fifteen feet in the air. A large truck of a variety that hauls refrigerated seafood sits about a hundred yards or more out in the marsh.

Charlo labors across the bridge and turns right, in the direction of a settlement known as Florissant, still some miles away. He plods along, gaining what he judges to be the centerline of the highway, past another quarter-mile-long line of ruins. Charlo has made this drive a thousand times from Hopedale to Chalmette and points beyond, and almost nothing about it is recognizable.

He picks his way slowly forward, his foot still throbbing, the sun baking him, his thirst gnawing at him like an abrasion in the pit of his throat. The highway here follows something of a ridge, which affords Charlo his only advantage: the water is shallower, having subsided to a point below his knees. It makes the going slightly easier, though he is also walking against an ebbing current as the last of Katrina's tides continue their retreat. He passes a large natural-gas processing plant sprawled above the marsh on the east side of the road. It would normally be bustling with workers, but it had been evacuated and sits eerie, flooded, battered, and empty.

Charlo presses on at an agonizingly slow pace. Most of the utility poles along this stretch are still standing, though stripped of their wires and in some cases knocked over at an angle. He measures his progress by the poles: he can hobble only the distance between two poles before he has to stop, catch his breath, and rest. At times he feels woozy and worries that he will fall. Only an iron will drives him onward.

He reaches the community of Florissant, a collection of maybe fifty houses strung out along a four-and-a-half-mile road known as the Florissant Highway. The place looks as if it's been bombed. Homes have been wiped clean to their slabs, their splintered remnants scattered in unrecognizable heaps on lawns covered in two to three feet of marsh mat and other debris. There are homes still clinging to their foundations but with giant holes punched through them, as if some massive fist had rammed the front door and come out the back.

Mangled houses are the least of his worries. Trees, limbs, power lines lie in a jumble across the road, every one of them looming as a formidable obstacle to a man in a severely declining condition. By the position of the sun in the sky, Charlo figures he's been walking four, five, maybe six hours by now, though he doubts he's covered four miles.

He presses on, hot, sweaty, his breathing labored, wondering how much farther he can go. At a clearing in the road, he comes upon two more formidable obstacles: huge alligators—one of them he estimates at eight to ten feet long—lolling in the shallow warm water atop the road about a hundred feet away. Charlo considers retreating but then thinks better of it. He's too exhausted, and anyway, where would he go? He moves cautiously forward, yelling out and clacking his poles together.

Gators here are hunted, so they're usually wary. These two take the hint and plunge off the road into the watery marshscape beyond, disappearing under the water. Charlo picks his way carefully past the spot where they fled, hoping he has really spooked them. If they should come after him, he's a goner. He's in no shape to run, and gators, over a short distance, are as quick as a horse.

The gators mercifully make no reappearance.

A half hour later, Charlo—close to collapse—is stumbling slowly forward, now almost oblivious to his surroundings, simply trying to will himself on, when a shocking thing occurs: he hears voices in the distance to the left of him. He looks that way and spots two men in pirogues, paddling amidst the ruins of a house.

Charlo calls out and the men look up, as startled to see him as he is them.

One of them paddles briskly over and introduces himself: it's Frankie Asevado, B.B. Nunnery's boyfriend, who rescued Matine and Neg Verdin from the barn loft on Bayou Road. He's paddled down here from the Florissant–Highway 46 junction to check on his house. He has his answer.

His house is gone.

The other paddler is his friend Chuckie Thurman, who also has a house at Florissant. His house has been destroyed as well.

Charlo is a mess: shirtless, shoeless, a web of welts, cuts, and abrasions on his arms, face, chest, and back. He's sprouting a beard, his hair is a disheveled mat. He looks like a bedraggled version of Robinson Crusoe. He spins out a brief version of the events that led him here, and

Frankie and Chuckie look at him with a mixture of disbelief and wonder. Having seen what Katrina did to the Florissant settlement, they have a hard time imagining that anyone in the maw of the storm could have survived.

Charlo bums some water and a cigarette from Frankie, who offers him a ride in the pirogue.

"Thank you, podnah," he says. "I know pirogues and I won't turn you over, but just don't ask me to paddle. I don't have the strength."

Frankie smiles and says he can paddle just fine.

He and Chuckie turn the boats in the direction of the Florissant–Highway 46 junction and paddle steadily till they run out of water. They have a shelter destination in mind, but it's two miles away and Charlo—who has traveled almost eight miles already—will have to walk.

With no choice, Charlo steps from the boat and hobbles onward. He can't remember ever being this tired in his entire life.

14. Cruel Tuesday

By late Tuesday afternoon, Ricky Robin is aboard a friend's airboat motoring through the vast, wrecked, debris-choked lake that St. Bernard Parish has become, heading east-southeast for his hometown of Yscloskey sixteen miles away. He's temporarily left the *Lil' Rick* and its ever-rotating roster of passengers in the capable hands of his cousin Dwight. His mission: to see how his house in Yscloskey, and that of his parents who live next door, fared in the storm.

The comings and goings of the citizens' flotilla at Violet Canal have brought snippets of news from many areas of St. Bernard Parish—all of it uniformly grim. But there have been no reports yet from the southernmost precincts—places such as Yscloskey, Shell Beach, Hopedale, and Delacroix Island. Ricky simply must find out what happened to the place that has sheltered so many generations of his family.

As for his house, surely, Ricky thinks, even this swift-moving, catastrophic flood couldn't have done much damage to a home perched and bolted on concert pilings set twelve feet above the ground? A house on a plot of land that sits relatively high for these precincts?

On the other hand, his parents' house sits at ground level: it's hard to imagine that it could have survived intact.

And as the landscape slowly slides by and the airboat moves deeper toward Lake Borgne and the gulf, a sickening feeling comes over him. The farther east and south he goes, the more profound the wreckage becomes. The fierce winds that threatened to upend the *Lil' Rick* at Violet Canal blew even more viciously down here, for not only are houses flooded to their roof lines: some have lost roofs and others have been simply flattened, lying in vast splintered rafts on the surface. He passes mobile home parks where trailers lie stacked up against one another and crushed like tin cans. Others have been torn apart and lie in unrecognizable heaps of twisted metal floating in the water. Off Highway 46, at a small settlement of camps set on stilts in a grove of woods, some of the camps have simply been blown away—their naked creosote pilings the only evidence that a dwelling once existed.

Ricky pushes deeper still, heading toward a wayside called Verret about ten miles below Violet Canal. It's there that the St. Bernard Parish levee protection system ends and the land opens up to its aboriginal state: implacably flat and sweeping marshlands etched with bays, lagoons, and sleepy bayous. As he nears Verret, the highway begins a long, slow, man-made rise to the top of the levee, perhaps twenty feet above sea level—a spot generally considered to be the highest in all of St. Bernard Parish.

It is along this rise that Ricky and scores of other storm-wise parish residents have parked some of their vehicles, believing they would be safe from any flood Katrina might throw at them. In Ricky's case, he's left his aging white three-quarter-ton Ford pickup on the eastern shoulder of the rise very near the summit; attached to it is his equally aging twenty-two-foot sportfishing boat. But as he nears the rise, he sees that many of the cars, trucks, and even a bus or two parked on the lower slopes are engulfed in water almost up to their windows. The summit proves no haven. Though his truck sits in only two feet of water, Ricky finds its top and hood covered in marsh grass—meaning that at some point the truck went completely underwater. He hops out of the airboat in disbelief, sloshes to his truck, and opens the driver's door.

Water and gruel-like marsh muck come pouring out.

Immersion in salt water is almost always fatal to truck and car engines, never mind what it does to vehicle bodies and cushioned interiors.

"Well, that was a nice old truck," he says to himself.

His fishing boat fared no better.

Ricky pauses and looks around, trying to get his mind around the breadth of this catastrophe. He peers across the road at a sturdy two-story fire station—whose builders had been mindful of its position in hurricane country—perched on the west side of the rise inside the levee. The station, normally manned by volunteers, is still standing but it is empty, wrecked, and forlorn, its bottom floor gutted by the surge and wind.

Ricky now realizes how far adrenaline has carried him and how deeply it has so far stanched his emotions. He's arrived at this point still trying to cling to his optimism, but he begins to feel it droop like the sagging sun above the surrounding marshy plain.

Ricky could hardly be blamed for his flagging spirits and energy. He'd spent most of Monday night dozing in his captain's chair aboard the *Lil' Rick*—his first sleep in almost forty hours. Keeping the trawler aright and his passengers safe had proven a grueling ordeal. Still, he'd awakened more refreshed than he thought he might be, and trying to look on the bright side. All things considered, the forty-five-odd refugees who'd spent Monday evening on the *Lil' Rick* had done so in relative serenity.

It had been a still night, a little on the warm side. Not much after dark, Matine and Neg Verdin had fallen into a bone-tired slumber in the *Lil' Rick's* two available bunks. But most of the passengers slept out on the hard aft and forward decks with little more to cushion and comfort them than the clothes on their backs or, in some cases, a life jacket or boat seat cushion they'd managed to come with. There was no privacy to speak of and the trawler's compact, barebones head was reserved for the long line of women and children; men were on their own. At least the refugees had eaten, and they had water and a safe place to sleep.

As daybreak arrived, Ricky's spirits had buoyed. He began counting his blessings. Susan and the family were safe nearby and would soon be ferried by small boat to join him on the *Lil' Rick,* and cousin Ronald was snug on the *Invincible Vance*. Ricky's parents, Charlito and Celie, now in their seventies, had ridden out Katrina with relatives in a subdivision down the road. He'd gotten news that they were safe, though not unscathed. As water engulfed their house, they had fled outside to the safety of a neighbor's raised porch. But the diminutive Celie was swept off her feet and almost taken under by what she described as a "wall of water" that swept around them. Only Charlito's quick action—grabbing her by the collar of her blouse—saved her from being washed away. They, too, would soon enough be brought by boat to the safety of the fleet at Violet Canal.

The bright dawn, however, also brought stark clarity mixed with continued chaos.

Just after sunrise, word began to filter in that Junior Rodriguez, the colorful, brash-talking longtime parish president, and his entire disaster-management team were trapped, with few resources save their dying cell phones and some flashlights, on the top of the flooded St. Bernard Parish government building in Chalmette. The sheriff's and fire departments, agencies that would normally be conducting frontline search, rescue, and evacuation, had all but been put out of business—squad cars, fire trucks, and ambulances had been destroyed or rendered useless by the flood, and practically every boat operated by the parish had been sunk. There were deputies and firemen eager to join search and rescue efforts, but few had any equipment.

At the same time, ever more refugees were crowding into Violet Canal, seeking shelter, food, and water on boats like the *Lil' Rick*. And by midmorning the encampment on the Mississippi River levee, still the only dependable high ground around, had swelled to more than a hundred people, including a large contingent of African-Americans who had been washed out of a decades-old black settlement down the road. They came bearing the disquieting news that a historic black cemetery near their neighborhood, a place holding scores of rough-hewn concrete tombs, had been so battered by Katrina's surge that coffins and bodies were strewn everywhere, some of them floating onto the flooded highway. Then came a group of nurses and nurse's aides, caregivers in a nearby nursing home, who were plucked from the catastrophically flooded facility by fishermen and ferried here in small boats. They began to tell an account so harrowing and shocking that people were having a hard time believing it.

As the morning wore on, Ricky, Ronald, and the other boat captains realized that their first priority was to bolster food and water supplies. The human surge was overwhelming the captains' abilities to provide for them all. The Robins had provisions calculated on the short-term needs of maybe a dozen people, not scores.

Scouting parties went out, raiding the cupboards of drowned convenience and grocery stores and breaking into flooded houses that they knew contained well-stocked freezers stuffed with still-edible gumbos, etouffees, soups, and other treasured local delicacies. (An astonishingly large percentage of residents throughout food-centric South Louisiana have a second large freezer tucked into their garages for the specific purpose of storing game and other goodies for the winter.)

This scouting expedition wasn't a simple task, however, since six to eight feet of water still lay over everything. In some cases, people were literally having to dive down in polluted, briny water for cans of food and bottles of water and wrestle them up to the surface. This search produced surreal moments, too, as when scavengers happened upon loaves of white bread, Little Debbie cakes, and Hostess Twinkies—their cellophane wrappers impervious to water—floating indolently in vast rafts on the surface. The nutritiousness of the offerings at that point was not an issue. They were harvested in great numbers with dip nets and brought to the grateful masses assembled at Violet Canal.

By midafternoon, this effort was well in hand and Ricky was feeling restless. The day had grown unbearably hot—not a hint of a breeze stirred. The crowd aboard his boat was beginning to get to him. He was the captain and everyone with a question posed it to him. But Ricky was out of answers. People were desperate for word of an evacuation plan; desperate to try to get messages out to relatives that they were safe. But Ronald Robin had one of the few working cell phones in the entire fleet, and he could get a signal only if he climbed to the tip-top of the boom of the largest shrimp boat in the harbor, and then only sometimes. In a torturous act of kindness, one of the last calls he was able to get out was to link a man to his son dying of cancer—a conversation that had to be carried on with the elderly man clinging precariously to the top of the boom. The rush and even euphoria of surviving the flood and being rescued had given way to a deepening anxiety and frustration, even anger, among many of the refugees.

Ronald could commiserate with Ricky. "It was all chaos and craziness, and the day—man, that sumbitch was hotter than a scalded dog," he recalls. "People were doing their best, but there was a lot everybody had to cope with."

Ricky, however, also recognized a deeper yearning than to take a temporary break from the demanding crowds. Their home here at Violet Canal that they had been sharing with Susan's father lay in watery ruin. Sooner or later this nightmare would end, the water would recede, and his family would need a place to live. "I had to go see my house at Yscloskey," he says. "I had to know if it survived."

His friend's airboat had appeared suddenly alongside the *Lil' Rick,* and Ricky had jumped at the chance to go—without having any time to discuss it with Susan, who was below. He could only hope someone on the trawler would pass word of his departure to her.

Now, here at the summit of the levee at Verret, he wonders how to complete his journey, the airboat owner having headed back to tend to his own family and friends near Violet. The water from the highway onward, unencumbered by levees, has retreated with the Katrina tides, but a foot or so still covers the road, making for a difficult slog if he has to walk.

Ricky looks around and spots his ticket: an abandoned pirogue on the downslope of the levee, a paddle lying alongside it. The highway may be too shallow to float a pirogue, but a ditch that flanks the highway's east side is plenty deep. So he pulls the pirogue to the ditch, hops in, and shoves off.

Debris clogging the water makes the going slow, although he's also helped some by a slow-moving current—the final ebbing of Katrina's high tides as they flow back toward Lake Borgne and eventually the gulf. This stretch of highway is devoid of residences or buildings until the junction of the Florissant Highway about two miles away. But Ricky has a hunch, based on what he's seen so far, that the tree-lined Florissant may have been left impassable by the storm.

He has an alternative route in mind. Just above Florissant junction, Ricky comes upon the entrance of an old man-made waterway known as the Toller Canal, which more or less parallels the Florissant as it travels in a slow five-mile oxbow toward Yscloskey. (Although no canal with that name appears on St. Bernard Parish maps, Ricky says this is what the locals call it.) He nudges the pirogue into the narrow mouth and, using the ebbing tide, makes his way slowly along, dodging numerous Katrina obstructions. Levees built from the dirt and muck removed during the canal's excavation line its banks. Stunted Spanish oaks, moss-draped hackberries, and other native species cloak the levees, and it's clear they've taken a beating. Trees toppled by hurricane

Tough Scenery: The Robin cousins, Ronald (left) and Ricky, at the bridge over Bayou La Loutre in Yscloskey nine days after Hurricane Katrina destroyed much of their historic fishing village. The far bank behind them had been lined with camps before the storm. (Photo by Ken Wells)

A Drive Through Hell: On the same day, the view from Ricky's van window of wreckage along the Florissant Highway. (Photo by Ken Wells)

Reunion: Ricky and Susan Robin in Ricky's FEMA trailer in spring 2006, during a rare visit from her temporary home in Tennessee. The Robins were not permanently reunited until the fall of 2007, more than two years after the storm. (Photo by Ken Wells)

Bayou Postcard: The *Lil' Rick,* Ricky Robin's handmade steel trawler, at the harbor on Bayou La Loutre in less turbulent waters about a year before the storm. (Photo by Monique Michelle Verdin)

Toughing It Out: Ninety-year-old Matine Verdin on the porch of the house that she, her two sons, and a nephew narrowly escaped. The house was eventually demolished, but Matine and her son Xavier are living in a modular home on the property. (Photo by Monique Michelle Verdin)

Sad Work: Herbert Verdin, who saved his mother and brother from the surge, tried salvaging items from the broken and flooded house but ultimately found little to save. He has since died of liver cancer. (Photo by Monique Michelle Verdin)

Xavier ("Neg") Verdin, Matine's disabled son, in front of his crypt in the historic Bayou Terre-aux-Boeufs Cemetery just up from the Verdin house. (Photo by Monique Michelle Verdin)

Miracle Man: Charles ("Charlo") Inabnet in front of the ruins of the storm-hardened camp on the Hopedale Highway he was tossed out of as Katrina blasted the area head-on. (Photo by Monique Michelle Verdin)

Grim Mementos: Photos tacked to the bulletin board of Charlo's trailer carry reminders of his harrowing brush with Katrina. (Photo by Monique Michelle Verdin)

Mobile Home: The Yscloskey house of Joe and Selina Gonzales in a thick field of marsh mat two months after being ripped from its moorings, spun around, and shoved some three hundred feet by Katrina's wind and water. (Photo by Ken Wells)

Solid Anchor: The *Joy Lynn*, an elegant sixty-four-foot oyster lugger that Joe Gonzales began building thirty years before, fared better than his house. Joe used multiple ropes to tie down the boat, which barely got a scratch from the storm. (Photo by Ken Wells)

Moving Day: Against all odds, the Gonzaleses, with the help of volunteers, were able to gut and stabilize their house, then pay a contractor to jack it up, load it on a trailer, and move it back to its original location. (Photo by Ken Wells)

Home Again: Selina and Joe in front of their residence after workers settled it back on its original slab. In the foreground are the large steel pilings on which the house now sits. (Photo by Monique Michelle Verdin)

Trashed: Most of the Gonzales family's Yscloskey neighbors had little to come back to. This house nearby was typical of the destruction. (Photo by Ken Wells)

Toying with Trucks: The violence of Katrina's wind and water was on ready display in neighboring Plaquemines Parish, where this multi-ton seafood hauling truck was tossed into an oak tree. (Photo by Ken Wells)

Boat Rescue: Thanks to their boat-handling skills, Ricky and Ronald Robin were employed for several weeks as part of a FEMA-financed effort to clear waterways of Katrina rubble and to recover sunken boats. Here, Ronald's boat, the *Evening Star*, tends a barge and crane lifting up a battered oyster lugger from a Plaquemines Parish harbor. (Photo by Ken Wells)

Oil and Water: A scene from a neighborhood near the Murphy Oil refinery at Meraux, where a Katrina-battered oil storage tank ruptured and soiled about 1,800 already flooded residences with thousands of gallons of crude. (Photo by Ken Wells)

Dog Day Afternoon: Animals were also victims of the spill. This forlorn Yorkshire terrier makes its way down Judge Perez Drive near the Murphy Oil refinery. (Photo by Aric Mayer)

Crushed: A once substantial house, flattened by the surge that overwhelmed levees protecting the Lexington Place subdivision. (Photo by Ken Wells)

Channel of Misery: St. Bernard's official memorial to its Katrina dead sits at the intersection of Bayou La Loutre and the infamous Mississippi River–Gulf Outlet (the MR-GO). The U.S. Army Corps of Engineers, which built the channel over local fishing and environmental opposition, has agreed to close it, but the funding to do so has yet to be appropriated. (Photo by Monique Michelle Verdin)

winds typically all fall in the same direction. But Ricky sees evidence of tornado damage—clusters of trees, most still upright, with their upper branches twisted and snapped into random shapes, as if some giant had flayed them with a crushing backhand.

With less than two hours of light left in the day, Ricky reaches a junction where the canal bumps back up against the highway a short distance above Yscloskey. The road is still covered in calf-deep water, easy enough to walk on but not quite deep enough to float the pirogue. He secures the boat and trudges onward, less than a half mile from home, peering ahead with both anticipation and dread.

What he sees, at the junction of the highway and a doglegged street that leads to his house, shocks him. He wouldn't normally be able to see his house from here, but he knows it is standing—because almost everything that once obstructed his view has been knocked down.

His parents' house is there, too—but not where it should be.

It's been lifted up and tossed against his own.

Even from this distance, Ricky can tell it's been battered and perhaps broken; it sits, part of it leaning over at an angle, its doors and windows blasted out or knocked awry. He thinks about what's in the house—all of his parents' possessions; all of his childhood memories; his father's beloved collection of the miniature fishing boats he's meticulously carved. He can only shake his head at having to bring this sad news back to Charlito and Celie.

A short distance behind his house, Ricky sees an object he doesn't recognize. He gazes at it for a long moment, his hands shielding his eyes from the lowering sun, to get a better view. *Ah, it's a boat—a big-ass boat.* Ricky judges it to be about thirty-five feet long. It's obviously been tossed up into his yard from nearby Bayou La Loutre.

Ricky shakes his head again, as if doing so might restore order to this catastrophic scene. But things only get worse. He gazes left, toward the entrance of an upscale development called Fort Beauregard Marina Estates, with large lots fronting deepwater man-made canals. About a dozen large and lavish weekend "camps" owned mostly by well-to-do New Orleans sportsmen stood here. Some of these "camps" are seven-thousand-square-foot mansions, done up in Creole and even Cape Cod architecture, and all of them are set up on elaborate twelve- to fifteen-foot high pilings of steel, concrete, or creosoted posts. Ricky does a quick scan and realizes most of the camps are simply gone. He counts at least five sets of forlorn pilings swept clean of the giant houses that sat atop them.

Katrina was an equal opportunity destroyer.

Ricky pushes on, moving past the junction and around a curve to the road, Robin Street, that leads to his house. A fallen tree and other debris have blocked a large drain, forcing Ricky to ford a short stretch of water, three to four feet deep, to get to his house just a long block away. He sloshes in and out of the Katrina-made pond, cutting through the yard he shared with his parents to examine their house first.

He peers through a battered window and what he sees sickens him: mud-covered furniture, clothes, and knickknacks spun together in an almost unrecognizable knot in the center of the room, as if the contents had been thrown into giant inward spinning whirlpool of mud.

Precious little can be saved here, Ricky thinks.

He turns and walks the short distance to his house, examining it as he goes. He's lost some windows and there's evidence that the house shifted slightly on its pilings, some of which have cracked. But the roof and basic structure seem to be intact. He mounts his front steps, trudges up, and enters through the front door.

The smell is the first thing that hits him: the unmistakable odor of lingering damp.

He peers forward in the fading light and quickly has part of the answer he came looking for: the dull brown but unmistakable line of a watermark sits three feet high on his walls. The line, he knows, is the indicator of where the water level finally *settled*, not necessarily how high it might have surged at any one moment.

There's plenty of evidence to suggest it got higher: pictures knocked off the walls, wet clothes hanging in closets at a level higher than the watermark.

Ricky is stunned. Even the hard-bitten seamen in him, who many times has seen firsthand the arbitrary violence of nature, can't imagine this much water piling in on top of his home place.

At least he has flood insurance.

Ricky has come with no provisions save a bottle of water and a flashlight. He has a long way back to anywhere, and part of that journey will be in the dark. He knows he should leave immediately. But he needs two more things: a drink, and more knowledge.

He goes to his liquor cabinet where he keeps a quart bottle of Jack Daniels on an upper shelf, fetches the bottle, uncorks it and takes two long drinks, chasing them down with a slug of water. He replaces the bottle, wipes his mouth on the back of his hand, and goes to a rear window where he has a semi-panoramic view of the rest of Yscloskey.

If the scene from his window is any indication, about 85 percent of what stood has been destroyed.

In the fading twilight Ricky trudges along in somber spirits—hot, sweaty, beyond tired. With tide and current still dropping toward the gulf, he decides his best bet is to gain the levee of the Toller Canal and walk back. The ebbing tide reminds him of the sole advantage that residents of Yscloskey and other burgs below the levee system will have: their disaster zones should dry out pretty quickly. But in most of St. Bernard Parish tucked in behind the levees, the very system designed to save them from floods is going to hold the water in for a long time; much of it, Ricky reckons, will have to be pumped out, or the levees will have to be dynamited or bulldozed in places to let it flow out.

Ricky's basic plan is to make it to the wayside at Verret, where he can only hope that he might run into someone patrolling for survivors and hitch a ride back to Violet Canal. On the other hand, he realizes that might be an improvident journey to undertake after dark, given the debris-choked waters. If Verret is abandoned, he can always camp for the night on the upper floor of the battered fire station.

Walking the debris-choked levee, though, proves tough. He's constantly tripping over roots and fallen limbs and having to dodge over, around, and under fallen trees. Broken, low-hanging branches claw and scratch as he slides by. It's painstaking, exhausting work. Less than an hour after he leaves Yscloskey, he feels he hasn't made much progress and his flashlight begins to dim, then dies. He stops to let his eyes adjust to the dark and get his bearings. The night is still, silent, stultifying. He trudges ahead, soon oblivious to everything save the will to keep moving, the enveloping dark, the sweat on his brow, the cadence of his labored breathing.

At some point, where the levee opens up and the ground grows soft, Ricky takes a step—and feels the earth move beneath him.

Startled, disoriented, he kicks forward, almost stumbling, as something big and strong squirms beneath his foot. Involuntarily, he cries out and begins to sprint away. A huge alligator, seething, darts toward the nearby water. Ricky's foot smashes into a root or a branch. He almost goes down—driving his big toe nearly through the top of his boot. (He'll lose a toenail over this.) He yells in pain, a shout that perhaps convinces the startled alligator that running was a wise choice.

Ricky sprints another twenty yards, obstacles be damned, just to make sure he is clear of the gator. He glances back, able to see little but pleased to hear the gator's noisy retreat through the underbrush. He stands for a while in the dark to catch his breath, calm his pounding heart, and recover his wits. He hobbles on, his toe throbbing, wide awake and keenly alert to the possibility of other gators. He encounters none and finally—close to four hours after leaving his house—he's within striking distance of the fire station at Verret.

The highway is dry now. Ahead in the dark, he is gladdened by the sight of lights flickering in the distance—others are at the fire station. He'll have company, maybe even find food and water.

Ricky quickens his pace and soon arrives, euphoric to have made it through a dark, long passage that had turned into an ordeal. There are maybe eight or ten people about. He first fixes his gaze on a tall shirtless man whose very demeanor gives away a bone-deep weariness. He walks up and introduces himself.

"I'm Ricky Robin," he says, "and I just walked all the way from Yscloskey."

The man grins and offers his hand. "I'm Charles Inabnet, though people who know me call me Charlo. And, funny, I pretty much walked here all the way from Hopedale."

Ricky looks him over—even in the inadequate glow of flashlights, he can see the welts, bruises, and abrasions on Charlo's arms and chest.

"Man," he replies, "it looks like somebody tied you to a tree a whupped you bad. What happened out there?"

"Katrina's the one that tied me to the tree," says Charlo.

"She took your shoes, too?" Ricky says, looking down and noticing Charlo's bare feet.

"My shoes, my shirt, even my doggone teeth," Charlo says.

"Aw, man, we got to find you some shoes somehow," says Ricky.

Doing what bayou men often do when they meet, they begin to swap stories, Charlo telling his first. Ricky listens intently, alternately laughing at Charlo's deadpan rehashing of parts of his ordeal and wincing at a great deal of the rest. When he is done, Charlo adds an odd coda. Thinking about it all, his greatest ambition (beyond a bath, a shave, finding some shoes, replacing his dentures, and most of all phoning his wife and daughter to tell them he is alive) is to go back down to Hopedale to check on his boat, the *Captain John J.*

A silence follows. Ricky Robin realizes he has tears in his eyes.

He can't readily explain them, for they are complicated. It's all too clear that the world he has known has been cruelly upended; indeed, the world of his childhood, the place that is the repository of his life's memories, may never be put back together precisely as it was. It is possible that the bayou way of life itself may simply not survive this blow.

But mixed in with this anxious grief lies something else: a tenacious optimism. Poor Charlo got washed out of two camps, tossed into the drink by a big-ass wave, spent a day roped to a tree in the company of raccoons, slept the night on a steel container, walked for miles barefoot on makeshift crutches, on the brink of dehydration, with a nail hole in his toe. Ricky himself has endured tornadoes and fierce tidal surges, the scary prospect of losing his family, the demoralizing flooding of both of his homes, and a harrowing encounter with an alligator. Yet here they both are, still standing, still able to laugh. And whatever happens—whatever grief, frustration, and anger lie ahead—they've got damned great stories, stories destined to become family heirlooms.

Down here, the power of stories can help keep you alive.

Charlo's rescuers, Frankie and Chuckie, are here as well. Between them all, they manage to find a first-aid kit in the fire station and treat, as best they can, Charlo's wounds, including his badly punctured toe. Shoes, however, are not to be found, though the men are able to improvise a quick fix, swaddling his feet in Ace bandages taken from the first-aid kit. Charlo can at least hobble around on the ground, still littered in many places with treacherous storm debris, with some protection against cuts and infection.

The strange serendipity of being storm-stranded in the South Louisiana food belt presents itself again when the bounty of the fire station's refrigerator and freezer are raided for a supper of shrimp and potatoes fried up over campfires on the adjacent levee. A stew of stories is swapped, the night grows late, and people begin to drag mattresses from the firehouse's upper floor out onto the levee.

This arrangement turns out to be short lived. There is a couple here that, snippets of overheard conversation reveal, has a drug problem. Absent their substance of choice, they quarrel and groan incessantly in low tones, making the situation uneasy for everyone. But no one wants to retreat into the stuffy, baking firehouse—until a snake invades the company and crawls over a woman sleeping atop a mattress. She shrieks out her discovery and the campers beat a hasty retreat to the firehouse's second floor. Ricky beds down in a corner; Charlo sleeps well off the ground, on top of an overturned refrigerator.

Still, things could be worse. While Ricky, Charlo, and the others at the Verret fire station try to catch some fitful sleep, Junior Rodriguez, the parish president still stranded on the roof of the local government office building in Chalmette, has been dictating a desperate plea for help via his cell phone to a resident outside the parish, who posts the message on an Internet forum. Junior wants the president of the United States to know that a lot of people in St. Bernard Parish remain in serious trouble.

Dear President Bush:

My name is Henry "Junior" Rodriguez and I am President of St. Bernard Parish Louisiana.

My parish is completely flooded from the recent passage of hurricane Katrina. The eye of the hurricane passed directly over my parish and has caused mass destruction and complete flooding.

Of our community of 67,000 citizens, many are surrounded by water and have no place to go. We have NO food, NO water, NO sanitation, NO power, and NO communication.

We have no way to rescue or recover our citizens.

Absolutely no attempt has been made to communicate with me regarding the catastrophe that has occurred to the citizens that I represent.

I cannot believe that in a country as sophisticated as the United States of America that the leadership in the White House cannot somehow communicate NOW with me and the local government that I represent.

This disaster is a direct outgrowth of the neglect of the Federal Government to address the costal erosion problem of southern Louisiana.

I implore you to please contact me directly or have the appropriate federal agency respond IMMEDIATELY to this disaster. I am in danger of having many citizens die if they are not rescued now.

On behalf of the citizens of St. Bernard Parish, Louisiana, I am begging for your help.

Sincerely,

Henry "Junior" Rodriguez

President, St. Bernard Parish, Louisiana

Junior posts his cell phone number at the end of the message. But it will be days yet before any agent of the federal—or state—government phones him back.

15. A Day of Reckoning

It's Wednesday, early yet, another cloudless day, the sun still tucked down behind distant trees, an ephemeral mist hanging over the water, the temperature tenuously cool on a day that by midmorning will again grow unbearably hot. Ricky Robin rises early from his mattress at Verret and bids his goodbyes to Charlo, Frankie, and Chuckie, who have decided to stick together. Ricky and an acquaintance named Huey, who has also spent the night at the station, find an abandoned motorboat inside the Verret levee and shove off in it. The water inside the protection levee has dropped some, but not enough yet to impede the borrowed outboard.

Ricky and Huey have a stop to make, for Huey has heard an awful story—one possibly involving the drowning of his grandmother—and he desperately needs to know if it's true. He has asked Ricky to divert the boat to investigate.

Ricky can't very well refuse, and anyway, he's curious. Huey's story is the same awful one that had filtered, in bits and pieces, through the Violet Canal flotilla on Monday night. It was almost too terrible to believe.

The place in question is St. Rita's, a nursing home off the four-lane Highway 46 about three miles below Violet Canal and an easy detour on the way back to Violet. The trip from Verret in normal times would take maybe twenty minutes by car, but given the need to motor through and around storm debris and obstacles, the route by boat takes more than an hour. The nursing home lies a long block down a spur road just off the west side of the highway.

Ricky spots the nondescript building, throttles back the outboard to idle speed, and noses the boat in a slow left turn toward the complex. It is still early, eerily quiet, windless, the water as still as the blue sky whose reflection it catches in openings between trees. The building stands as if some surreal still life: a drab apparition, water etched up to the bottom of its lower windows, trees standing like pickets in mirrored water, the roofs of drowned cars and trucks mounding up on the unruffled surface like giant turtle backs.

A frisson of foreboding shudders through Ricky. He thinks about turning back, but he knows Huey needs to look inside this building for himself. Ricky steers the boat toward the nearest window; they are at eye level when they arrive. They look in.

What they see doesn't quite register at first. It doesn't seem to make sense. But clarity comes like a jolt: it's a pair of feet, ghostly white, sticking up out of the water, the toes pointed toward the ceiling.

Whoever they belong to must have gotten trapped, somehow, below the five to six feet of water that still lies atop the nursing home.

Huey breaks down and cries. Ricky has seen enough.

Ricky backs away as Huey begins to tell what he's heard. About sixty mostly elderly and frail patients, including his grandmother, waited out the storm there. Plans to evacuate them somehow never materialized. The water came seemingly out of nowhere in one or two battering waves. Nurses, other personnel, and a few citizens who had come to stay with their relatives during the storm tried frantically to rescue them, but many of the elderly drowned in their beds and wheelchairs.

Huey's heard that at least thirty people are dead, maybe more, and they are all still inside. He's heard the story of a fisherman who was able to save his ailing brother by floating him out on a mattress—yet had no choice but to let another feeble patient drown because he couldn't get back before the water engulfed the place. Many of the survivors are said to be in critical condition, most having lost their medications or, in some cases, having been disconnected from oxygen bottles and the like. They've been taken to an impromptu shelter where there is simply no medical care beyond what volunteers can offer. The beastly hot temperatures are only making their situation more precarious.

Ricky can only shake his head.

They pull slowly away from St. Rita's and continue on toward Violet Canal.

Susan Robin is ecstatic to see her husband. And, yes, she knew where he was all along: the airboat operator who had dropped him off at

Verret had swung back through Violet Canal to tell Susan of Ricky's plans to paddle or walk to Yscloskey. Knowing the distances involved and the time Ricky was dropped off, she calculated that he probably was held up by dark and had to spend the night someplace.

Still, Ricky has arrived not a moment too soon. Susan is now in a great deal of pain from her recent back surgery; her father, Sidney T., isn't doing well. Her daughters are growing anxious, as are other passengers aboard the trawler. Matine Verdin, in between fretting over the traumatized Neg, alternates between stoicism and despair. Last night, Susan reports, she insisted on giving up her bunk to "the old man"— Susan's father, though Matine is older than Sidney T. She slept seated in a folding chair next to Neg's bunk. She also surrendered her meal of spaghetti to Neg, fearing that the modest helping he got wasn't enough to sustain him. Susan worries that Matine herself may become undernourished. Other times, Susan encountered her crying softly, begging in her limited English to go home.

Susan could only hug her and say, "You have no home, cher. Sorry, but none of us have a home."

It's become plain to Susan that waiting here much longer isn't a viable option. People are starting to fall apart. A way out has to be found, and soon, too.

To make matters worse, the nearby Mississippi River levee has become increasingly crowded with refugees, and for all of the efforts to scavenge some food and share what people are finding, the results are uneven. Some people aren't doing well on their rations and are growing quietly desperate. A certain rowdy element, fueled by beer and whiskey, frustration and the heat, is beginning to make its presence known. Quarrels and near fights have broken out, and some of the more beaten-down levee dwellers are beginning to feel fearful and anxious. A man in a flatboat appears alongside the *Lil' Rick* in the afternoon asking for Ricky, and bearing a sheet of paper. It's a petition, signed by 150 levee dwellers, appointing Ricky "the marshal of Violet Canal."

Ricky shakes his head when the man explains the problem, not sure what to say. He's not a cop, has no cop training, has no weapon and, petition or not, no actual authority beyond the bounds of his boat. But he says he'll see what he can do.

Later in the afternoon, another man arrives at the boat with more optimistic tidings. There are reports of efforts to organize boatlifts from one or two places on the Mississippi River levee above Violet Canal. One of the staging areas is opposite the Kaiser Plant, a large industrial complex on the river a few miles west and north of Violet that has also taken in a large number of the refugees. Some survivors are heading there by boat. But the levee is also being used as a roadway or footpath for those who can find a way to get to it.

Matine Verdin overhears this conversation and talks it over with Ricky. With Susan's declining condition, and worries about Sidney T., Ricky reluctantly decides he has his hands full, and that Matine and Neg would be better off getting out now. They would at least have a chance of reuniting with relatives who by now are surely searching for them.

Matine nods in agreement. She expresses as best she can her gratitude to Ricky. "When this is over, come over. We'll get together and cook a gumbo," she says.

"That would be nice," Ricky replies.

Matine and Neg board the flatboat, wave goodbye to Ricky and Susan and the others still aboard the *Lil' Rick,* and make the short journey to the Mississippi River levee, where they are helped out of the boat. From their perch on the *Lil' Rick,* the Robins can see them plod up the levee, a harder climb now that the water has dropped appreciably. Other evacuees are turning right, in the direction of a large truck that has materialized to take refugees to the boatlift collection point. But Matine, tugging on Neg, goes left, in the direction of Bayou Road—in the direction of home.

After a few steps, though, she stumbles, rolls a short distance down the levee, and gets entangled in some loose strands of barbed wire— debris left by the receding waters. Her cries bring attention and she is soon helped up, extricated from the wire and eased gently to the top of the levee again. As helpers tend to her cuts and scratches, she assures everyone she isn't badly hurt. She slowly regains her composure, smoothes her dress, and begins with Neg to plod, resigned, toward the truck.

They are helped aboard and the truck trundles off toward a staging area, where they will board a barge loaded with St. Bernard refugees headed for the west-bank town of Harvey. They are finally leaving their stricken homeland—though it will be days before their ordeal is over.

As much as her pain is driving her to leave as well, Susan Robin is still reluctant to forsake the basic safety and comfort of the trawler and Ricky's presence, and Ricky feels he can't go just yet. For one thing, a boat the size of the *Lil' Rick* still can't get out of Violet Canal, clogged as it is with other boats, some of them sunken, and storm debris. He won't leave the *Lil' Rick* behind unsecured. The trawler may be the only useful possession they have left. And, amid the lingering chaos, he takes seriously his presence as a stabilizing influence here.

But a serendipitous event changes Susan's mind. In the evening, a kid aboard the *Lil' Rick* climbs up to the top of the raised booms with Susan's cell phone and gets a signal. He dials out to a phone number that Susan has given him, the number of her grown son by her first marriage who had evacuated to Tennessee, and miraculously gets him. He has been frantically trying to reach Susan and the family and has already hooked up with a doctor who owns a sportfishing boat docked on the north side of Lake Pontchartrain. The doctor has expressed willingness to attempt the forty-mile, debris-choked trek south across the lake to fetch Susan, her father, and whoever else wants to leave. A nurse will accompany them.

The Robins talk it over. It's a no-brainer.

On Thursday morning, the boat arrives and Susan, Sidney T., and her daughters say their tearful goodbyes to Ricky. They strike out up Violet Canal to the MR-GO, and up that until they reach Lake Pontchartrain, which they cross and eventually make their way out of the Katrina zone, driving with Susan's son to Tennessee. Ricky's parents, Charlito and Celie, will endure a similar odyssey as they flee the hurricane's damage. Later, Ricky's cousin Tee-Tee and his son, Dwight Jr., also depart, joining the escalating crowds of refugees boarding ferries that local and state officials have finally been able to organize to carry survivors to drop-off points across the Mississippi River. There, buses await to take them to places as far away as Dallas.

By the time on Thursday afternoon—four and a half days after the storm—that the National Guard and the Coast Guard splash into Violet Canal aboard military trucks on roads still covered in a foot of water, the encampment here has pretty much emptied out. A straggling group of refugees refer the caravan commanders to Ricky Robin, the marshal of Violet Canal. Ricky will have a hard time articulating what went on here, and he is too modest to tell them that he and the other captains at Violet have already done much of the work that the military has finally arrived to do.

As for that rowdy crowd on the levee, Ricky handled that, too. Listening to weather reports on his transistor radio, he heard that another hurricane had formed in the deep gulf. Although it isn't expected to pose a threat to the Louisiana coastline, he wandered into the group— knowing they didn't have a radio. He solemnly reported the grim news of another storm, suggesting they decamp down the levee to join the crowds trying to get to the rescue ferries.

In an hour, the levee was empty.

PART TWO

Aftermath

16. Nine Days Beyond the Flood

It's Thursday, September 7, another cloudless, hot, and muggy day. I'm driving with my new acquaintance, Ricky Robin, in the Katrina-dented van that saved Susan Robin and her family, through the mud-splattered, wrecked, and by now largely empty and mildewing precincts of St. Bernard Parish.

We motor slowly past the rows and rows and streets and streets of battered, silent houses with mud caking their lawns, waterlines up to their eaves, and storm drift (and sometimes boats) on their roofs; past fallen trees, upended utility poles, downed power lines lying like uncoiled dead snakes on the shoulder; past cars decorating fences and in some cases leaned upright against the sides of houses, or stacked like bricks atop each other; past the wind-ravaged, flood-soaked, sometimes gutted facades of gas stations, restaurants, and convenience stores, their parking lots often littered with debris and drowned cars; past the ubiquitous sportfishing boats now sitting high and dry on the roadside and in some cases in the middle of the road, boats that once ferried refugees back and forth to safe havens like Violet Canal, now abandoned and in some cases cracked and broken as if they'd had a hard landing; past the hollow-eyed and raw-ribbed stray dogs occasionally tumbling out of the wreckage or venturing from the yards they still intended to protect, dogs on the edge of going feral, too many days beyond food and care.

We've traveled several miles already from an emergency operating center on the southwestern edge of Chalmette, headed in the general direction of Violet Canal, where Ricky says we will pick up his cousin Ronald Robin and go on from there. Yscloskey is our hoped-for destination, though there is only faint hope of getting there. Ricky keenly wants to show me the ruins of his hometown, but the Florissant Highway, when he checked a day ago, was still closed by storm debris to traffic.

So far on this journey I've yet to spy a single car, truck, house, or commercial building—not one structure or man-made thing of any kind—that had been spared the destruction of Katrina.

That's because for all practical purposes, except for the shrimp and oyster boats that Ricky and other captains saved at Violet Canal, there pretty much won't be any.

"Incredible, huh?" says Ricky. "You have to see this to believe it."

He stops. "That sumbitch even drowned the Wal-Mart," he says.

I could already appreciate Ricky's gallows humor. "Incredible" actually seemed an understatement.

My reporting duties for the *Wall Street Journal* had not yet taken me to the destroyed Mississippi Gulf Coast, but until arriving in St. Bernard Parish I thought I'd already seen the worst of the storm's ravages in Louisiana. I'd watched from the opposing bank as throbbing Huey helicopters tried desperately to seal the vast, raw gash in the Seventeenth Street Canal levee in New Orleans, where water five days after the storm was still coursing, like some untamed whitewater river, into the posh Lake View neighborhood. You could plainly see the cleaved-open houses and the cars, buses, and trucks wrapped up into tight scrums by the currents.

I'd kept a reporter's vigil for an entire afternoon on an oven-hot off-ramp of I-10 just a few miles west of downtown that had been turned into a boat launch area to search the sprawling lake that much of New Orleans had become. It was all too surreal: the constant coming and going of oversized pickup trucks towing skiffs and airboats manned mostly by volunteers come to look for survivors. The crews—owing to disturbing reports of gunfire on CNN and the like—were heavily armed. I watched a man in camouflage fatigues, carrying a heavy-duty shotgun and sporting a bandolier of ammunition around his chest, easing into a boat with four other volunteers. He looked like he was out for an invasion of a small country instead of a mission of mercy. Boats like his had to pull away slowly; the near waters were clogged with semi-submerged vans and cars that clearly had been abandoned, most likely in a moment of panic when the waters abruptly rose, smack in the middle of the freeway. I'd seen survivors brought in that a volunteer emergency medical technician later would tell me were "too dehydrated to cry." I'd even hopped into a canoe and gone on a grim paddle looking for a body when EMTs on the ramp, who were under orders not to leave their positions, thought they spotted one bobbing up against a partially submerged railing of the eastbound freeway about a hundred yards away. There was no one else who could go, so I volunteered; to my relief, it turned out to be a deceiving cluster of debris.

I'd driven to the point where the St. Claude Avenue Bridge over the Industrial Canal plunged abruptly into the becalmed, dark, stinking lagoon that the Lower Ninth Ward had become. Houses from this vantage point still stood window deep in water. I interviewed two exhausted African-American ministers who, on their own, had been paddling the neighborhood in a leaky canoe on the off chance of finding more survivors; the police and the National Guard, having searched once, had moved on. One of the ministers, lacking a proper paddle, had simply been pushing the canoe with his hands. He had raw, bleeding sores in the crooks of his arms, from the constant rubbing against the canoe's rails, to show for it. They'd waded ashore, barefoot, in this putrid stew. They had scant food and water and were sleeping in the soggy, cramped, hot loft of a nearby flooded church. Theirs was one of a seemingly inexhaustible supply of stories—most tragic, some heroic—I was collecting.

I'd taken a rented SUV and driven up the soggy median of the flooded ramparts of Esplanade Avenue, the boulevard forming the lower boundary of the French Quarter, to interview wary refugees, many of whom had fled the misery and anarchy of the nearby Louisiana Superdome and returned to their flooded houses rather than face another day in that place. They straggled out of second-story apartments, wading through foul waist-deep water to seek food, drinking water, and most of all a way out of town. A jacked-up pickup truck manned by Alabama volunteer policemen (one keeping watch with a shotgun) handed out bottled water, energy bars, and oranges to all comers until their provisions were finally gone. I witnessed perhaps the oddest line of the post-Katrina experience: a dozen people, standing in knee-deep water at Esplanade and North Robertson Street, fondling sweaty quarters and waiting to use the only working pay phone for blocks around.

I'd been on the ground at the infamous New Orleans Convention Center, a shelter that was never meant to be, when the National Guard had finally gotten control of the place and was emptying it out. The scene was of a street fair gone horribly awry: lines of bedraggled, exhausted survivors waiting wearily in line for buses that had been promised for days; a frail elderly black woman needing medical care being wheeled to a National Guard truck on a delivery dolly, the only surrogate for a gurney or wheelchair available; a block-long row of angry Lower Ninth Ward evacuees, camped out on the sidewalk, eager to tell the story of how they had to commandeer an abandoned city bus and drive themselves to safety when the buses and drivers promised by the city never materialized. Now here they were, in this hellish place without food, water, plumbing that worked, or order of any kind; a place where rumors of crime ended up being more menacing than the crime itself. Mounds of garbage littered the streets and sidewalks and the blindingly acrid, rancid smell of the center—detectable from six blocks away, if the wind was right—filled the air. Despite that, I had, out of journalistic curiosity, gone in to check out stories of an impromptu morgue on an upper floor, but was knocked back, gagging, from a doorway by the odor. Eventually it required workers in hazmat suits to clean the place up. Among other things, they had to rip out a million square feet of stinking, sodden carpet.

I'd also watched as the last few hundred poor souls stranded in the wretchedness of the Superdome had been corralled into long, temporary paddocks on the outdoor mezzanine for *their* bus ride out of hell. Each pen, crafted from steel fencing and numbered, held fifty-six people, a bus worth's. Shade didn't exist. A helicopter hovered over the crowd to provide ventilation.

The scene seemed proof of the egalitarian nature of Katrina's misery. In the pen on the far left milled an orderly if beaten-down group of European tourists, Scandinavians judging by their blond hair and accents, who had not heeded evacuation warnings and had seen far more of the underbelly of New Orleans than they'd intended. They sat with remarkable patience, sipping bottled water and fanning themselves with hands and improvised bits of cardboard, waiting for a big-voiced National Guard solider to bark out their number so they could board a bus. In the pen on the far right: a hapless group that seemed to represent a final police sweep (of humane intentions, one could only hope) of the stricken city to evacuate the last of its drunks and the homeless. A third of them lay sprawled and dozing in the stifling heat; half of those awake seemed incoherent; the rest stood, calling out to anyone in earshot, asking for money and cigarettes (the guard had given them food and water). I couldn't help but wonder where this busload was headed, and how they would be greeted upon arrival.

Still, I also knew that New Orleans, for all the tragedy, natural and man-made, that had befallen it, had a beating pulse. Early on I'd ventured into the historic French Quarter and found it basically unscathed save for some downed trees in Pirates Alley and Jackson Square and some roof and facade damage here and there. The adjacent Central Business District, including world-famous Canal Street, likewise had suffered some moderate flooding and wind damage, but a great deal of it was still intact. I'd driven out along St. Charles Avenue, the storied boulevard running through the city's scenic Garden District, and found a great deal of it had also been spared. I'd checked with some trepidation on a friend's just-renovated house and found that, other than a missing shutter and a downed magnolia tree in the side yard, the place seemed unharmed. St. Charles Avenue's old and glorious oaks had taken a battering, as had the overhead electric grid of the city's fabled streetcar line. Some peripheral streets off the St. Charles Avenue ridge had flooded, but all in all it was clear that the treasured attractions of New Orleans remained essentially in one piece. The city had a core from which to rebuild.

But as I drove with Ricky Robin through the dispiriting streets of Chalmette and beyond, I'd not seen evidence of a surviving core so far in St. Bernard Parish. As we trundled past the wreckage, Ricky explained the ID around his neck. The National Guard had finally arrived in large numbers a few days before and was just beginning its massive house-by-house parishwide search for Katrina victims. Checkpoints were springing up, and moving around was proving to be tricky. Ricky had appropriated this ID from a buddy who had in fact been deputized by Junior Rodriguez, the parish president, to work the parish equivalent of homeland security. Junior was so desperate for manpower than any able-bodied St. Bernard resident who showed up and was willing to stay on to help with disaster relief got hired. Ricky himself was on the payroll and was waiting for his own badge to be printed up. Meanwhile, his pal's ID would get us past checkpoints without having to do a lot of explaining. After what he'd been through, Ricky wasn't of a mind to justify himself to National Guard guys from Arkansas or wherever, though he was happy that help had finally arrived. The receding waters had made it painfully obvious how thoroughly decimated St. Bernard had been left by the storm. "Recovery" seemed like such a hollow word when there seemed to be so little that could actually be recovered.

At the grove of oaks just above Violet Canal, where Susan Robin had run into the Industrial Canal flood, we encounter the first National Guard presence I've seen: two trucks, one of the amphibious kind jacked up on giant tires, rumbling up the St. Bernard Highway, American flags flapping, carrying wide-eyed soldiers through this strange and battered landscape. We don't hit the first checkpoint until Violet Canal. Ricky pulls over and we hop out to find Ronald Robin sitting in the sparse shade of a portable white canvas awning the guard has erected on the shoulder of the highway. Ricky's already sketched a bare-bones biography of Ronald for me, but even with his minimalist description of his older cousin I'd conjured up a somewhat flamboyant character.

I'm not disappointed. Ronald smiles brightly and rises as Ricky introduces me. He's wearing a white ball cap with parish president Junior Rodriguez's name printed in red block letters across the front, a pink V-neck tank top, baggy brown shorts, his bare legs stuffed into white shrimper boots identical to Ricky's pair, his white socks protruding over the boot tops. Accompanying this outfit are dark dime-store sunglasses and an ornate gold chain around his neck, accented by a bejeweled gold anchor (a good-luck charm given to him by his late wife, I learn afterward). Ronald is sipping from a bottle of orange Gatorade and is being kept company by a pack of dogs, including an auburn-colored pit bull mix whose ribs are starting to show. Ronald and the Guardsmen are feeding them the best they can; the diet includes military MREs, the packaged dehydrated food whose acronym means Meals Ready to Eat. Animal rescue groups, when they finally arrive in St. Bernard, eventually come bearing dog food. The dogs are wary of new company but settle in under the shade at our feet as Ronald, Ricky, and I chat. Ricky explains my mission and Ronald gives me an annotated version of events, including the fact that his house on Oak Ridge Street, about two miles above Violet Canal, got flooded almost up to the roof line and still has a foot of water in it. Ronald says he would show me his house today, but many of the streets in and around Violet have now been barricaded by the National Guard as they conduct their house-to-house searches.

The parish is indeed drying out but there are still large neighbor-hoods where ponds and pools of water, beyond the reach of pumps, will simply have to evaporate. It's been beastly hot since the storm, with temperatures soaring to the nineties, and relief workers who have en-tered a few soggy homes report that almost all of them already reek of mold and mildew. I could only think of the thousands upon thou-sands of closed-up, catastrophically flooded houses filled with damp furniture and muddy, wet carpets, where mildew and mold were having a field day.

We're soon under way again and quickly reach the next checkpoint, where the St. Bernard Highway bends around to become a four-lane artery. It's manned by grim-looking National Guardsmen and deputies of the St. Bernard Parish Sheriff's Office. We soon find out why. Ricky knows a deputy, who agrees to let us through—so long as we don't stop up ahead where we will see a gathering of ambulances and police vehi-cles. "They're finally trying to get the bodies out of St. Rita's today," the deputy tells Ricky.

At this point I'm oblivious to this catastrophe, and when we've driven out of earshot I ask Ricky, "What bodies?" He fills me in as we drive slowly by a line of recovery vehicles. From our distance, St. Rita's looks like a building in a generic office park and shows no readily transparent damage, except that its parking lot still has a foot of water in it. It could even pass for an ordinary business day, since some cars and trucks that had been driven there by caretakers and people staying with their relatives still litter the parking lot. I ask Ricky why it's taken so long to recover the bodies; he doesn't know, but Junior Rodriguez later tells me that the local owners of the place were under criminal investigation for not carrying out an evacuation. The nursing home had become a crime scene. And by this time, the condition of the bodies inside had so deteriorated that the police were forced to hire an outside contractor who specialized in these kinds of recoveries.

We continue east-southeast on the St. Bernard Highway, Ricky and Ronald offering a running commentary of what we're seeing. We pass a cluster of large suburban tract houses—mini-mansions, of a sort— with flooded yards and battered exteriors. The largest of the houses has simply been decapitated by the wind. I begin to understand that St. Bernard really is a small community when the Robins can frequently point out the ruined houses of acquaintances, old friends, and near and distant relatives. "That's Sylvia Park," says Ricky of a newish looking development of large brick homes that looms up on our right. Houses here go for $300,000 and up. "My sister lives in there—she got six feet of water in her house," he says.

We hit another snag—not a roadblock but driving conditions. The farther we go, the messier the St. Bernard Highway becomes. Here, the eastbound side of the four-lane is still shut—two feet or more of storm muck and drift cloak the roadbed like crusted gray icing on a cake. We navigate into the westbound lanes, where only one of two lanes has been cleared. Ahead of us a giant road grader is slowly plowing the muck off the road, kicking up a cloud of dust in its wake. We're forced onto the shoulder at one point to allow more National Guard trucks to rumble by.

Soon we come upon a long line of drowned cars and trucks parked on the east shoulder of the highway—it's the rise in the road at Verret where Ricky had left his truck and boat during the storm, hoping the elevation would save them. He points them out as we drive by. "All those people like me who thought our stuff would be safe up here, well, they're gonna be surprised when they come back."

It wasn't until some weeks later, when I returned for a reporting visit, that Ricky related to me his overnight stay in the Verret fire station and his encounter with Charlo Inabnet. Only then did I realize how many threads there were to his Katrina story.

We drive on to the intersection of the Florissant, Ronald noting the wild sweep of the marshes on either side of the road, the opening up of the land beyond the levee system. "This is God's country down here," he says.

We expect our journey to end here, but the roadblocks are down and the highway is open. "Damn, Ronald, look at that," says Ricky. "Maybe we can get to our hometown after all." Ronald hasn't yet come down this way and is eager to see what Katrina has wrought.

We pull into a parking lot for a moment to contemplate the wreckage at the intersection: a service station and convenience store utterly flattened, its twisted metal awnings and roof lying in random heaps. A Robin cousin owned this business. Across the road, a sign still stands, directing drivers to a seafood outlet in Yscloskey, another business owned by cousins.

As we head down the Florissant, I'm shocked by what I see, and so are the Robins: the staggering violence of the wind that blew here becomes evident in the unrecognizable scrums of twisted debris that once constituted homes. We come upon a yard with a green metal stairway to nowhere: the house it once belonged to lies pulverized in the background. Later there's a room ripped from a log home. It sits canted against a tree on the roadside, as if someone had roughly dismantled a dollhouse and thrown part of it away. We see the foundations and pilings of homes that simply have been blown into the ether.

"Damn," says Ronald, "this place got bombed. Yscloskey's just like this, Ricky?"

Ricky nods grimly. "Pretty much."

We drive slowly, the Robins pointing out again where friends and relatives once lived on large lots now holding only rubble. I count a mere three houses still standing, and two of those appear badly damaged, where perhaps fifty existed before Katrina. We encounter more road graders ahead, and squeezing onto the shoulder of this somewhat narrow two-lane highway is difficult. There's debris—including tire-gouging nails, splintered wood, and jagged metal—everywhere, some of it concealed in drying mud that looks like the cracked hide of a giant prehistoric alligator. A couple of flat tires and we'd be stuck.

Ricky navigates us successfully through, and we arrive at Yscloskey, its water tower rising up on our right. Ricky actually hasn't been past the intersection of the Florissant and the road that leads to his house, so we drive on a short distance to see whether the bridge over Bayou La Loutre is open to traffic. If it is, we can cross over the bayou and see the eastern half of Yscloskey, and perhaps get all the way down to the end of the road at Hopedale. As far as Ricky knows, no one has been down that way.

But even the short drive to the bridge is jolting for the Robins—so little is recognizable amid the splintered wreckage. Ricky points out a historically significant loss: the brick foundation of the parish's (and perhaps the region's) oldest trading post lies among downed trees and the twisted metal from destroyed mobile homes, reduced to a pile of broken bricks. Ronald's brother had a house on this stretch of road. It's gone. A little farther down, a jaunty red metallic two-story building holding an ice factory and shrimp processing facility, one of two serving Yscloskey, has been kneecapped. The entire first floor is ripped away except for its steel framework, and the guts of its second floor—cables, electrical wires, fiberglass insulation—sag exposed and morose from above. Katrina necklaces—tarps, trawls, blankets, clothes, plastic bags, wire-cage crab traps—drape trees in the background.

The bridge can't be crossed. The vertical-lift span has been jacked up by Katrina's surge a couple of feet above the roadbed, creating an impassable gap. We linger here for a while, the Robins looking around, trying to make sense of things. The far bank heading toward Hopedale ought to hold a line of camps, but they're gone. The view across the bayou toward the village is equally disconcerting: docks, houses, the small village store, a second icehouse, all knocked down or so badly battered that they will have to be torn down.

Soon we leave so Ricky can double back and show us his house and his mother's house and the calamity that befell his neighborhood. But before we depart, Ricky turns to Ronald in a moment of understandable defeatism. "What we got left here, Ronald?" he says, gesturing toward the ruins of a town. "The family seafood business? Gone. The icehouse? Gone. The store? Gone. Momma's house? Gone. This bridge? Broke. Who's left to buy our shrimp and our oysters? Well, the oyster beds are probably gone. And where's our market? It's gone, too. I got no choice. I think I gotta leave."

We drive the short distance toward Ricky's house but find the lane blocked by a lingering flood. Ricky points in the direction of his place and his parents' house tossed up against it. Robin Street looks like the scene of an artillery battle.

Ronald can just look out and stare.

On the route back to Violet Canal, near the Florissant–St. Bernard Highway junction, the Robins find one mildly cheering sight: San Pedro Pescador Catholic Church, known here as "the fishermen's church." Katrina battered the sanctuary but didn't knock it down.

Ricky explains that every early August here, the church presides over the blessing of the shrimp fleet. Priests say mass and sprinkle holy water on a parade of brightly decorated boats. Hundreds attend, and then the throngs head for community centers, backyards, or bars to eat seafood, drink beer, and dance. Ricky wonders about the fate of this decades-old ritual in the face of Katrina's devastation.

Ronald shakes his head. "This is God's country," he says, "and God's taking it back."

17. The Imperfect Storm

Anatomy of a Not
Altogether Natural Disaster

Two days later, I'm driving through the community of Meraux, named for a St. Bernard physician, plantation owner, and sugar baron, in the north central quadrant of St. Bernard Parish. My tour with the Robins had mainly taken me along the west side of the parish, save for our eastern jog along the Florissant Highway into Yscloskey. I'd not seen St. Bernard's most populated areas: Meraux, and the enclaves of Arabi and Chalmette, which sit just below the Lower Ninth Ward, encompassing the parish's elongated commercial and industrial heart along a four-lane boulevard known as Judge Perez Drive.

I'm getting an eyeful. Looming ahead are the smokestacks and vast crude-oil storage tanks of the Murphy Oil Company refinery, the parish's major employer and, at this moment, its major polluter. In graphic testimony to the power of Katrina's surge, one of the tanks—left partially full upon the approach of the storm—was actually lifted up and heeled over slightly, severing its connection to feeder lines. More than a million gallons of toxic crude gushed out and ran unchecked on Katrina's brutal tides until the tank was empty.

I'm here with some *Wall Street Journal* colleagues, including Doug Blackmon, the Atlanta bureau chief running the post-storm coverage. The *Journal,* based on my verbal report to Doug about my day with Ricky and Ronald Robin, was actively interested in a St. Bernard story. I needed a fuller picture to fill in the context. This turned out to be one of numerous return trips I made over a four-month period following the storm. Fortuitously, the roads in from New Orleans had reopened the day after my helicopter journey, and we were able to get past check-points with our press credentials and a special pass given to me by Junior Rodriguez.

We go looking for the stricken Murphy Oil tank, and it's surprisingly easy to spot among the large number of lookalike hulking white tanks in the Murphy Oil battery: it's the one clearly listing to the side. It sits about fifty yards away in a shallow lake of oily water, wearing a broad bathtub ring of crude three or so feet up its side. We have unfettered access—the place is abandoned—and with hip waders we might have made it to the wrought-iron lattice of stairs that climbs one side to the top, though I'm pretty sure, even with hip waders, I would not have tried such a journey. The area still reeks of crude—the lake before us is more oil than water.

All around are signs of the height and intensity of the flood and the path the escaping oil took. A modular building of the kind that might hold a temporary office bears an oil mark above the top of its windows—a full eight or nine feet above the ground. Dikes meant to contain a spill have been breached and overrun. Just outside the dikes is an abandoned twenty-foot sportfishing boat named the *Reef Relief*. Its true color is white but its hull looks as if it has been smeared in crude oil with a heavy brush. A five- or six-foot-deep drainage canal along a perimeter of the tank battery remains filled with thick sludge; dead, oil-soaked vegetation fans far out from each bank.

We move on to nearby residential neighborhoods to get some idea of how far the oil tide ranged. The answer is far. Neighborhood after neighborhood in the vicinity of the refinery got double-whammied—houses flooded, often to their rooflines, with briny water, then drenched in smelly oil like some toxic icing on a cake. With the water now receded, these neighborhoods look like the set of some eco-horror movie. We drive deserted streets, cloaked in a foot of drying, cracked oil mixed with marsh mud. In some places, the oil hasn't evaporated yet, leaving shimmering puddles. Trees are already dead; shrubs are either coated in oil or strangely mummified into a brittle amber color, as if they'd never possessed life at all. It's late afternoon, still unrelentingly hot, a waning sun casting slanting auburn rays across a distant bend in the road. It's a place consumed in an arching silence, a place exuding an eerie toxic glow as oil-vapor dervishes rise up in ghostly dances. The air is damp, fetid, and smelling of petroleum.

The houses on either side of us stand as time capsules of the disaster. Nothing man-made has moved since the water went down. Clearly, no one has been here; this oil-caked street and many others are unmarked by tracks, save the ones we are making and, now and then, prints of some hapless dog left behind and forced to wander this poisoned wasteland. It's in these neighborhoods that Katrina has created some of her more mesmerizing sculptures. We come upon a single-story orange brick ranch house with a washing machine atop it. So much marsh mat sits on the roof that it looks as if it's wearing a fringed grass skirt. A red sedan, its make obscured in marsh grass, is *vertically* blocking the front door, its rear tires snagged on the roofline, its front bumper on the lawn.

On a street nearby, what appears to be the recreation room of another ranch home has been severed from the house, stripped of its roof, accordioned into an odd shape, and tipped forward so that we're looking through exposed beams and the metal strips that formerly held one of those suspended ceilings. Plainly visible are an overturned refrigerator, a picnic table, folding chairs, a rug, a white wall phone jarred off the hook, and a shower stall whose top has been pried off. There's something mildly pornographic about this, as if someone's private life had been abruptly laid bare. More disconcerting: a golden retriever stands silently guarding the gaping entry. On yet another street, a jaunty twenty-foot white fishing boat has been ripped from its trailer and deposited halfway up on the roof. On other streets, cars are stacked atop each other like firewood.

The tragedy of and anger over this will be exacerbated when returning residents, let back in for the first time nineteen days after Katrina's landfall, learn that the damaged tank flunked Murphy Oil's own hurricane-precaution protocol. Upon the approach of a hurricane, tanks are supposed to be either emptied, so there is no oil to spill, or pumped full of water so their weight renders them impervious to the storm's ravages. The tank that ruptured contained at least 25,000 barrels of oil, however, and that oil slimed about 1,800 homes, polluted area canals, and turned a square-mile residential zone into a toxic waste dump. The spill was the subject of about 130 individual lawsuits, most of which were eventually merged into a single class-action suit in New Orleans federal district court. In January 2007, the federal judge overseeing the case approved a $330 million settlement between Murphy Oil and the vast majority of plaintiffs, though some residents who opted out of the class-action suit still have claims pending against the Arkansas-based oil company. The spill provides yet another example of how man-made folly, error, and miscalculation, including engineering and environmental mistakes dating back decades, greatly aggravated the blow Katrina delivered to coastal Louisiana.

Another case in point is what befell the residential enclave of Arabi, which sits in the upper quadrant of St. Bernard Parish on what, for these precincts, amounts to high ground. The burg holds the economically lower end of St. Bernard's blue-collar demographic, its dwellings a mixture of compact pre–World War II Creole cottages and shotgun houses in neighborhoods that have seen better days, and small postwar ranch and prefab homes in various stages of upkeep. Arabi's basic misfortune was to sit just south of the Lower Ninth Ward, meaning it bore a full frontal assault from the breaches in the Industrial Canal levees. Those ruptures were at least abetted by questionable design of the embankments and extra pressure on the levees as the Mississippi River–Gulf Outlet magnified the surge.

In our drive through Arabi, we simply couldn't find a house that had been spared. On a narrow lane that ran roughly parallel to a protection levee, Katrina had committed incredible mischief. For about six blocks, every other house had been pried from its slab and moved, as if by design, into the middle of the road.

Past Arabi, we entered the commercial hub of Chalmette, also perched on relatively high ground in the parish's upper north central quadrant. It had fared no better. I'm no fan of the strip mall and the way such cookie-cutter developments have spread their garish, blocky clutter and sameness to seemingly every corner of the nation. Still, it was shocking to see what had happened along Judge Perez Drive, the parish's major four-lane commercial artery that runs east of and roughly parallel to the St. Bernard Highway. The drive curves like a teapot handle through Chalmette, Meraux, and other waysides for about twelve miles before it ends at Bayou Road near St. Bernard High School. On the

Saturday morning before Katrina, Judge Perez Drive had been mobbed with traffic—the vehicles of those leaving, the vehicles of those staying but trying to load up on last-minute provisions.

Now it was a corridor of mass destruction. Ricky Robin was right: the Super Wal-Mart *had* drowned, as had the huge Home Depot store, along with the Rite Aid pharmacy, every restaurant, every service station, every food store, every bank. Everything that sold anything had gone underwater or had been flooded *and* thrashed and broken apart by Katrina's gales. The swath of unrelenting damage was punctuated at one point by the fire-gutted remnants of a shopping center on the eastern side of Judge Perez. The fire was presumed to have been started by Katrina as well, from either falling, sparking power lines or a ruptured gas main that blew up. I could only think that the owner had at least been spared the grim job of tearing the place down.

Midway down Judge Perez, opposite a storm-ravaged McDonald's, stood Lexington Place subdivision, a fairly new, expensive enclave of perhaps a hundred 3,000- to 5,000-square-foot homes set in an expanse of land hard up against the substantial levees of the Forty Arpent Canal (sometimes called the Florida Walk Canal). Part of the Meraux enclave, Lexington Place lay far enough east of the Murphy Oil refinery to have escaped the spill. But that was of little solace. Katrina stomped the place just the same. A dozen or so large houses on its eastern flank near the levee were either blown down or washed away, or so incredibly broken as to be unidentifiable as houses. Most stunning of all: the surge, clearly flowing from the east, had ripped from its slab a four-bedroom brick house and pushed it more than a block up the street, crushing cars, utility poles, and anything else in its way.

I drove around St. Bernard Parish for days looking for pockets that had escaped the storm, but could find none. Its fifteen public schools, its libraries, all of its churches, its public buildings—everything had suffered major to catastrophic flooding.

If errors, engineering miscalculations, and past environmental follies played a major role in St. Bernard Parish's destruction, they didn't fully explain what had happened here. The more I delved into Katrina's track and history, the more I came to realize that it was the Imperfect

Storm—huge, erratic, and meteorologically singular. That Katrina mod-
ulated into a Category 3 hurricane as it made first landfall at Buras,
Louisiana, across Breton Sound in Plaquemines Parish, was wildly over-
sold. The storm was still a monster who had primed her victim long
before striking, and arrived pushing a Category 5 surge. Human mistakes simply aided and abetted the disaster. A critical component of
Katrina's destruction was the sheer size of the hurricane. On Saturday,
August 27, as the storm was approaching Cuba as a low-level Category
3, it began to gain in intensity but, more ominously for the South
Louisiana–Mississippi region, nearly doubled in size before the day
was over. Tropical-storm-force winds now extended an astonishing 140
nautical miles from the center, according to a National Hurricane Center
report published four months after landfall and updated in August
2006. At this point, forecasters still believed—as did many in the South
Louisiana–Mississippi region—that Katrina was a Florida-bound storm
that would thrash itself out somewhere above Miami.

But Katrina only nicked South Florida as a Category 1 hurricane,
tracking west-southwestward across the state. Then, middle-to-upper-
atmospheric steering currents that had kept the storm on that course
began to retreat eastward. A mid-latitude trough popped up over the
north-central United States, and as the storm moved around the periphery of the retreating high-pressure ridge, it shifted course to the northwest. By early Sunday, the eyewall had contracted into a sharply defined
center and—in less than twelve hours from Saturday to Sunday—Katrina
escalated from a low-end Category 3 storm to a Category 5. The storm
now packed peak sustained winds of 160 miles per hour and moved
within 170 miles southeast of the mouth of the Mississippi River. All day
Sunday, however, the storm continued to grow in breadth. By late Sunday, hurricane-force winds extended 90 nautical miles from the center
while storm-force winds extended an astonishing 200 nautical miles in
every direction from the eye.

Two full days ahead of landfall, then, the storm was already pushing
up abnormally high tides all along the south-central and southeastern
Louisiana and Mississippi Gulf Coasts, priming the area for the killer
surge yet to come. As it intensified to Category 4 and then Category 5,
the hurricane also began to generate what the National Hurricane

Center report calls "large northward-propagating swells, leading to sub-stantial wave setup along the northern Gulf coast." For St. Bernard Parish, this meant that its outer band of hurricane protection, par-ticularly the seventeen-foot-high levees along the west bank of the MR-GO, began to feel the effects of high tides and battering waves long before the main fury of the storm arrived. This wave setup proved even more devastating for the obliterated portion of the Mississippi Gulf Coast, which was pounded by a twenty-five-foot surge. And consider-ing the waves generated by Katrina, no wonder. A buoy sixty-four nauti-cal miles south of Dauphin Island, Alabama, recorded a wave height of fifty-five feet as the storm veered toward the Mississippi coast Monday morning—tying the record for the highest wave ever measured by a National Data Buoy Center marker.

Thus, concluded the National Hurricane Center report, "the mas-sive storm surge produced by Katrina, even though it had weakened from Category 5 intensity the previous day to Category 3 at landfall in Louisiana, can be generally explained by the huge size of the storm. . . . Though Hurricane Camille (1969) was more intense than Katrina at landfall while following a similar track, Camille was far more compact and produced comparably high storm surge values along a much nar-rower swath."

At 6:10 a.m. on Monday, August 29, Katrina's eyewall slammed into Buras on the west bank of the Mississippi River, not far from the harbor at Empire where stood the boat captain who gave Ricky Robin his frantic radio report of the cataclysm of wind and water that was befalling the place. Katrina's winds were blowing at a sustained 125 miles per hour, but the National Hurricane Center noted that, given the storm's massive size, there was a good chance that Buras was being pummeled by even stronger Category 4 gales—150 miles per hour or better—an hour or two before official landfall. Plaquemines Parish's western hur-ricane protection levee actually withstood Katrina's initial surge, but the storm was only toying with the place. As the eye moved over land, Katrina's counterclockwise rotation generated violent gales from the northeast. A surge estimated at twenty to twenty-five feet high swept over the eastern protection levees, eventually swamping the western levees as well. The Mississippi River levees were also overtopped and breached in several places. Structures that had survived the brutal winds were flattened or inundated by killer tides. The very mouth of the Mississippi River was rearranged.

Buras and a number of small towns above and below it—Port Sulfur on the north and Venice to the south near the river's end—were practically obliterated. When I drove through lower Plaquemines Parish after St. Bernard Parish I could only stare in disbelief. The Buras water tower had been decapitated and its huge blue and white tank cast into someone's backyard, its spindly steel legs lying broken and crumpled all around it. It sat there sullen like a toppled Cyclops. A multi-ton ten-wheel truck of the kind that hauls refrigerated seafood was hanging, impaled by stout branches, from a sturdy oak tree by its back wheels. Huge oceangoing fishing boats had been tossed up on area highways. An amateur video taken at the nearby Empire Marina after the storm had moved on toward St. Bernard Parish showed two men, washed from a sinking boat, literally crawling across this soggy, buoyant mass to the shelter of another boat, so thick was the debris and marsh mat. They were fetched from the drink covered head to toe in diesel from a spill of unknown origins.

It took about two hours for Katrina to cross the open water of Breton Sound and come ashore in St. Bernard Parish between Yscloskey—near where Charlo Inabnet was holed up—and Delacroix Island to the south. But the storm was creating trouble long before landing. Around 4 a.m. on Monday, steadily rising tides roaming up the MR-GO pushed into the Industrial Canal, leaking into New Orleans neighborhoods on either side, an omen of very bad things to come.

By 5 a.m., the MR-GO had been turned into a long frothy, seething corridor for Katrina's surge, and although the roaring tides hadn't yet crested its tall levees, the levees were already taking a pounding from the five- to seven-foot waves kicked up by gale-force winds. By dawn, as the surge began to build and quicken, the levees started to erode and fail. By the time Katrina's eye passed over Hopedale and grazed Violet Canal, entire sections of the levees were already disintegrating. The outer defense line protecting eastern St. Bernard Parish was compromised and the surge rushed across the marsh, piling up behind the inner ring of smaller levees along the Forty Arpent Canal. These levees, integrated into a pumping system, were built to rid St. Bernard of localized flooding caused by heavy rains. They were never meant to block violent hurricane surges.

By 6:30 a.m. Katrina began pounding violently on St. Bernard Parish's northern side, pushing what some have described as a large wall of water into the upper reaches of the MR-GO where it intersects and merges with the Gulf Intracoastal Waterway before heading into the Industrial Canal. This created what is called the funnel effect. The surge, squeezed into this narrower, combined channel, mounded rapidly and began to overtop and erode protection levees both east and west. It unleashed a devastating flood into the eastern upper corner of St. Bernard, basically destroying the Bayou Bienvenue Marina and sinking dozens of commercial fishing boats there, and flooding every business along a busy four-lane north–south thoroughfare known as Paris Road. The same flood poured westward into sprawling New Orleans subdivisions on either side of the Interstate-10 corridor, where tens of thousands of homes and hundreds of businesses were overrun and ruined.

The worst was still to come. A little before 7 a.m. the funnel began pushing exaggerated tides into the already swollen Industrial Canal, and water topped floodwalls and levees on either side. By 7:30, the surge had pounded a massive breach in the Industrial Canal levee between Florida Avenue and North Claiborne Avenue, sending water cascading into the Upper Ninth Ward of New Orleans and the neighborhoods of Bywater and Treme flanking the French Quarter—a flood that reached eight feet deep in parts and continued unabated for about fifteen hours.

By 7:45 this levee-killing surge committed its most violent act: the tall, steel-reinforced I-wall levee where the Industrial Canal courses through the Lower Ninth Ward was overrun and undermined in two places, creating catastrophic gashes on its eastern side and sending a virtual tsunami into the hapless Lower Ninth, where scores of people were riding out the storm—most of them by this time thinking the worst was over. Two separate waves crashed over the place, flattening houses, killing some occupants, and creating vast scour zones where nothing remained but the slabs of houses. Along the edge of these zones lay hulking piles of twisted debris—house and car parts, furniture, splintered utility poles, masses of power and phone lines all knotted together in unfathomable sculptures by the raging waters.

This was the same surge that overran Arabi, helped drown parts of Chalmette, threatened Susan Robin and her family in the van near Violet Canal, and, by some estimates, coursed with diminishing fury all the way to the wayside of Verret, where Ricky Robin later encountered Charlo Inabnet.

Around 8:15 a.m. the National Weather Service issued its first flash-flood warning for Orleans and St. Bernard parishes, based on eyewit-ness accounts of the Industrial Canal levee breach. It urged all remain-ing residents to "move to higher ground immediately"—a warning that came far too late for most. By 9 a.m. most of the Lower Ninth lay under six to eight feet of water, with more coming.

As late as 8:30, St. Bernard Parish officials, hunkered down in the multistory parish government complex off Judge Perez Drive, remained oblivious to the unfolding catastrophe, thinking they were home free. But they started to fret when they heard the first scattered reports of rapidly rising water in Arabi—this was the Lower Ninth Ward flood bullying its way into St. Bernard Parish. They also didn't know that by this time, the MR-GO levees had been breached in twenty separate places—miles-long sections of it were simply gone. A huge surge, loosed from the MR-GO, was bearing down on the nine-foot-high levees of the Forty Arpent Canal. These levees didn't fail—they were simply overrun, setting up the destruction of such enclaves as Lexington Place, the battering that tilted the Murphy Oil tank, and the swift-moving, west-ward flowing part of the surge that overran Violet Canal.

Bob Turner, director of the Lake Borgne Levee District, a state-created agency that oversees St. Bernard's levee system, had been up all night monitoring the parish's pumping stations, some of which are manned. When 8:30 arrived and there still wasn't a hint of serious trouble, Turner began to think about breakfast and then a long nap. The early calls from Arabi were disturbing, but more chilling for Turner was a call at about 8:45 from employees manning the parish's public works complex on the east side of Paris Road. "Help us!" a caller cried out over a cell phone. "The water is already over the levees. We're on the second floor and water's already up to the second floor. We're moving to the roof soon if it doesn't stop."

The water, of course, didn't stop, and a handful of employees scrambled onto the roof—parts of which soon began to be peeled off by Katrina's howling winds. (The employees were not rescued for many hours.) "By the time I got that call, I knew we had a major flood on our hands," Turner recalls.

Indeed, almost nothing in St. Bernard's flood protection system was able to stanch the flow of Katrina's killer surges. A huge, fortress-like lock and floodgate ostensibly meant to control storm tides at the intersection of the MR-GO and Bayou Bienvenue proved no match. Its heavy steel-plate doors were ripped away. Giant barges were tossed atop it, jamming the lock even further. In the late afternoon of Katrina's landfall, when Turner and others went to check on the Bayou Bienvenue lock, they couldn't even find it—the structure was totally underwater.

How rapidly the water came depended greatly on elevation and proximity to the major levee breaks. But descriptions of the storm given by the Robins and others at Violet Canal mesh closely with eyewitness accounts from areas in the direct line of massive breaches in the MR-GO and those who stood directly downstream from the scour zones created in the Lower Ninth Ward by the Industrial Canal levee breaks. In some cases, as at Violet Canal, hapless residents got caught in the path of three floods—the Industrial Canal surge from the northwest, the Lake Borgne and MR-GO surge from the east, and a smaller but still damaging surge caused when the Mississippi overran its bank in several places.

The experience at Chalmette High School off East Judge Perez Drive was typical of the chaos and horror of the deluge. The two-story high school had been opened as a "shelter of last resort" for residents, which meant that most of the five hundred or so who showed up there were the frail and elderly without relatives to look after them, or the poor (some of them also elderly) who simply had no means to evacuate or who feared their houses or mobile homes wouldn't stand up to hurricane winds. Doris Votier, the parish's superintendent of schools, was in command of the shelter and had endured a rough night: some windows had blown out, rain had blown in, the school had lost power, backup generators couldn't be started, and she'd watched in awe and dismay as the roof on the elementary school across Judge Perez Drive had been methodically ripped away by Katrina's gales. Chalmette High itself had suffered some roof damage. Still, when daylight came, Votier took relief in reports that Katrina would dodge east.

Then came a call about water in the streets of Arabi, and Votier and Wayne Warner, the school principal, took quick action, moving food, water, and the elderly up to the second floor as a precaution. But with Katrina's winds diminishing, no one was prepared for what happened next. "We looked out down the main thoroughfare that the school sits on and we see a wall of water coming," Votier recalled. Within fifteen minutes, Chalmette High had five and a half feet of water in it—well, not just water. "It was a mixture of marsh bottom mud, oil and gasoline, fish, and grass"—all pushed by an alarmingly strong current, said Warner. And more was still to come.

At St. Bernard High School, about seven miles southeast, where Herbert Verdin and Mike Vetra briefly sought shelter, school workers manning the emergency shelter set up there were shocked to see a swift-moving flood running directly toward them from the east. They ran outside, hoping to move their trucks out of harm's way, but by the time they reached the parking lot the vehicles had already been swamped. The flood was moving so rapidly that they were unable to battle the brutal currents to get back to the entrance. On the verge of panic, they broke a window and made their way up to the second floor as the surge rushed in.

Another witness to the rapidity of the flood was a remote security camera operating on backup batteries at the transmitting tower for Fox 8, a New Orleans area TV station. The tower sits off Paris Road about a half mile from the MR-GO levees near the channel's intersection with the Gulf Intracoastal Waterway. The camera was pointed east, toward the MR-GO. At 8:24 a.m. it picked up a frothy white line moving in the distance. By 8:30, the line had grown more pronounced and was just outside a chain-link fence surrounding the transmitter tower. By 8:37 the camera recorded four feet of water coursing around the transmitter footings; twelve minutes later the water was twelve feet deep.

Amateur videos also captured the timeline and the terror. In one, a man aimed a handheld camera out a rain-streaked front window in a dwelling identified as the Vaccarella home on Tracy Street in Meraux. The time stamp on the video marked it as 8:39 a.m., and the scene showed howling winds and wind-whipped trees—but the only water on Tracy Street was from sheeting rain. "There goes Momma's roof," said a man on the voice-over, training the camera on a single-story house across the street as shingles were being ripped away. Ten minutes later, the man added, "There's a terrible situation here"—but still Tracy Street remained unflooded.

The next shot showed a time stamp of 9:59 a.m., and by then circumstances had turned ominous. Choppy waves slapped at the window line of the house across the way. "Look what we've got," said the man on the voice-over. "Our trawls, our vehicles, our whole livelihoods—everything's flooding out right here."

By 10:44 a.m., the next time stamp, Tracy Street had become a seething lake. Water clawed at rooftops, the wind continued to howl, and whitecaps roiled across the angry surface. The handheld camera panned to two men trapped on a nearby roof desperately trying to get into a storm-tossed boat that had extended a long rope their way. The man holding the camera tried to yell helpful instructions but the men couldn't hear him. After five fretful minutes, they plunged into the choppy water and pulled themselves along the rope to the safety of the boat.

A final scene, taken from the roof of the house, where the camera operator had fled, panned across a sea of submerged houses to a strip mall in the distance. "Good Lord," said the man. "Look at that shopping center over there. It looks like it's destroyed." A minute later he added, despondently, "This is unbelievable. How do you prepare for something like this? You can't be a hero. We thought we could save something, but what could we save?"

There is no time stamp on the video shot by Fabian Guerra and his wife Pam of their substantial two-story house at 2434 St. Marie Street in the hapless Lexington Place subdivision. But their ten-minute movie is utterly unsettling testimony to how quickly the morning turned terrifying. An opening shot, through a water-splattered glass front door, was uneventful: a car on the street outside, swirling wind, pelting rain. In the next shot, though, water was running rabbity across their front lawn.

"Oh, God, please let it stop," pleaded Pam. "It's gonna be in our house in a few minutes, Fabe."

The next shot was taken from the stairwell leading to the second floor. "Oh, God, I can't believe this," said Pam. The camera showed water about three feet deep swirling through the hallway. The Guerras' dog, Hop, swam frantically, trying to mount a floating and very obviously moving wooden coffee table.

"Look at me, Hop!" Pam cried out. "C'mon, Hop!"

Despondent, she said to Fabian, "She's trying to get on the table and can't!"

In the next shot, Fabian pointed the camera out a hole they had cut through their roof from the attic. Their second floor was underwater. Low clouds raced past. Wind gusts rattled the rafters and drowned out some of the audio. The camera panned to a silver sedan—on their neighbor's roof.

Fabian said: "I've made a few bad mistakes in my life but this has got to be the worst mistake anybody could make." He swung the camera east, in the direction of the levees over which Katrina's surge came, capturing a sea of rooftops, floating debris, and wind-whipped water all the way to the horizon.

He then panned the camera to Pam, staring in shock at the distance. "Me and my wife survived," he said in a stricken tone. "But only by God's will did we survive. . . . The water came up and it went from the ground to the roof in three minutes."

By 11 a.m., Katrina's inbound surges were beginning to slow, but 95 percent of St. Bernard Parish was already underwater, eight to ten feet in most places, twenty feet in some. All roads were impassable, all power out, all landline phones dead. Cell phone service was sketchy. Towers that survived operated on backup battery power, but they too went dead over the next several days.

By 1 p.m., while Ricky Robin and the Violet fleet continued to battle gusty winds and vicious currents to pick up survivors, the situation was turning grim at places like Chalmette High School. The five hundred original evacuees had swelled to as many as fifteen hundred as the Violet flotilla and other rescuers with boats ferried shell-shocked flood victims to the school. They used the concrete awnings attached to the second floor as landing ramps. Most of the refugees came with only the clothes on their backs, severely testing water and food supplies. The plumbing had stopped working. There were no usable bathrooms.

Votier and Warner recalled how eerie it was to sit in the building filling with refugees and look out on the vast lake that Chalmette had become, hearing the faraway and desperate cries of the stranded in the distance. With cell phone service sketchy and transistor radio news reports still not attuned to the breadth of Katrina's deluge, school officials were still in the dark. "At a time when you can talk on video phones from Afghanistan, we couldn't talk to our leaders a mile away," Warner said. They had no idea that 80 percent of New Orleans was underwater or that eighty thousand people were trapped there. "We didn't realize the magnitude of the event. We couldn't understand why nobody was coming to help us," said Votier.

As darkness began to fall over Chalmette High, the shelter's plight turned nightmarish. A man wet and shivering came in: he said he was unable to live without dialysis, and every day that passed he reminded the staff how many days he likely had left to live. Other people needed oxygen, including a man who arrived with only a twenty-four-hour supply. "There we were in the middle of an eight-foot toxic lake in a totally devastated community, needing oxygen to save lives," Warner recalled. There was, of course, no way for them to get oxygen, or anything else.

Back on St. Marie Street in Lexington Place, Fabian and Pam Guerra remained trapped in their attic, with darkness an hour away. "This is Fabian," Guerra said in a bleak tone as his camera revealed the flood below him. So much storm debris had gathered between his house and the house next door that it looked as if you could walk across the water. "I'm back on the roof. We're hoping we'll get help soon. . . . There's people all over calling for help. There's an elderly man . . ." What he said next is unintelligible; feedback from a howling gust of wind distorted the audio.

He continued: "There are a lot of people hollering for help across the way. They sound like they're in the attic. A lot of people are injured, and no doubt, quite a few people are dead. God forbid."

He added: "This is facing toward the Gulf Outlet, toward Lake Borgne to the north, and all I can see is water. . . . I thought I was safe, but I was stupid. . . . It's getting late, there's snakes on the roof. There's nutrias. There's muskrats. . . . We're hoping we don't have to spend the night like this, with snakes crawling on our roof."

He turned the camera on Pam, who was trying to call out on their cell phone. "We're running out of battery. Why don't you turn it off, Pam?"

He panned to the attic, focusing on their dog. "I hope they'll let me take him. He's like my son. We got another dog in here with three puppies. I don't know how she found us but she did. They deserve to live, just like us."

He then turned the camera on himself, his face exhausted and in shock. "This is Fabian. I'm glad to be alive. And I'll never stay through another hurricane again. I will run."

18. Pioneers in
the Rubble

I lost track of Ricky and Ronald for a few weeks after our tour of St. Bernard, except for a photograph that someone emailed me in mid-September. George W. Bush had paid a visit to the New Orleans region on September 12 and stopped off briefly in St. Bernard Parish. The photograph was of Ricky, in a T-shirt, jeans, and his white shrimper boots, and the president having a chat before Bush hopped back on his presidential helicopter. The president had also stopped in to see Junior Rodriguez, the parish president. Junior is a large, flamboyant man who walks with an ornate cane and is known for speaking his mind, and not always in polite English. Though there was no account of what went on in the meeting, I figured Bush had gotten an earful, given what I knew were Junior's feelings about the federal response to the storm.

I could only wonder what Ricky had told the commander in chief, but I'd misplaced Ricky's cell phone number. For all I knew he had made good on his musings to leave St. Bernard Parish.

And, anyway, the Katrina story had moved on from the drama of the first week to post-mortems on the failures of various levels of government to manage the crisis, to the continuing grim hunt for the dead (whose numbers, though woeful, were not anywhere near the early dire estimates), to the political promises—and broken promises—of recovery. I contributed energetically to the *Journal*'s coverage. But as compelling as the New Orleans story was, there was no danger of it being undertold. The entire world press corps was fixated on it. As often as possible, I would slip away from the pack and return to bayou country, looking for stories about people on the margins.

Sometimes inclinations are productive in unintended ways. My early ramblings in St. Bernard and Plaquemines parishes first tipped me off to Katrina's serious environmental consequences. Besides the six billion gallons of increasingly toxic water trapped behind levees in New Orleans, and another few billion in St. Bernard parish, that was slowly being pumped back into Lake Pontchartrain, Lake Borgne, and other area waterways, Katrina had set off a large number of oil spills. The Murphy Oil tank was my first clue. But driving lower Plaquemines with my photographer friend and colleague, Aric Mayer, in the second week after the storm, we came upon a cluster of workers, dressed in white biohazard suits, paddling in small boats and tossing out large circular absorbent cotton pads onto an oily pond off the roadside. We learned that the oil had gushed from a twenty-inch-diameter pipeline ruptured by a Katrina-caused fissure in a Mississippi River levee. The next day, on an airboat tour of the battered southern end of Plaquemines, we kept running across sheens of oil, out-and-out oil slicks, and dead, oil-covered birds, notably pelicans.

I ended up spending a few days querying the Coast Guard, the federal agency tasked with monitoring maritime oil spills, and state pollution-control agencies. I uncovered unsettling statistics, which I reported in the *Journal*. Katrina had set off forty separate spills—ten of them large enough to be classified as major—and unleashed an estimated 190,000 *barrels* of oil and other petrochemicals into towns, bayous, and marshes mostly in and around St. Bernard, Plaquemines, and Lafourche parishes. How serious was this? The infamous Exxon-Valdez tanker spill in Alaska in 1989 only topped this amount by about 50,000 barrels. And only 40 percent of Katrina's spilled oil had been recovered, meaning the remainder still lay scattered in neighborhoods, bird-rich marshes, and area fishing grounds.

Katrina's enormous saltwater surge also had done major damage to diminishing stands of freshwater marshes and swamps in these parishes, even inundating vast upland ridges, known in these parts as *cheniers*, sheltering oak, hackberry, and other soil-stabilizing trees. Soon, "saltwater burn" began showing up, as grasses, shrubs, and trees turned an orange-rust color and the more fragile plants started dying off.

Conventional wisdom holds that salt-burned marsh and even upland woodlands can recover over time. But conventional wisdom perhaps didn't apply here. No hurricane to date had delivered such a powerful, far-reaching surge, and the area had never experienced flooding that had taken two weeks to pump out. What most certainly *wasn't* going to recover was the multimillion-dollar citrus crop in lower Plaquemines Parish that stood within the surge zone. On our airboat tour, we motored past dozens of vast orange groves—still submerged in four to five feet of salt water—where thousands of trees laden with fruit about a month away from harvesting were already dead. I picked an orange and it seemed petrified.

On Halloween day, I found myself in a rental car driving slowly through parts of Chalmette with a vague idea that I might try to make my way down to Yscloskey—maybe I'd find Ricky down there. Two months had passed since the storm, and I was mostly interested in knowing whether stricken St. Bernard Parish was showing any signs of life. My answer came soon enough: it barely had a pulse.

Residents had for about six weeks now been allowed to trickle back in for visits, but the parish was still under dusk-to-dawn curfew. It was, save for generators, still without power. Its sewers had been so badly clogged by marsh muck from Katrina's surge that it would take months to pump them out and get them fully functioning again, which meant that essentially St. Bernard had no plumbing. In New Orleans, a fair number of restaurants and bars on Bourbon Street and in the French Quarter had sprung back to life. But here not a single business had reopened.

And for all the soothing, reconciling talk that had come out of FEMA when agency officials finally arrived, FEMA trailers were vaporware—people had heard of such things, but nobody in St. Bernard had seen one. In fact, it would be December before the first of these trailers made an appearance in the Louisiana Katrina belt. Junior Rodriguez and his coterie of workers were living and working in modular housing the parish had bought from commercial dealers. Early on, Junior had asked FEMA for permission to buy sixty-five hundred similar trailers he'd located on the open market, with hopes that he could quickly jumpstart the monumental task of housing displaced residents who wanted to return. FEMA said no: he'd have to wait for the official FEMA issues, which were not yet off the assembly lines.

This would be one of the first, but hardly the last, example of FEMA's implacable inflexibility in the wake of this monumental disaster. Legions of pages, and at least one entire book, have been given over to FEMA's post-Katrina performance. Suffice it to say here that blue-collar, independent-minded St. Bernard Parish would find itself woefully unprepared for the depths of pettifoggery to which FEMA subjected it and its citizens. It's not that FEMA did no good; it just did its good in an agonizingly slow, frustrating manner.

On this mild, sunny late October day, I'd driven through the desolate Lower Ninth Ward, crossed the St. Claude Avenue Bridge, and entered St. Bernard at a checkpoint now manned by parish sheriff's deputies, joining a short line of vehicles, most of them pickup trucks carting ladders and building materials, heading into the suburban wasteland of Chalmette. Once past the checkpoints, the vehicles dispersed and disappeared, leaving eerily empty streets.

What struck me, as I passed businesses and detoured through residential neighborhoods, was how little had been disturbed since Katrina blew through. There were simply few people about. One explanation, when I stopped by to visit with parish officials in their modular offices, was that many residents were still stuck in far-off temporary shelters, in some cases without transportation, and had not yet made it back. Many who had returned saw how grievously their houses had been wrecked. They turned around, got in their cars, left the mess behind.

Still, I did find a pocket of life as I pulled off the St. Bernard Highway onto Jean Lafitte Parkway in western Chalmette, what once must have been a pretty tree- and shrub-lined residential street that winds its way east–west to the commercial hub of Judge Perez Drive. It was pretty no more. Lawns, trees, and shrubs were dead; the median was a hump of muck and debris. Katrina-killed cars sat mournfully in driveways or along the street where they had gone underwater. One was so covered in marsh mat that at first I didn't recognize it as a car. This was a neighborhood of substantial brick houses, many of them two stories high. Few showed outward signs of damage except for busted windows, crushed awnings, or ripped-up roof shingles. But they all bore other grim reminders of Katrina's visit: spray-painted search dates on their doors and watermark necklaces below their second-story windows.

I noticed a shiny pickup truck pulled onto the shoulder before a gabled red-brick house. Out front stood a mound of debris—pink-rouged insulation, mud-splattered furniture, soggy carpets, water-logged, mildewed photo albums and knick-knacks. I pulled over to see if anyone was about. Inside the house, its front door gone, I found Mike Bertel, an affable twenty-three-year-old college student, and his pal, Cole Crocker, also twenty-three, pounding away with crowbars and hammers.

The house belonged to George and Lois Cramond, a retired couple who were neighbors of Mike's grandparents. Until the storm, they had lived across the street. Mike, born in the New Orleans suburb of Gentilly, knew the Cramonds from the time he was a toddler, having spent considerable time at his grandparents' house before moving to Colorado as a teenager.

Mike and Cole, it turned out, were St. Bernard pioneers, of a fashion. They were among a vanguard of workers who would tackle the arduous job of gutting reparable Katrina houses—essentially stripping the interior of water-damaged, moldy Sheetrock or plaster so that only bare studs remained. Mike had spent his teen years working construction with his dad in Colorado and was handy with a hammer and saw. He had moved back to Louisiana to attend the University of New Orleans. He was a junior enrolled in business classes there when Katrina struck—drowning his own rental apartment in the Lake View district, destroying most of his possessions, and flooding the University of New Orleans campus.

With his school closed and no job prospects, he'd volunteered to gut his grandparents' house and that of another St. Bernard relative when the Cramonds called to ask if he'd take on their house as well. (This soon became a full-time business for him.) Having done his relatives' houses, Mike already knew the grimy task he faced: demolition was the easy part. Carting out mud-caked, stinking, waterlogged furniture, carpets, rugs, and drapes—not to mention freezers and refrigerators wafting the unbearable stench of long-rotting food—was the dispiriting, backbreaking part of the job. He'd enlisted Cole, a high school buddy from Colorado, to come down and help him.

Later I interviewed the Cramonds, who had evacuated ahead of the storm and already moved to temporary housing well above New Orleans. They had no thoughts of returning. In their late seventies, they had already been washed out of one house in 1965 by Hurricane Betsy and had spent thirty-eight years here, at 2508 Jean Lafitte Parkway, thinking they'd never have to move again. But Katrina wrecked those dreams in about fifteen violent minutes when the surge overwhelmed their neighborhood.

The Cramonds were well-to-do by St. Bernard standards—George was retired from Shell Oil Company after a long white-collar career, and Lois had retired from teaching with a nice pension. They had already bought a lot on high ground above Interstate 10 in the Baton Rouge area and were contracting to build a house there. But having come once to visit the place where they'd raised three children and entertained friends and neighbors over crawfish boils and seafood suppers, they simply couldn't bear just to walk away, leaving the place to rot until the wrecking ball arrived. So they were paying Mike $6,000 to gut it—hoping that, in time, perhaps someone looking to repopulate St. Bernard might take it off their hands. The house had been appraised at $285,000 a few months before Katrina struck; the Cramonds were asking $60,000 for it now, although it seemed to me, at this moment, impossible to say whether it had any value at all.

If, as the parish estimated, 95 percent of St. Bernard's housing stock had been flooded—and a high percentage of that catastrophically—then a huge number of houses here would have to be gutted or knocked down. Surely, many others like the Cramonds would declare St. Bernard no longer worth the risk and pack up and move. This portended a scenario in which you'd end up with a glut of gutted houses in emptied-out neighborhoods where weeds occupied the vacant lots of the tear-downs—not an appealing notion of community.

When I met them, Mike and Cole had already cleared the bottom floor of the Cramonds' house, carting out the ruined furniture, pictures, and other keepsakes to the curb, shoveling out eight inches of hardened muck from the floor and removing a dead snake from the family room. Katrina had also performed one rather fantastical act, moving a fully loaded freezer from the house and wedging it in so tightly between the Cramonds' Lincoln Continental and their garage ceiling that neither could be moved. A tow truck had to be summoned to winch the car out.

They took me upstairs where they had just begun gutting the second story. Besides the musty odor, the first thing that struck me was Katrina's water line, etched three feet up on the wallboard, and the spreading stains of mold crawling up the walls. This meant that the water here had *settled* at about fifteen feet above the street but probably got higher than that. No one could say precisely how fast Katrina's surge had arrived or how high the water actually went on and around Jean Lafitte Parkway. A woman named Carole Spano, who had stayed behind in a one-story house on a side street two blocks away, did not survive to tell what she saw—she'd apparently drowned. A grim sign spray-painted on the remnants of a wooden fence propped up in her driveway spoke volumes about the reality facing survivors. It read: "St. Bernard Killed Carole. Can We Rebuild That?"

Mike showed me into the Cramonds' master bedroom, reeking of mold. He pointed to a small pile of things sprawled on a mildewed mattress: three metal folding chairs, two badly mildewed wooden end tables, a cypress porch swing caked in mud, Mr. Cramond's water-stained fifty-year-old baseball uniform from his days playing first base for Shell Oil's company team, a leather German officer's overcoat, a souvenir he'd brought back from World War II. Other than some photographs taken from the walls on the second floor, these represented all the salvageable items from the Cramonds' entire store of possessions. "That's not much to take away considering everything they had and all the time they lived here," Mike told me.

Later I followed Mike around as he cleaned out other houses, collecting anecdotes for a story I ended up writing for the *Journal* about post-Katrina house-gutters. Mike told me more than once that it wasn't the mold, the stench, the dead animals, the muscle-numbing task of wrangling fetid, muck-covered carpets up from the floor, that got to him. "The hardest part," he said, "is to toss out people's possessions—lifetimes—onto the curb."

I pressed on, taking in the depressing scenery, driving past the grim memorial to the deceased Carole. Every so often I would meet a passing car or run across a pocket of activity, mostly house-gutters like Mike

Bertel or patrolling sheriff's deputies. It appeared that I was one of maybe fifty people in all of St. Bernard Parish.

The farther south and east I went, the emptier the landscape became. At Verret, where Ricky met Charlo and spent the night in the fire station, the line of dead vehicles, including Ricky's truck and boat, parked on the high ground where the flood protection levee met the highway, remained untouched. Some of the older vehicles had begun to rust.

I reached the stricken Florissant Highway and motored through terrain that seemed frozen in time—save for the weeds that had begun to choke some lawns and cover up hurricane debris, little had changed since I'd driven through with Ricky and Ronald more than six weeks before. It was still a tableau of crushed houses, blown-apart camps, splintered, downed trees, and smashed-up mobile homes.

I entered Yscloskey in the middle of the afternoon and found it a silent, ruined ghost town—the blasted waterfront, the wrecked icehouse, the crumbled old trading post, the debris clinging to trees and utility lines, the truck tossed into the far-off marsh: it was all still there. As I drove toward the Bayou La Loutre bridge, I could see Ricky's house across the bayou in the distance, through a clearing of downed trees and houses.

But one thing had changed: the bridge was now open to traffic, so I crossed it and turned left, angling for the small residential cluster that lined the banks of Bayou La Loutre before it empties into the MR-GO less than a mile away. This was the part of Yscloskey I'd not yet seen.

Almost nothing along this short route, where the road closely hugged the bayou bank, looked salvageable. Some houses had been blown to smithereens and lay in heaps. Some that were on stilts remained standing but had been eviscerated by wind and water—their innards sagging from blown-out windows, doors, or cavernous holes gouged in the walls. I wondered if tornadoes had roamed this place.

The road made a sharp right turn. About three long blocks beyond that I came upon a startling sight: a man, slight, with frizzy gray hair protruding from a blue cotton-and-mesh ball cap pulled down low on his forehead, stood with a garden rake before a set of concrete steps framed by a railing—steps that apparently once led to something but now stood in a moat of rubble disconnected from anything else. He was methodically raking storm debris into a pile. I pulled over, got out, and introduced myself.

"Joe Gonzales," he said. "Nice to see ya. This is where I live."

I peered around, thinking he must have meant this is where he *used* to live, since no house stood on this spot. His lawn looked like mischievous giants had run through, ripping branches from trees, pulling houses apart into piles of splintered wood, and scattering debris—tin from gutters, broken furniture, metal tools, plastic gasoline jugs and lawn chairs, cement building blocks, bits of rope, tattered clothes, pots and pans—everywhere. This all sat on, or was partially covered by, a topping of dense marsh mat that Joe would later discover was three feet deep in some places.

"I'm tryin' to find my driveway first," he continued. "It's under here someplace. But my house—it's still here. It's just not where it used to be."

He pointed to my right and sure enough, about three hundred feet away, seemingly afloat on a raft of undulating wheat-brown storm mat, sat a white clapboard house with a jaunty aqua-green roof and matching shutters. Katrina had banged it up as it ripped the house from the three-foot pilings it used to stand on. The back end had been cleaved open, exposing bare stud walls. There were two major gashes in the tin roof, and the storm had knocked out a window, frame and all. The house had been spun around and what had been the front porch was now facing the back yard of Joe's neighbor's property, where the dwelling finally settled. Just off the battered porch was what remained of the neighbor's house: a small section holding a window, part of a roof, and some siding. The rest of it was gone.

I tried to imagine the combination of wind and water that could perform such a feat. But having seen how Katrina dislodged the four-bedroom slab house in Lexington Place and drove it a block up the street, I was no longer jolted by anything.

"She's busted up," said Joe, "but she ain't broke. Me and my daddy built that house with our own hands when I came back from the war and I guess we built it good. Come see."

We waded gingerly through the storm mat, Joe admonishing me to be careful. There were lots of boards about with long nails protruding from them. We reached the house and I peered through the missing window. All I could see was a tangle of mud-caked furniture and appliances, most of it unrecognizable, corkscrewed into the center of the room by the spin-cycle effect of the flooding. To my untrained eye, the house looked like a candidate for the bulldozer.

Joe, however, had a decidedly different opinion, as he went through the checklist he'd made in his own mind. The exterior walls were made of native cypress, impervious to rot; the interior stud walls were made of longleaf pine from two-by-fours that, though rudely exposed by the storm, seemed remarkably free of aging and wear. He'd sized up the house from every angle he could access. As far as he could tell, she was still plumb, the floor and ceiling joists having done their job of keeping her squared up.

"Look at that," he told me, peering through an opening in a wall torn away by the storm. "Solid pecan floors. You can't get lumber like that anymore. And look at this storm sheeting." Joe reached in and knocked on the inside of an exterior wall to show the diagonal planking, exposed when Katrina ripped away wallpaper and plaster, that tightly bound the stud walls and kept them from shifting.

"Nobody puts in storm sheeting like that anymore. That's why this house stayed and a lot of others didn't," he said. "Them new houses, shuh, they build them with nail guns and cheap lumber. That stuff just don't last. Go look at them fancy camps over there—some of them cost a million dollars and you can't even find a stick of wood from them. They're gone. When me and Daddy built this house, we didn't have power tools. Everything was done by hand. Every board you see, we sawed by hand. Every nail, we drove with a hammer. We designed everything and we made everything—the windows and the shutters and the doors. We did it all."

Joe turned, looking off toward the horizon as if in thought. "That's why I can't just let her go. We got too much in it, though it didn't cost that much in today's dollars. When we built it, in 1946 or '47, we had thirty-eight hundred dollars worth of materials in it. If it wasn't my daddy's house, maybe I wouldn't care so much."

He patted the house as though he were patting an old friend on the shoulder. Then he shook his head and said, "If I can get it moved back for twenty, twenty-five thousand dollars, I'm going to put it right back where it was."

I dutifully wrote all this down in my notebook, though I can't say I shared Joe's optimism, even as I admired it. We spent a little more time poking around the house. Joe pointed out mud-caked pieces of furniture that he told me he would restore once he got them out of the mildewing mess. Assuming you had the time, patience, and talent for removing old varnish and paint, sanding interminably, then recoating the object of your desire with varnish, shellac, or paint, Joe assured me you could restore many things that looked hopelessly damaged.

"C'mon, come meet the family," Joe finally said. "We're all on the boat." He pointed to nearby Bayou La Loutre.

We waded through the marsh mat, past the rubble of Joe's former porch strewn with the concrete blocks that once formed it, and crossed the narrow road over to a dock where sitting moored was the *Miss Carol,* a handsome fifty-foot oyster boat on loan from Joe's grandson-in-law. There I met Selina Gonzales, Joe's wife of sixty-one years, and their disabled son, Richard Joseph, and began to gather their story.

Joe Gonzales was seventy-nine years old, retired a decade or so from oyster fishing. He'd grown up here, as had his father, grandfather, and great-grandfather before him. His family had been early Isleño pioneers to the area. Save for the two years he spent in the Pacific and Korea at the close of World War II, he'd never lived anyplace else, nor ever wanted to. Selina was seventy-eight and also came from an Isleño family that had been in St. Bernard Parish forever. Neither family had much money —"When we met," Joe told me, "Selina didn't own a proper pair of shoes." Many of the Isleño families of that generation might, by today's standards, be considered subsistence hunters, fishermen, and gatherers. But it was a poverty invisible to them, since the bayous, marshes, and sea kept food on the table; nobody went hungry or *felt* poor.

Joe had dredged oysters all his life, a skill he'd learned from his father. But he'd also prospered as a boatbuilder, sketching out boats in his head and painstakingly building them on blocks in his backyard. He'd built more than thirty oyster and shrimp boats, mostly for other Yscloskey fishermen, and gained a reputation as a master craftsman. If you wanted a boat fast, you didn't call up Joe Gonzales. But if you wanted a beautiful, superbly crafted vessel, he was your man.

Selina was a traditional Isleño housewife, which meant that she was a fantastic old-school cook (I was gratefully introduced to her skill on several extended visits). She could also pluck ducks, peel shrimp, pick crabs (the local term for tediously removing the meat), shuck oysters, clean fish, and plant a garden. In the early lean days of their marriage, she'd sometimes sewed and made their clothes. The lot they'd built their house on measures one hundred by three hundred feet, and it originally cost them $750 (before Katrina struck, similar property was going for $100,000). They'd raised two children in the house, Joy Lynn, who died suddenly in the late 1980s and left two children of her own behind for Joe and Selina to care for, and Richard, now sixty, who in 1981 was struck by a drunk driver as he walked on the shoulder of the road just out in front of the Gonzales home. He lost a leg above the knee and the wound never properly healed. He eventually developed bone-marrow cancer, and doctors were forced to amputate the leg at his hip. Richard had tried a titanium prosthesis, but the pain and discomfort made wearing it unbearable. The leg gathered dust in a closet. He'd now spent more than a decade hobbling around on crutches.

Richard had fished oysters with Joe when he could and now and then captained his own boat when he was feeling up to it. He was also a skilled carpenter and mechanic. He'd married, raised three daughters, got divorced, and for the last several years had lived with Joe and Selina here in Yscloskey.

In 1998, Selina fell ill with stomach cancer and survived radical surgery after radiation and chemotherapy, but she had not been totally well since. Her restless energy and enthusiasm made up for the drag the illness had put on her life. But Joe had been forced to sell his working oyster boat, the *Lady Desiree,* to help pay for Selina's extensive treatments.

Then Katrina struck. They'd all evacuated to what they thought was higher ground—the house of Richard's daughter Gretchen Nicosia and her husband Mike, a substantial two-story ranch in an enclave known as South Lake about midway between Yscloskey and Violet Canal. But they felt less safe when a wave battered down the door, broke windows, and drove them up to the second floor. "When the water first came and we looked outside, we thought we were looking into a goldfish bowl out the windows," Selina told me.

They held out in the house for a day, then made their way down a ladder poked through the second floor window into a tiny flatboat owned by a friend. It was crowded with other refugees, and Selina ended up sitting in the bottom of the boat in a puddle of water. But she was happy to be out of the flooded house. They found a more substantial powerboat at a neighbor's house, managed to get it started, and, in the dark, made their way through the treacherously flooded landscape, dodging floating debris and downed power poles and lines, to the harbor at Violet Canal. There the *Miss Carol* lay at the dock, having miraculously survived the storm even as many other boats had been sunk. They boarded the boat, which had been stocked with food and water, and parceled out what excess provisions they could spare, giving away fifty cases of bottled water to those in need. They watched in shock and amazement the rescue efforts by the Violet fleet and citizens' flotilla, their son-in-law, Mike Nicosia, joining in. In the scrum of the harbor, where it was hard at first to move around, the Gonzaleses came to learn of the pivotal role of one of their neighbors, Ricky Robin. They never saw or spoke to Ricky while at Violet, but they knew him well. Charles Robin, Ricky's father, was Selina's first cousin.

They stood at Violet for four days, and then Richard, at the helm, guided the *Miss Carol* with some difficulty up a little-used local bayou to the battered Bayou Bienvenue Marina. There they docked for another day amid the wreckage of dozens and dozens of boats that lay overturned or sunk in the harbor. By then, the enormity of the catastrophe that had befallen St. Bernard was abundantly clear, and a nephew, tracking them down in his powerboat, advised them to leave. The entire parish was under an evacuation order. Replenishing their supplies might become impossible.

They took his advice and set out on a fretful odyssey that would take them away from Yscloskey for about six weeks. They crossed Lake Pontchartrain and spent a night in the battered community of Slidell in the house of a friend of their nephew. Then they motored by car to

Baton Rouge, where they spent three days in an apartment provided by another of Richard's daughters. Leaving Baton Rouge, they returned south to spend a week with Richard's third daughter, who lives in the Lafourche Parish town of Larose, about a hundred miles by car from St. Bernard. Meanwhile, Hurricane Rita was making its way toward the Louisiana coast. They were forced to evacuate again, this time for a couple of days to Butler, Alabama.

They returned to Larose for another week; then, one day, Joe had had enough. He felt terribly lonesome for his bayou home, though he worried that it no longer existed. Still, the tug back was as inexorable as the tide, and by this time the *Miss Carol* had been moved to a dock on Bayou Lafourche near Larose. They loaded her up with enough provisions for a couple of months and motored down Bayou Lafourche toward the gulf, heading for the entrance of the MR-GO. Seven hours later they were docked on Bayou La Loutre across from their home in Yscloskey, emerging from the boat to see for the first time the wreckage all around.

Selina, who had not been feeling well since the storm, cried. At that moment she would have been happy had they turned the *Miss Carol* around and headed back to Lafourche Parish, where at least a real bed awaited them. But Joe was determined to stay. His nomadic post-Katrina tour had convinced him that at this stage in his life he simply couldn't live anyplace else. It would kill him. Richard's daughter in Baton Rouge had offered to give them a house there, but Joe declined.

"What would a man like me do in Baton Rouge?" he asked me bluntly in the broad, Cajunesque accent common to these bayous. "The noise, the traffic, man. It's quiet out here. Anyway, I don't know anything else."

When I caught up with them, the Gonzaleses had been at anchor on Bayou La Loutre for about two weeks, and it was certainly quiet now. Not a single other person inhabited Yscloskey at the moment, though a part-time resident had pitched a pup tent in the rubble of his fishing camp and came to visit from time to time. Except for a trickle of other house and camp owners driving by to see their properties, however, and parish cleanup crews that came sporadically to remove downed trees, the Gonzaleses had Yscloskey to themselves. Power, phones, and gas remained out of service throughout St. Bernard Parish, and nobody had a clue when they might be restored. Joe and his family were fifty miles away from the nearest operating laundromat and supermarket.

The *Miss Carol* was a handsome boat, broad at the beam with a sun-shielding canopy covering her long open deck, a good thing to have, as the fall weather here can often wax quite warm. But the boat wasn't much of an apartment. Joe showed me the quarters: three rough-hewn rack bunks wedged into a tight cabin. The Gonzaleses did their cooking on a propane stove and shared a bathroom so cramped that a person with his elbows out would scrape the walls. There was no shower. A small droning generator supplied electricity for a tiny air-conditioner to cool the cabin as needed and run what lights they required at night. They had cell phones but the service was fitful.

The Gonzaleses had plenty to eat, supplementing the supermarket provisions they'd brought along with speckled trout—a species many think is the best eating fish in the bayous—that Richard caught from time to time by casting lures off the *Miss Carol*'s fantail. But it struck me that they were not so much living here as camping out. They intended soon to join the lines of refugees applying for FEMA trailers. But so far there had not been a sign from anyone in any official capacity that temporary shelter would be arriving anytime soon.

Joe and I walked back to his rubble-strewn yard where he further sketched out the economic realities. He owned two other houses on property next door. One he used for storage. The other was a rental house that had supplied a few hundred dollars a month in income. Both lay wrecked beyond repair. Now, he and Selina's only income was an eight-hundred-dollar-a-month Social Security check. Joe carried modest flood and homeowners insurance for both his house and the rental house. But when he did the math on his damages—houses, their contents, a truck and car, not to mention a shed that harbored his extensive woodworking tools—he figured his losses at half a million dollars, well beyond his insurance coverage.

We stood near the disconnected stairs that once led to his front porch. Joe pointed out where the tool shed used to be. He told me it would take the equivalent of a bulldozer to scrape the mat and storm debris off his property. But before that happened there were things he wanted to account for. "You wouldn't believe the tools I had," he said. He ticked off a partial list: band saws, table saws, lathes, sanders, grinders, chisels, even high-end welding equipment. Katrina's flood ruined everything electrical and buried most of it in debris to boot.

Joe picked up his garden rake and scratched away some marsh grass. A mud-encrusted object emerged: a router, a tool used to finely mill wood. He broke off some of the dirt, holding the object up for inspection. "Well, you can replace tools," he said. "I guess I'm going to have to."

He paused, then looked at me. "Want to go see my boat?"

I thought I'd seen his boat, but he wasn't referring to the *Miss Carol*. He pointed to our left; sitting not far away in the cluttered debris field was an elegant planked oyster boat, painted white, trimmed blue at the waterline and red along the gunwales and the bow sprit. Somehow, riveted as I was by Joe's story, I'd completely missed the impressive presence of the boat. It sported an unfinished metal-framed canopy and a rounded cabin aft. We walked over as Joe explained that she was his last major boat-building project. He'd already invested about thirty years and $200,000 in her. "The *Joy Lynn*, named for my daughter," he told me. "I tied her down for Katrina with four big ropes and she stayed put—well, she got knocked off her building blocks but that's all. The storm got my house but it didn't get my boat. She hardly got a scratch on her."

When I thought about it, I realized that Joe had started building the *Joy Lynn* around the same time that Ricky Robin was laying the keel for the *Lil' Rick*. (And it was only later that I realized this was the same Joe Gonzales who had praised Ricky's crafting of his boat all those years ago.) He later told me that he might have finished the boat already save for the expensive and morale-sapping episode of Selina's bout with cancer, which had prevented him from working on it except occasionally for the past seven years.

We came up alongside the boat and ascended a battered aluminum ladder that Joe had dug out of the marsh mat and propped up along the port side. He climbed the ladder first. I followed. I'm no marine architect, but even a layman could marvel at the *Joy Lynn's* clean, flowing, elegant lines and the obvious craftsmanship that had gone into her.

Joe gave me the dimensions. The boat was sixty-four feet long and twenty-two feet wide at the beam, built for stability and capacity, not speed. Oyster boats are designed to work the inland bays and lagoons that hold most of the oyster reefs here, and it's not unusual to see them puttering to the docks loaded to the gunwales with hundreds of burlap sacks filled with oysters. "Every nail, every screw, every bolt. I did all that," Joe said as we clopped across the spacious deck.

We went aft, where he opened the door to the cabin trimmed in milled red cedar. Joe explained what remained to be done: some trim work on the cabin, completing a fully furnished bedroom designed for four bunks, and a galley. When all that was finished, a company that specializes in such things would come and lift the *Joy Lynn* from his yard and find a way to ease her gently into the bayou across the road. Once she was afloat, Joe would drop in a powerful diesel engine and rig the clutch, hydraulics, and the oyster-dredging winches and motor off toward the nearby Gulf of Mexico.

How long would all that take?

Joe looked around, as though for a moment he could actually shut out the reality of the disaster all around him, and smiled.

"I don't know, but I've got to take a ride on her before I die."

19. Dancing
with Boats

Where the Mississippi makes a sharp bend known as the English Turn, State Highway 39 exits St. Bernard Parish and dives, hugging the river, deep into the eastern side of Plaquemines Parish. A few miles in, the road leaves the clutter of development and the land opens up, the high, grassy levees of the river on the right, sprawling farmsteads and fields on the left, broken now and then by woodlands. There are no actual towns here. But the road wanders, curling with the river, through sparse and sometimes faded settlements still clinging to the place names of the grand eighteenth- and nineteenth-century sugar and cattle plantations that once defined this area: Braithwaite, Dalcour, Bertrandville, Carlisle, Davant, Phoenix. At one lonesome straightaway stretch, an impressively long white stockade fence rises up, framing a gorgeous expanse of property—an arbor of perhaps fifty towering live oaks, planted long ago in a handsome alignment, set on a green, close-cropped pasture speckled with yellow wildflowers. Surely here once stood some grand antebellum mansion. On this late March day cloaked in an azure sky, temperatures in the middle seventies, buttercup and goldenrod setting the greened-up levees and fields ablaze, it's hard for me to conjure the fury with which Hurricane Katrina roared across this land seven months before.

But I'd just left behind stark reminders of the storm, having motored through numerous Chalmette neighborhoods that looked far worse than when I'd seen them on my last visit in December. On Jean Lafitte Parkway, where I'd witnessed the Cramonds' house being gutted, the curbs were piled so high with ruined furniture, lumber, and broken-up drywall that the rubble sometimes obscured the houses. Later I learned that the FEMA-sponsored cleanup had ground to an abrupt halt a couple of weeks before over a payment snafu involving the federal pay-master and the main contractor. St. Bernard would have to endure being one vast, sprawling trash dump until the matter was cleared up.

But even out here, in this pastoral, sparsely populated land, re-minders of Katrina crop up from time to time: blue-tarped roofs of houses still under repair; decimated mobile-home parks with crushed, rusting trailers still lying in ruin; the morose slabs of what once were houses hemmed in by spring weeds; and now and then, dense clus-ters of FEMA trailers marking the resettlement of the displaced and dispossessed.

South of Phoenix, the road gently wanders away from the river. A man-made protection levee rises up on the left to guard the narrow alluvial ridge holding what few settlements there are before this higher ground surrenders to a flat fetch of brackish marsh fanning out to the far horizon. I pass a white wooden plantation home fading to ruin. Later, adjacent to a graceful old brick Catholic church stands an abandoned green store, a sign next to it reading incongruously, "Bail Ponds—24 Hr. Service." A light breeze carries a hint of the Gulf of Mexico about twenty-five miles away.

The road finally plays out at a dead-end about sixty miles from the St. Bernard Parish line at a wayside whimsically named Bohemia. Al-though my destination is a commercial fishing marina about five miles above Bohemia, I've never traveled this road and can't resist driving to the end to see what Bohemia looks like.

The answer is that on this fair morning Bohemia is a gloriously wild and largely empty place, populated only by a rough, storm-damaged hunting camp on the outside of a flood protection levee. The camp is set in scrub woodlands on the verge of a small swamp tucked into the wide marsh beyond. Buttercups and dandelions paint the grassy levee slopes. A narrow slough, surrendering to something of a drought that has gripped the region since Katrina passed, tracks the inside of the levee. Its cracked-mud banks hold dwarf cypresses, alder, bull tongue, and an astonishing profusion of the most exotic wildflowers found in these climes—water-loving spider lilies. They sport ephemerally white conical flowers, set in a brace of deep green leaves, their cones framed by other-worldly six-inch white tendrils that resemble spider legs.

Doubling back, I come upon my destination, a spur road over the protection levee at a place a highway sign marks as Pointe-a-la-Hache (Ax Point in English). The top of the levee reveals a panorama far less pastoral than the view at Bohemia: it is strewn with a half dozen storm-damaged boats, including a once handsome oyster lugger, the *Mister Rabbit,* easily fifty feet long. It remains tethered to the giant piling that once held it at dock in the harbor about two hundred yards east—until Katrina ripped them up and tossed them to this levee peak at least fifteen feet above the water. Beyond the *Mister Rabbit* is a small work barge that was treated just as rudely. The prize, though, belongs to a shrimping skiff, the *Captain Gator.* At least thirty feet long, the skiff lies, its rigging battered, on the dandelion-choked banks of a shallow canal clear across the highway behind me.

Ahead sits a rectangular-shaped harbor, a place that might once have passed for scenic with its gleaming white boat sheds, wide-planked wharves jutting into the water, crisp-cornered slips berthing mostly hand-hewn oyster luggers, and shrimp trawlers decorated with bright flags and pennants. All of it is set at the foot of a pretty bayou meandering through a spring-green marsh. But the harbor is a postcard of disaster: the boat sheds are unidentifiable, reduced to random mounds of crushed metal siding, broken cement bricks, and rusting, twisted beams exposed to the salt air. Whatever boats remained within had no chance of survival.

The banks out from the wharves are littered with broken boats and boat parts bulldozed into large, unsightly piles. The harbor looks like it could accommodate at least a hundred decent-sized commercial vessels, but there are only about a dozen afloat and tied up here now, all of them oyster luggers, and not many of them operative. Some bear the red spray-painted identification numbers that designate them as boats that had sunk at their moorings and were pumped out and refloated or lifted up by crane from where they lay. Others wear more obvious scars—gashes in their cabins, bows, and railings, broken rigging, mud-smeared decks. The scars mark them as boats recently fetched from the bottom where they had been driven down by the overpowering flood.

I'm looking for two specific boats, however, and from the top of the levee I spot one of them tied to a catwalk at the southeast corner of the harbor—the jaunty, upturned bow of Ricky Robin's trawler, the *Lil' Rick*. Despite his morose vow that day on our tour of Yscloskey to abandon battered St. Bernard Parish, Ricky had a change of heart. He simply couldn't leave the *Lil' Rick* behind, trapped as it was for a while in the rubble-filled, silted-in bayous left in Katrina's wake.

I know Ronald Robin's boat, the *Evening Star*, is also somewhere in the harbor. But I don't immediately see it until I fix my eyes on the most prominent object afloat: a massive rust-colored barge, at least a hundred feet long, easing wakeless across the flat brown waters of the harbor. Atop it sits an impressive yellow dragline powering a four-story black metal crane, an American flag flapping at the top of its boom, a giant sling, attached to a two-inch steel cable, dangling just above the water. Supplying the locomotion for this behemoth is the thirty-eight-foot *Star*, its bow lashed to a stanchion on the barge's aft port side. It looks like a dolphin pushing a whale.

Normally a barge of this size bearing a crane with seventy-ton lifting capacity would be pushed by a proper tugboat. But these still aren't normal times. There were no tugboats with drafts shallow enough to make their way through the Katrina-made chokepoints into these remote bayous. After all the calamity that has befallen them, Ricky and Ronald have stumbled upon some luck. By keeping their boats safe and sticking it out here, they've found a profitable use for their considerable maritime skills.

The barge and crane are part of a FEMA-funded boat removal and recovery operation to clear St. Bernard and eastern Plaquemines parishes' stricken waterways of sunken boats and other obstructions, including houses, fishing camps, and whatever else Katrina might have blown into them. The barge is owned by an old friend of the Robins, Donald Merwin, who operates a boat-repair yard at Violet Canal. They have been working methodically from one stricken marina to another for about six weeks now, getting $750 per boat per day, plus overtime on some days. I know this because Ricky briefed me after I'd phoned to tell him I was moving to New Orleans to do more research for this book. "C'mon down," he said, "and we'll catch up."

I drive over to the *Lil' Rick*, tied up on the southeastern corner of the harbor. I spot Ricky wearing a white hard hat, T-shirt, and jeans pulled over black rubber boots, seated in a plastic chair on the partially shaded aft deck of the trawler. My presence is announced by the gruff but harmless barking of Lulu, his black-and-chocolate Labrador retriever mix. A delicious aroma is wafting from the trawler's galley.

"Lulu, baby, it's a podnah," Ricky says as he shushes the dog and welcomes me aboard the trawler. He rises, smiles, and greets me warmly. Lulu, who was plucked from the roof of Ricky's Violet Canal house the day after the storm, comes over to check me out.

"How I'm lookin' since you saw me last?" Ricky asks jovially. "At least we're not eatin' that FEMA food anymore. No more MREs."

"What's in the pot?" I ask.

"Chicken stew," he says. "Stick around tonight and you can have some."

Ricky points out in the harbor toward the barge. "It was Ronald's turn to move it. We just picked up a boat on this corner and now we're goin' after one over there. I said I'd help him but he said it was OK. Look at him go out there. You know, the thing about pushin' that barge is that you don't have brakes. Just because you want to stop doesn't mean the wind stops. If that thing gets away, it can cause real damage. So you gotta be real careful—and you gotta know what you're doin'.'"

Over coffee, Ricky gives me the up-to-date narrative on everyone. He and Ronald now have FEMA trailers, his in the yard of his home at Yscloskey and Ronald's in the yard of the home of his son, Van, near Violet. But because they are working seven days a week in the boat-recovery operation, a job that includes pushing the barge on long, slow trips from harbor to harbor, they mostly sleep on their boats and spend little time in the trailers. It's just as well, in his opinion. St. Bernard remains a debris-choked wreck and the large majority of residents are still gone. And while a handful of bars and some convenience stores have reopened, the parish doesn't yet have a proper supermarket, laundromat, or doctor's or dentist's office, though there is a clinic set up by volunteer doctors on the site of the drowned Wal-Mart. Thus it remains a rough place to live.

Meanwhile, Ricky's wife Susan, her two daughters, and her father Sidney T. are living in Tennessee, where they ended up after their boat evacuation from Violet Canal. They were essentially adopted by the congregation of the Salem Baptist Church in Trenton, Tennessee, a town of forty-six hundred about 110 miles northeast of Memphis. They were offered free use of an unfurnished house that the church owned. When word spread around town that a family of Katrina refugees had arrived needing shelter, donated furniture and appliances filled up the house in a day or two. Sidney T. and Susan had both found good doctors, and with a return to his regimen of medication he was doing somewhat better. Susan's back was still giving her fits. But, all in all, they were counting their blessings.

Of course, Ricky tells me, everyone is miserably lonesome. "Susan keeps wanting to come down, but there's still nothing down here to come to, and I'm planning to go up there but so far I haven't made it. We're lucky to have any work at all, so it's hard to leave. I'm figuring I could drive up there—drive eight hours straight, stay twelve hours, then drive straight back—and maybe I wouldn't be missed. I'm gonna have to do that soon before Susan forgets what I look like."

At that moment, Ricky's cell phone rings. It's the IRS.

"Yes, this is Mr. Ricky Robin. What can I do for you? No, sir, I haven't filed taxes since 2005. We have a problem with that because we lost everything in the house in Katrina and we don't have nothin' to go by. But, listen, would you get back to my wife on this? She has all the information, such as we have. OK, thank you."

Ricky hangs up and shrugs. "What can you do?" he says. "The man still wants his money, no matter what happened to us down here."

After the National Guard arrived in the parish, Ricky and Ronald got put on the St. Bernard Parish payroll for a while. "The parish had no personnel," Ricky says. "Hell, we heard some of the prisoners became policemen. They opened up the jail and I think some of them got a check. We did what we could do, helpin' out here and there." Among other things, they inspected broken levees, providing what advice they could to parish officials coordinating with Army Corps of Engineers personnel, who by that time were in the parish in full force starting to rebuild the badly battered levee system.

Ricky continues: "I'm glad I've come down here. I'm actually feeling better since I left St. Bernard. With all the house-gutting going on where we are, the air down here is cleaner. And it's quiet—man, when you come down here you've got to bring your own noise."

Ricky glances out toward the barge, which has come to rest about three-quarters of the way up the harbor. The dragline's boom is swinging around and beginning to lower its giant sling toward the water, preparing to launch another boat-fetching operation. An aluminum oyster lugger, maybe forty feet long, sits capsized in fairly shallow water there, its bottom poking up from the murky depths. Beyond the barge, far off its port side, a boat under power makes an appearance—a scenic white lugger, trimmed red along the water line, sacks of oysters stacked high on its deck, puttering slowly toward a dock.

"Look at that li'l boat loaded with oysters," says Ricky. "That's sweet, huh? That's the way I like to come in—loaded. That's a couple of thousand dollars he's got there."

An irony of the post-Katrina world is that commercial fishing stocks in St. Bernard and Plaquemines parishes have made a startling comeback. Although Katrina buried thousands of acres of oyster reefs in sludge, those that were untouched are producing bumper crops. And the estuary shrimping grounds, where the storm provided something of a service by stirring up and scouring out bottom sediments, are also producing a bountiful shrimp crop.

Of course, this means there are more oysters, shrimp, and crabs to be harvested than there are boats to gather them, Katrina having decimated the local fleet. Ricky offers graphic testimony. "I pity these poor fishermen down here—half their boats have been lost. So what we're really trying to do is to save the boats we can. Instead of being in a hurry to raise a boat, we try to bring it up slow and careful so that if it's not already broken we don't break it. It takes a lot longer, but it's the difference between putting people back to work or putting them out of business."

Ricky offers more anecdotal evidence of what went on here. Katrina's eye went right over the place. One boat from this harbor washed all the way to Horn Island, Alabama, about a hundred miles east. A giant shrimp trawler disappeared altogether. A half dozen houseboats docked here ended up tangled in some cypress trees about six miles away. Boats got sunk atop other boats. "When we think we have a good idea of how many boats we're dealing with," Ricky says, "we come up surprised. We pulled one out today and found another boat on top of it. This place got hammered."

Ricky pauses, then adds: "It's unreal—it's rough you know. I see a lot of good people come down here and they start crying. They've lost their boats, they've lost their houses; they've got nothin'. We're tryin' to help them out as best we can. That's why every boat we save is important."

Ricky's phone rings again. It's Susan, on speakerphone.

"Well hello, my sugar," says Ricky. "Whatcha doin'?"

"Hey, baby. I'm waiting at the doctor's office with Daddy and everything looks fine so far. They took some more blood work."

"What happens if his blood works isn't right?"

"Well, they'll have to give him another blood transfusion."

"Oh, well," says Ricky. "I'm just hoping his blood work holds."

"So what you doin', Ricky?"

"I'm b.s.in' with my podnah, Mr. Ken Wells, and enjoyin' the nice breeze of the day."

"Well, that's good, Ricky. I won't keep you. I was just missin' you, is all."

"Well, I'm missin' you, too."

Ricky hangs up. "I don't mind workin'," he says, "but every once and a while I need a break. I think I'm just gonna sneak out—put a mannequin in my place. Put some sunglasses and hat on it, and they'll never know I'm gone."

He looks out toward the harbor again.

"He's eighty-five years old, Susie's dad," he says. "It's good to know that the shots are still workin' for him. They're better off up there. Just the idea of goin' to the hospital here is unreal. We had a nice hospital, but . . ." Ricky's voice trails off.

In the distance, the *Evening Star* has disconnected from the barge and is making a slow turn this way. "Ronald's coming back," says Ricky. "That means the barge is gonna be there for a while."

About three hours later, the sling on Donald Merwin's barge emerges slowly from the murky depths with a big fish—a gray, aluminum-hulled

oyster boat. It comes up canted to the starboard side, an artful position-
ing of the sling by the crane operator so that the ton or so of sludge and
water trapped inside will slowly start to drain out. From our position,
maybe three hundred yards away, the boat looks to be in one piece. If it
doesn't have gaping holes punched in the bottom, it should float again.

I leave the *Lil' Rick* for a walk around the marina's perimeter to get
a closer look at the operation. I run into Aurora Frederick, a forty-
something African-American woman who has a deeply personal interest
in the rising vessel. It's her boat.

"I can't believe I'm seeing it," she says. "I left it here in the storm and
when I came back at the end of September I just couldn't find it. It was
tied up over there"—she points to a dock space nearby—"so I wasn't
looking for it out there."

She made a return trip a little later with a friend who scanned the
water with her and said, "Oh, look out there. Is that an island?" Aurora
looked and said, "No, that's the bottom of my boat." Katrina had swept it
from its tie-down position and flipped it over.

A couple of years earlier, Aurora, a resident of nearby Davant, invested most of her savings—seven thousand dollars—in the boat after
learning to dredge oysters by apprenticing with friends. It's not the
fanciest boat in the world. But for Aurora, a divorcee, it represented a
new lease on life, an opportunity to rise from menial jobs to meaningful
self-employment. Pre-Katrina, during a good season, she would harvest
up to fifty sacks of oysters a day. "I was making good money," she says.

Out in the harbor, the crane lifts the boat higher above the waterline. Sludge and water continue to pour out. I see the *Evening Star*
headed for the barge. Ronald Robin soon edges the trawler up to the
barge's port side, where workers secure it to a stanchion with fat yellow
ropes. The barge, to the audible straining of the *Star*'s engine, then
begins a slow, graceful pirouette. Aurora's boat, dangling above the
water, glides slowly toward the near bank here.

We're joined by Donald Merwin, the barge's owner, who gives Aurora the preliminary report. They've drained most of the water out of the
boat but a great deal of heavy black sludge remains. And there are big
holes in the hull below the waterline. Their best bet, Merwin tells her, is
for the crane operator to deposit the boat on the bank.

Aurora mulls the situation over. She will have to move quickly to perform any repairs since the boat, once out of water, will begin to rapidly rust and deteriorate. And she'll have the additional expense of hiring heavy machinery to relaunch it.

Aurora nods. "OK," she says. "I understand."

In a few minutes, the barge, under Ronald's skillful navigation, has slipped into position to pivot the boat onto shore. The crane slowly swings around and Aurora Frederick's boat is eased gently, as though it were a fine piano, onto solid ground.

From this close the boat looks like a wreck. A gaping gouge runs along the port bow, and metal decking has been torn away in several places. A ring of rust girds the hull. A barge worker comes over to say that it will be a monumental task just to shovel out the thick sludge filling up the engine room.

Still, Aurora thanks Merwin profusely for the care his men have used in recovering the boat. She walks over to it as if she'd spotted a long-lost friend. "If I can just save my engine," she says, "I'll be OK."

I ask Merwin how the job in general is going so far. "We're about 85 percent done," he tells me. His crews started in Violet and recovered thirty-two boats; they picked up another thirty-six in Bayou Bienvenue; and they've gotten to seventeen here so far. Given what he's witnessed to this point, he counts the recovery of Aurora Frederick's boat as one of the success stories.

"It gives her some hope," he says. "And these people down here could use some hope."

Ronald and the *Star* have returned to the dock near where the *Lil' Rick* is moored. I cross over a plank positioned as a walkway and step aboard.

"How you makin' out?" Ronald says cheerily through his open cabin door. "C'mon in. I've got some coffee."

He fetches me a cup and then introduces me to his dog, Sophie, a tiny and timid Yorkshire terrier with a ribbon in her hair. I go over to say hello to Sophie, who is seated in a chair next to Ronald's captain's chair.

She trembles as she sniffs my hand.

"That's daddy's girl," Ronald says gently and playfully to the dog.

"That's a thousand-dollar dog, no lie. When my last wife was alive, that dog went to the beauty parlor every Thursday. Sometimes I took her, 'cause I knew she was Momma's baby, yes, she was. Ain't that the truth, Sophie?"

Ronald gives Sophie a pat.

Given Ronald's background, I figured him for a pitbull—or at least a hunting hound—kind of guy. But he's clearly crazy about Sophie.

I ask if it's fun moving that behemoth of a barge around.

"It's a challenge," says Ronald, "but little by little we're gettin' it." The big worry, he says, is the strain the pushing and towing is putting on his engine. "We're underpowered for a job like this."

At any rate, Ronald says, wrangling boats off the bottom helps break up the monotony of a job involving a fair amount of down time, though now and then the tedium is punctuated by moments of oddness and hilarity. During a break, for example, Ronald and Ricky were walking the bank near the stricken Bayou Bienvenue Marina when they stumbled upon an extremely curious mound of storm debris. It turned out that Mr. Binky's on nearby Paris Road—St. Bernard Parish's only X-rated video and sex-toy store—had lost its inventory to the flood, and a great deal of this merchandise had apparently washed up near the marina. Ronald dug a couple of things out of the muck, only to realize that they were very large sex appliances of the kind that are advertised on late-night cable TV. "Ricky found one that took two batteries. I found one that took four—can you believe that?" Ronald tells me, unable to suppress a grin.

"Well?" I asked.

"I got one at home in my FEMA trailer—it cleaned up nice," says Ronald. "Now, Ricky, him, he asks me, 'What you want that thing for? You could put yourself out of business, Ronald.'"

Ronald (who later introduced me to his girlfriend, also a dispossessed St. Bernard resident, about half his age) smiles. "I told Ricky I didn't think that would happen."

Our conversation is interrupted by the squawking of a walkie-talkie on the cabin console, summoning Ronald to move the barge again. The traffic also includes orders for Ricky to relocate a large storm-damaged oyster lugger tied to a nearby dock. The lugger is jutting out into the harbor, where it could prove an obstacle as the barge comes by. Merwin wants it moved out of the way into a slip.

"We can maneuver in pretty tight spaces," explains Ronald, "but you don't want to take any chances. You clip that boat with the barge and the boat's done."

I hop off the *Star* and join Ricky on the *Lil' Rick*. His son Ricky Jr. happens to be aboard—Ricky got him on as a deckhand with the barge crew. Ricky disappears down below to crank up the *Lil' Rick*'s engine, barking out orders to Ricky Jr. to untie the trawler. He comes out on the aft deck, commandeering the big steel aft wheel. Their target, an aging white lugger painted powder blue at the waterline, lies about twenty yards up harbor.

Ricky deftly moves the *Lil' Rick* alongside it, tying on to a metal rigging post midway between the lugger's bow and cabin and lashing a tiger-striped rope to a port aft cleat of his trawler. The idea is to swing the lugger out toward deeper water so that her stern is lined up with one of the empty slips, then pivot the *Lil' Rick* around and nudge the lugger slowly into the slip. This sounds somewhat simple save for a couple of issues: the slip is only about two feet wider than the oyster lugger, and a stiff breeze has sprung up, greatly complicating steering the lugger in a line that will avoid a damaging collision with the dock, even at low speeds.

Ricky turns this into motorized ballet, finessing throttle and wheel in a noisy, fluid synchronicity to send the lugger into a slow pirouette— all the while barking out orders to Ricky Jr., who has hopped aboard the other boat and rushed to its stern. His job is to signal, as the lugger gets close to the slip's opening, how far off line she might be and, if necessary, to use leverage on the tall pilings marking the opposite corners of the slip's entrance to muscle the boat back on course if it seems to be drifting awry. The wind could make this both necessary and dicey.

About six minutes into this exercise, the lugger's stern is dead on to the slip—but coming in a little high. Ricky shouts out, "Catch the piling!" Ricky Jr. steps as far out on the boat's stern as he dares and uses his gloved hands and muscular arms to correct the drift off course by stiff-arming the piling and pushing away.

The lugger slides gently into the opening, scarcely nicking the piling, before straightening out. Ricky gives the *Lil' Rick* a burst of throttle, then throws the trawler momentarily into neutral. He hustles over to the tie-on cleat and uncouples the boats so that the *Lil' Rick* won't get dragged into the slip behind the lugger. Back at the throttle, he throws the *Lil' Rick* into reverse as the lugger glides noiselessly in, coming to rest about a foot from the slip's bulwark.

"How 'bout that?" says Ricky. He looks at his son. "Next time, I'm gonna let you try it."

Ricky Jr. laughs and throws up his hands. He admires his father's skill and craft. But later, over a bowl of chicken stew, he will declare that he still wants to be a drummer in a rock-'n-roll band, not a shrimp-boat captain.

The day wears on, the wind drops, the sun begins a slow surrender from the pristine sky. Marsh birds flying in formation carve a dark V on the luminescent horizon. Gulls squawk and glide nearby. An easy tide moves into the harbor, murmuring and curling around boats and painting the mirrored surface with colors that don't have names. In the middle of the harbor, baitfish skitter across the surface, followed by the telltale sign of marauding speckled trout looking for a late-afternoon snack. A person with a rod and reel and the proper bait could easily catch supper.

The barge has found its next project, but has quit for the day. It sits empty and at rest in the distance, the flag atop the crane hanging limp.

Sitting out on the aft deck of the *Lil' Rick,* an hour before sunset, Ricky and Ronald have found a moment of peace. A pastoral quiet has settled in, the aroma of chicken stew wafts from the galley, Lulu the lab lies at Ricky's feet. The Robin cousins are sipping cups of freshly made coffee. Under more normal circumstances—say, if we were at anchor after a day of fishing—you'd be tempted to say it doesn't get any better than this.

Ricky is telling me the story of meeting President Bush during their brief encounter back on September 12, in the early days after the storm. "I kinda felt sorry for the man, actually," says Ricky. "He's was catching some hell, I know that."

"What did you say to him?" I wanted to know.

"I told him I was a fisherman—a proud fisherman—and that all these fishermen down here were already in trouble before the hurricane. I said we needed help—we needed him to buy our shrimp. I told him, 'I know you'll give us a good price.'"

Ricky smiles at the thought. He's savvy enough about Republican free-market politics to know that George W. Bush isn't likely to rescue Katrina's beleaguered commercial fishermen by subsidizing the price of shrimp.

Even for those fishermen lucky enough to still have their boats, Ricky says, problems abound. Katrina destroyed the commercial fishing infrastructure—mechanized loading docks and ice plants were simply wiped out. For a long time, temporary facilities, such as they were, were being run from expensive generator power. Ice had to be trucked in. At the same time, the unexpectedly large run of shrimp had turned out to be a fickle bonanza because the New Orleans seafood market, the biggest buyer of St. Bernard seafood, was still in a post-Katrina slump. This meant shrimp had to be marketed and shipped farther afield, further raising processing costs. As a result, dockside prices, which ought to have been up, were depressed. At the same time, gas and diesel prices were flirting with three dollars a gallon, greatly raising boat expenses and making it hard for the captains to make much of a profit. "You could make money on shrimp at four to five dollars a pound," says Ricky, "but not at the dollar to two dollars a pound the shrimpers are getting now. And I'm talkin' two dollars a pound for jumbo shrimp."

Ricky goes quiet for a while. I'm wondering if this diversion to the sad state of his lifelong occupation is giving him second thoughts about staying in St. Bernard. But he surprises me. "The thing is, I gotta get back out there," he says, pointing in the general direction of the gulf. "I gotta get back to shrimping."

So he's not leaving the parish after all?

Ricky has to think this over. Then he shakes his head and smiles. "We're here, huh, Ronald?"

Ronald nods. "We're here."

20. A Short Journey of Hope

On a sunny midmorning in early June, more than eight months after Katrina, I drove through the lingeringly bleak streets of the Lower Ninth Ward, where the traffic lights were still out, the potholes were still unfilled, the houses were mostly still abandoned, rotting, and forlorn, and headed down the St. Bernard Highway for Yscloskey. The tableau in St. Bernard was not much cheerier, though there was more life.

House gutting was in full bloom; pickup trucks stacked with building materials stood in modest lines at reopened gas stations; Family Dollar on the St. Bernard Highway was doing a brisk business in bottled water and cheap canned goods; giant tanker trucks, to the unceasing rumble of diesel engines, were pumping out still-clogged sewer lines; the sounds of hammering and sawing filled some neighborhoods.

I made no stops, oblivious to a route whose smallest features I'd practically memorized by this time, until I crossed the Bayou La Loutre bridge, rounded the sharp right-hand curve in Yscloskey Highway, and pulled onto the narrow shoulder just beyond a mailbox with hand-painted red lettering that read, "1921/Gonzales." I'd arrived in the nick of time.

A small group of workmen, two of them bare-chested, sweaty, and well beyond grimy from a morning's exertion, clustered around an imposing yellow John Deere dozer-loader and a ten-wheeled red Mack truck. The truck was coupled to a seventy-foot-long iron-red double-axle trailer, and upon this trailer sat a remarkable thing: the house of Joe, Selina, and Richard Gonzales, poised for its three-hundred-foot journey back to the slab from which Katrina had so rudely tossed it.

I waved to the workers and made straight for Joe and Selina's FEMA trailer, which had been relocated a short distance east to make way for the move. I rapped on the rattle-prone metal door, calling out a greeting, and the Gonzaleses, whom I had visited many, many times by now, beckoned me in.

"So is today really the day?" I asked Joe as soon as I cleared the door.

"They say so," Joe replied, "but they've said that a lot of times. I sure in the hell hope so."

After my visit to the Gonzaleses at Halloween, I'd written a story about their saga for the front page of the *Wall Street Journal*. A group of engineers in Baton Rouge read the piece and, moved by Joe's declarations that he wanted to restore his house to its original location, made the hundred-mile trip to pay him a visit. Around the same time, John Ratcliff, a commercial air-conditioning salesman from, incredibly, Gonzales, Louisiana, a hamlet just east of Baton Rouge, drove through this stricken bayou country where he sometimes fished. An evangelical Christian driven by his religious obligations and compassionate nature, he wondered what he could do to help. He came across Joe, Selina, and Richard when he saw them clustered aboard the *Miss Carol* and found his answer, motivated not just by their story but by their irrepressible determination to reclaim their home and their lives despite formidable obstacles. John more or less adopted them and began to marshal a network of volunteers, most of them evangelical Christians, that he'd tapped into with his own determination. Soon, Joe's house-saving mission was no longer the lonely crusade and sentimental longing of an elderly, storm-traumatized man.

The Gonzaleses settled their insurance claims, getting $87,500 for their house and $50,000 for its contents. Money, materials, and help from outside started pouring in. The engineers—who had confirmed Joe's diagnosis that his house was structurally sound—drew up elaborate plans for elevating and anchoring the dwelling to make it as flood- and hurricane-proof as possible. They did the work for nothing. A volunteer welder came all the way from Texas to construct the pilings, made from ten-inch-diameter, fifteen-foot-long steel pipes, on which the house would sit. John Ratcliff, sacrificing numerous weekends, assumed the arduous task of clearing the Gonzales lot of three feet of storm debris and downed trees, and bulldozing away the rubble that surrounded the house.

Driving down Interstate 10 in New Orleans one day, John encountered two vans filled with students whom he was certain were volunteers. He followed them to their headquarters, a garishly painted building off the main drag coursing through the Lower Ninth Ward and the hub of an evangelical relief group called the City of Light. He parked and approached the students, clustered under a tent, and made an appeal. The restoration of the Gonzaleses' dwelling, and their life, he told them, could not begin until the onerous work of gutting the house was done. And Joe, Selina, and Richard were financially stretched and simply not physically up to the task.

The group's leader was gone, but John pressed a map with directions to the Gonzales house in the hands of a student, got in his truck, and prayed. A couple of days later, eleven students from Truman State University, a small liberal arts college in Kirksville in north-central Missouri, arrived at Joe and Selina's doorstep. In two days, the Gonzales house was cleared of muddied furniture, dead appliances, and marsh mat. The first day, Selina made sandwiches for everyone; the second, with more notice, she cooked a giant pot of her locally famous jambalaya. The kids had never tasted anything like it.

With the house cleared out and plans approved to resettle it on the steel pilings anchored to concrete footings, in early May Joe contracted with a Mississippi house-moving contractor, who had come down to work the Katrina belt, to tackle the tedious and technically challenging task of jacking the house out of the seven-month-old bog in which it sat. This proved to be slow and frustrating work, partly because the contracting crew, divided between other jobs, often didn't show up. Joe had given the company twenty thousand of the twenty-five-thousand-dollar fee up front and wondered many a day whether he'd been taken.

Slowly but surely, though, the house rose from the mud on large wooden cribs—six rectangular stacks of eight-by-eight-inch crossties placed strategically under the house—as about a dozen synchronized pneumatic jacks lifted the structure a foot at a time. When the house had been raised about three feet, the contractor, employing the giant

Mack truck, skillfully backed the long steel trailer under it. Then, using the jacks again, he began gingerly disassembling the cribs and lowering the house onto the trailer bed. This was a nerve-wracking operation, for if the house came down too fast, or settled misaligned in some way, it could easily break apart under its own weight.

Joe's house held fast.

But it sat there, proud on its cribs, for about three weeks before the operator ever came back to attempt to move it. By then Joe—who every day, heat or not, spent tedious hours in and around the house doing minor preparatory repairs such as stripping out the old wiring and yanking out exposed nails—was beside himself. He'd studied the nearby ground and believed it hadn't dried out sufficiently to move the house without bogging it down, unless supporting materials, such as planks or plywood, were laid carefully in the path that the trailer was to take. I was there the day the operator showed up and told Joe he had nothing to worry about. The truck, he said, was plenty powerful enough to pull the house out of the muck without getting stuck.

He cranked the Mack up, put it in gear, gunned the engine. The trailer bearing Joe's house swung around, rolled about three feet—and sank in the mire like a boulder in quicksand, burying the trailer so that Joe's house once again sat on the ground. They chained the giant big-tired John Deere machine up to the truck, hoping to pull truck, trailer, and house out of the muck—but couldn't budge them.

Joe walked away. He was so disgusted he couldn't even yell at the guys. "I told them fellas that was gonna happen," he fumed. "They should've listened to me."

The crew would have to come back the next day and start all over again, jacking the rig out of the mud, high enough so that Joe's initial suggestion—putting down planking as a roadbed—could be carried out. Under cloudless skies with temperatures in the low nineties, this part of the project took another couple of days of exhausting, mud-splattered work. Then the workers evaporated to other jobs, and Joe's house sat there again for a while, like an abandoned ship.

Today, though, was supposed to be the day. The crew had been on-site since early morning, checking the position of the house on the trailer and the condition of the ground. They swore another attempt would be made before the day was over, which is why I'd driven down as quickly as the speed limit allowed.

Joe, Selina, and I had been chatting for a few minutes in the cramped living room of their FEMA trailer when I heard the deep rumble of the John Deere's engine come to life.

"Hhm," I said to Joe. "You think they're ready?"

Joe seemed afraid to answer that question. There had been too many disappointments already. He'd even had bad dreams about the house, waking up sometimes in tears.

"I'll go see," I said. Joe followed me out the door.

It was about 11:30 a.m. I rounded the corner of the FEMA trailer and walked toward the commotion around the Deere. Just then, the Mack truck's engine rumbled to life, too. As I got closer, I could tell that the operator wasn't taking any chances this time. The Deere had been coupled to the Mack truck with a steel cable, and they were both going to be doing the pulling. And covering the first boggy fifteen feet of the route out was a path laid with heavy planks. Beyond that, the ground had been leveled and compacted by the constant coming and going of the heavy Deere machine and the Mack.

Suddenly the show commenced. Engines revved and strained. The house and trailer creaked and groaned as they began to swing around under the tremendous torque of the pulling machines. The trailer lurched forward, the house swaying atop it, slowly, surely, grindingly making its way out of the bog. As the truck and the Deere gained traction, house and trailer picked up speed.

In less than two minutes, the Gonzaleses' house was halfway to its destination.

The truck and the Deere braked. Workers decoupled the Deere and the Mack truck took over. The driver gunned the engine and pulled the house—it seemed like at fifteen to twenty miles an hour—bouncing it across the yard to a spot where it could be lined up and backed over its original slab.

Joe grimaced and so did I. A bouncing house could break apart. But Joe's was built as solidly as his boats. It didn't suffer so much as a crack.

It took another hour or so to clear away a tree that blocked the final path and to disconnect the temporary sewer lines, also standing in the way, that ran from the slab to the FEMA trailer. But before long, on a gloriously sunny day, the driver slowly and painstakingly backed the house onto the slab.

Joe's house was home.

"Oh, Lord," said Joe, with a mixture of relief and joy. Even he couldn't seem to believe it. "Who the hell would have ever thought this house would ever get back here? An old house like this?"

Selina had nothing to say for a while. She had stayed inside the FEMA trailer and couldn't bear to peek out the window to look.

But when word came that there had been no disasters, that her house was safe where it belonged, she peered outside to make sure it was true. And then she cried.

She emerged later in the afternoon to finally have a look.

"It's wonderful," she said. "Just wonderful."

21. Hard Realities of the "Federal Storm"

The journey of the Gonzales house is as close as I can come to finding a happy ending in post-Katrina St. Bernard Parish. The Gonzaleses, when the new year dawned in 2008, were still not moved in. It took about three more months, and another $8,500, to slowly jack the house up to its final elevation more than thirteen feet above the ground, and another month or so to affix it to the steel pilings. But these days the house sits jauntily bolted to its impressive metal stilts, a proud monument to the family's determination, even obsession, and the generosity of their helpers.

With the aid of many volunteer carpenters and tradesmen from as far away as New Jersey and Pennsylvania, including a group of Princeton University maintenance workers, the house has a new rear wing, serviced by an elevator that will spare Selina and Richard, who are not as spry as Joe, the arduous walk up their wide and graceful exterior stairway. The house also has a new roof, new windows, new wiring, new insulation, new hardwood floors, new appliances, and a new central air conditioning unit. The interior drywall is in. It still needs paint inside and out. But from their front porch, they now have a lovely view of Bayou La Loutre across the road, slightly obstructed by the graceful Spanish oak in front of the porch. And Joe plans to add a back porch, which will also give them a view of the pretty meandering bayou and marsh that sits a quarter mile behind them.

But the semi-happy ending for the Gonzaleses is the exception, not the rule. Joe has saved his house and preserved a gem of blue-collar bayou architecture. But all around him in Yscloskey, and throughout the bayou belt, lovely self-built homes damaged or mowed down by Katrina are being replaced mostly by trailers and modular housing. The aesthetics of this bayou region are being radically altered.

For many people, that's the least of it. Well more than two years after the storm, St. Bernard Parish remains a place badly bruised and utterly changed by Katrina's wind and water—its population and tax base depleted, its white-collar ranks decimated, its economy struggling to recover, its social fabric torn. It is still, even now, a community marked by rotting houses awaiting demolition, emptied-out neighborhoods, temporary trailers camped in the side yards of houses still under repair, and ubiquitous FEMA trailer parks.

FEMA, meanwhile, in a move designed to prod residents into permanent housing, declared in late November 2007 that it would close all of its trailer parks throughout the Louisiana storm belt by the middle of 2008. The announcement, however, resulted in a wave of protests from residents and low-income-housing advocates. Then, in the spring of 2008, FEMA further declared that the trailers, owing to a defect in their manufacturing process, contained unsafe levels of formaldehyde and posed a potential health hazard to their occupants—thereby presenting a more urgent reason for residents to vacate them. Still, it seems a safe guess that FEMA's trailers will be around for at least another year, perhaps longer.

Perhaps the most vivid description of what befell St. Bernard Parish came from Michael Brown, the controversial director of FEMA who was fired within two weeks of Katrina's landfall (either in disgrace or as a scapegoat, depending on your point of view). Brown, after touring the parish shortly after the storm, told the Associated Press, "I put St. Bernard almost on the magnitude of what I saw in South Asia [in the wake of the tsunami there in December 2004], where it is just utter destruction."

Still, I wouldn't count the place out. What will save it, if it is to be saved, is the pioneering spirit that founded it and the gritty blue-collar pluck that has nurtured it for most of its long history. The core of St. Bernard's resurrection will be the bayou people—people like Ricky, Susan, and Ronald Robin, Joe, Selina, and Richard Gonzales, Frankie Asevado, B.B. Nunnery, Charlo Inabnet, and the Verdins—who are slowly and often painfully clawing their way back to the places that they love.

Sorrow remains palpable here. Katrina is blamed directly for the deaths of 132 people in St. Bernard Parish, including a baby swept from its mother's arms; Carole Spano, whose grim spray-painted memorial marked the Cramonds' Chalmette neighborhood; an elderly, infirm man found in the lap of his dead elderly wife who would not leave him behind; and 35 mostly elderly residents of St. Rita's Nursing Home. But that hardly tells the tale. If you spend any time at all among residents, everyone has a story of deaths that, though not statistically tied to Katrina, they put into the Katrina column. These include many ill and infirm people who, separated from their doctors and medicine for far too long, died days or weeks or months afterward, never having fully recovered. It includes scores of the elderly who, seeing their homes destroyed beyond reclamation, simply gave up wanting to live. Ricky Robin himself had such a story, though in his grief he couldn't bring himself to tell me until some time after I arrived to collect the tales of those who survived. His father and mentor, Charles "Charlito" Robin, had suffered on and off with illness and depression before the storm. After surveying the loss of his house, many of his prized boat carvings, and his way of life, he took his own life in January 2006. He was seventy-five years old. He was buried in St. Bernard Catholic Cemetery in Violet after a mass at Our Lady of Prompt Succor Catholic Church in Chalmette. "I'm just sorry I didn't record more of his stories," Ricky says.

The deaths at St. Rita's will haunt the parish for a long time. The facility's owners, Sal and Mabel Mangano, were indicted by state authorities a month after the storm on thirty-five counts of negligent homicide and twenty-four counts of cruelty on the grounds that they failed to carry out an evacuation that would have saved their mostly infirm patients. They pleaded not guilty. Their defense rested in part on the fact that St. Rita's, built more than twenty years before Katrina, was erected on ground that had escaped flooding in Hurricane Betsy in 1965 (again, before St. Bernard had a unified hurricane protection levee). Their lawyers also made the argument that the Manganos had been so confident of their location's safety that they remained in the nursing home themselves, and many friends and staff members accepted their invitation to use the place as a hurricane shelter as well. Finally, they invoked actions of the state itself as evidence of their innocence, noting that the state's attorney general had filed a $200 billion lawsuit against the U.S. Army Corps of Engineers. The suit alleged that the corps' substandard levees were largely responsible for most of Katrina's flooding deaths—an argument that has caused many local residents to label Katrina "the federal storm." Thus, their lawyers maintained, the Manganos were victims of federal negligence, not criminals.

In early 2007, a judge ordered their case moved to a state court in St. Francisville, a jurisdiction near Baton Rouge. After a nine-day trial that began in late August 2007, around the second anniversary of Katrina's landfall, the couple was acquitted by a six-person jury on all counts. Despite the verdict, the deaths continue to cut like a sharp knife through a community where the owners, before Katrina, were held in considerable esteem. Many of the relatives of St. Rita's victims remain despondent and angry, and the Manganos still face some thirty civil suits related to the storm deaths. Others see the drownings as a tragedy that destroyed far more than the thirty-five people who died there that awful day.

The parish marked its Katrina deaths by placing a memorial, on the first anniversary of the storm, at the end of the Yscloskey Highway, about a quarter mile east of the Gonzales house where the road meets the MR-GO. It consists of a granite obelisk on which are inscribed the names of the victims and an ornate bronze-colored, seven-foot-high iron cross with a Picassoesque metal face of Jesus welded to the cross's junction. The cross is planted on a concrete foundation in the waters of the MR-GO.

The builder-artist is a welder and beer-drinking friend of Ricky Robin's named Vincent LaBruzzo, an imposing, long-haired, bearded man fond of biker attire who crafted the cross in his machine shop. A couple of hundred people attended the ceremonies. Ricky came to play trumpet; LaBruzzo came wearing jeans, biker boots, and a custom-made red-white-and-blue sleeveless shirt; and Junior Rodriguez, the parish president, came to give a speech, though he made no mention of a brief controversy over part of the monument.

The New Orleans affiliate of the American Civil Liberties Union, alerted to the plans to install the cross, had some weeks before pointed out in a letter to Junior and other parish officials that the Christian icon, with Jesus attached, perhaps amounted to a violation of the principles of separation of church and state. To which Junior, never one to mince words, advised the ACLU, in a comment to a reporter, to "kiss my ass." The head of the ACLU, in turn, in a rather measured and politic response, suggested that Junior would be better off "kissing the constitution" and obeying the law.

Junior's defense was that the memorial was built with money raised from private sources and placed on private land—though it seems a stretch to argue that the shallows of the MR-GO, a federally funded waterway, aren't public property. The ACLU, perhaps in deference to the deeper sensibilities of citizens trying to make their way back in the grief-stricken parish, didn't sue, though it is likely the law was on the organization's side. Even without abandoning my position as a First Amendment hawk, I could still muster some sympathy for the visceral reaction of the locals.

What is both endearing and off-putting about St. Bernard Parish—indeed, South Louisiana in general—is that it is one of the last truly unselfconscious places in America. It is inhabited by people of strong beliefs and opinions generally unfiltered by the homogenized political and cultural bromides that inform polite conversation and political discourse in much of the rest of America, and especially urbanized America. I doubt it ever occurred to Junior that his comments could be viewed as oafish or ignorant in the wider world. Here, owing to centuries-old Catholic roots, religion is the same as Catholicism, even as, paradoxically, evangelical churches have become in recent decades a strong presence in the old South Louisiana Catholic belt. It is part of the fabric of life—along with sin, cooking, drinking, eating, fighting, fishing, sex, and love. In the local mind, these things are inseparable. It is possible that you might not even believe in God, or be a Catholic, but you would not have second thoughts about putting the Catholic-inspired cross and Jesus in the MR-GO. The religious symbol is a deep cultural marker—in the local view, the right thing to do.

A more prosaic (and certainly more humorous) example of that unselfconsciousness was a sign I saw outside a newly opened bar called the Wherehouse just off the St. Bernard Highway where Ricky, Vincent

LaBruzzo, and I went to have a beer one day. It read: "Double Trouble Thursdays. Men: All U Can Drink, $20, Ladies drink free." In an age when even beer companies spend millions of dollars annually on "drink responsibly" campaigns, it's hard to think of a brighter red flag to, say, Mothers Against Drunk Driving, than that sign. Yet no one here thinks of this as other than the shrewd capitalist instincts of an entrepreneur trying to win back some of the lucrative beer-drinking market.

St. Bernard's misery and prospects can't be measured without taking stock of the bigger picture. Katrina is blamed for 1,464 deaths in Louisiana, most of them in New Orleans; it displaced an estimated 1.4 million people, a figure that represents an unprecedented storm-related diaspora. The storm damaged or destroyed about 217,000 homes and about 18,000 businesses. A report by the American Insurance Services Group in 2006 put insured losses, including damages in other states in Katrina's path, at $40.6 billion. It estimated actual losses at $81 billion. More recent figures have upped that estimate to more than $100 billion. "This figure makes Katrina far and away the costliest hurricane in United States history," a report on the storm by the National Hurricane Center said in August 2006.

St. Bernard has marked its slow crawl back in mundane milestones. The first year was fitful, with fewer than 20 percent of residents returning. The flooded Home Depot store on Judge Perez Drive reopened about four months after Katrina landed and was the first major retail business to do so. Residents would have to wait almost a year before Winn-Dixie reopened the parish's first major supermarket. But in between, a handful of gas stations, mom-and-pop convenience stores, roadside food stands, and a smattering of restaurants and bars shrugged back to life. As an example of the deeply ingrained, perhaps even unconscious, local priorities, a place serving boiled crawfish, crabs, and shrimp opened long before a laundromat did. A one-stop volunteer medical clinic sprang up, though for serious matters people were forced to go beyond even New Orleans, and its own stricken medical system, to gain proper care. Living in St. Bernard was flirting with being tolerable—but even today it's not easy.

Several sets of statistics tell why. A post-Katrina census by the Louisiana Recovery Authority, the state agency monitoring Katrina rebuilding efforts, published in August 2007 shows that about fifty thousand St. Bernard residents—about 75 percent of its population—had moved elsewhere, more than eighteen thousand of them to the three contiguous parishes north of Lake Pontchartrain. The census was taken a year after the storm, and parish officials later told me that they were seeing some resettlement back into St. Bernard from those nearby parishes, particularly by people who had maintained jobs here and grown tired of their ninety-minute commutes. They estimate the parish has regained about half to 60 percent of its pre-Katrina population, but those are still discouraging numbers.

That shift is certainly mirrored in school statistics. Before Katrina, the parish had 8,800 students scattered in fifteen parish schools. Katrina destroyed five of them and damaged all of the rest. Doris Votier, the superintendent, heroically reopened the schools in November by consolidating grades K–12 in the undamaged portion of Chalmette High School—334 students enrolled. At the start of school in the fall of 2007, the enrollment had grown to about 4,000. Remarkable as that sounds, it's still less than half of the pre-Katrina levels. (Votier, for her efforts, received a John F. Kennedy Profiles in Courage award in 2007.)

"It confirms what I feared," says state senator Walter Boasso, who channeled his frustration over the state and federal response to Katrina into an unsuccessful run for governor in the fall of the same year. "Many of the people who can afford to leave have left and are simply not coming back." Boasso's interest is far from just political. A St. Bernard native, he is the founder and chief executive officer of Boasso America, an industrial tank fabrication concern headquartered in Chalmette, that remains one of the parish's biggest employers.

As discouraging, that same census showed that Orleans Parish, of which New Orleans makes up about 80 percent of the population, had suffered a net loss of about 233,000 people—about half of its pre-Katrina population. Historically, the economic fortunes of St. Bernard have been inextricably tied to New Orleans. The continuing woes of the city—its politics are a mess, its rebuilding efforts are haphazard, and it remains ringed with huge, abandoned, catastrophically damaged neighborhoods—bodes poorly for St. Bernard's own economic recovery.

On May 10, 2006, St. Bernard demolished the first of an estimated eighty-four hundred houses it intends to tear down; the actual number is constantly in flux, since in many cases it depends on the willingness of homeowners to return and undertake gutting operations. Originally, the parish had decreed that any Katrina-flooded house that hadn't been gutted by the first anniversary of the storm would be condemned. But it eased off when some homeowners pointed out the financial and logistical hardships of returning to the parish.

The operation began, perhaps fittingly, in Lexington Place subdivision, where Fabian and Pam Guerra survived that harrowing day on their rooftop, and where Katrina moved the four-bedroom home down the block and into the middle of the street. The floated house, because it blocked the street, became the third or fourth one to be demolished. As of the end of 2007, the parish was about halfway through the list of eighty-four hundred. The operations could take another year, perhaps longer. The demolitions are expected to eradicate about 30 percent of the housing stock in Chalmette, St. Bernard's largest town.

I stood for about three hours watching the demolitions on the lower end of Bradbury Drive on that pristine, cool May morning. It takes about six months to build a house and a couple of hours, sometimes less, to tear one down, depending on how badly damaged it is. It's a fairly simple process: one or more bulldozers rumble in and strategically smash down the walls, causing the roof to collapse. Then, the dozers slowly push the pile of rubble toward the curb. There, a loader with a giant mechanical arm grapples the rubble and tosses it into dump trucks or the cavernous metal rubbish containers loaded on the backs of one of several eighteen-wheelers lined up along the road. It's a noisy, dirty process, with the constant groan of machinery, the loud splintering of houses being torn apart, the air constantly filled with dust from crushed Sheetrock, insulation, glass, and other debris. A house is reduced to a clean slab after about ten truckloads. All of this debris heads for a landfill off Paris Road, which, during spikes in gutting and demolition operations, grows into a kind of depressing Pikes Peak of crushed dreams.

On that day in Lexington Place, I had company. Donald Arceneaux, a forty-something salesman for a Budweiser distributorship serving the New Orleans area, lived up the street until the storm. He had come, in his white shrimper boots, Nike sweatpants, ball cap, and T-shirt, to watch his neighborhood undergo the start of its Katrina cleansing. He was like a lot of St. Bernard residents—undecided about moving back. Roughly every other house in the block below his had been marked for demolition; every house on his street had badly flooded.

He'd gutted his home of seventeen years, partly because it pained him to simply let it sit and fester, partly in hopes that he at least might be able to sell it one day. For now, though, he and his family had settled in a mobile home in Kenner, near the New Orleans airport, where they were watching and waiting as they considered their options. "This was a place where everybody knew everybody, a good place to raise a family. It's hard to see it like this," Donald told me.

We walked back to his house, a bruised brick ranch typical of most of the Lexington Place dwellings: three or four bedrooms and two bathrooms on compact lots. I stepped inside for a moment and a familiar odor arose—the fetid smell of mold and mildew. "Watch for the rattlesnakes," he'd admonished me. I had heard other stories of snakes invading Katrina houses, and I'd also heard from workers that residents spread such tales to keep out looters. Looking at this house, it was hard to see what was left to loot. About 95 percent of Donald's earthly possessions were strewn in an anarchic pile on the curb.

Besides coming to watch the demolitions, Donald had a specific mission: his wife had asked him to see if he could recover some decorative wedding glassware from a hutch that sat in the rubble, but which he had reason to believe had not been terribly damaged. Donning a Home Depot facemask and gloves, he got down on his knees and began painstakingly picking through the debris—the matted, mud-splattered insulation, the broken picture frames, the smelly sofa cushions, until he finally found the hutch. Ten minutes later, after breaking a glass panel, he in fact recovered some wine glasses. Their discovery, he told me before he drove away, would give his wife one of the few reasons she's had to smile since Katrina blew through and upended their lives.

22. The Toll upon the Land

The MR-GO Must Go

"It's hard to believe, huh?"

The speaker is Gatien Livaudais (pronounced GAYshun LIVohday), a St. Bernard landowner from an old-line parish family that had acquired about twelve thousand acres of wetlands in the eastern part of the parish long before the MR-GO. I'm traveling with Gatien and some friends in his sturdy aluminum outboard down Bayou Dupre, the ancient natural waterway whose man-made appendage is Violet Canal. We've motored several miles already in the direction of Lake Borgne to the east, traveling through pockets of trashed marsh out of which Katrina took giant bites. As we approach the intersection of Bayou Dupre and the MR-GO, the sight isn't a pretty one. Pre-Katrina, two thriving settlements of weekend fishing camps stood here, one called the Horseshoe for the slow bend in the canal along whose marshy shores the camps were built, and another below us called Happiness Bayou. It was named, the local story goes, by a couple who lived out here almost full time and considered the place the happiest on earth.

There is no happiness here now: both settlements are in ruin. Most of the camps simply have been flattened; others, pried from their stilts, lie broken on their sides or upended on their roofs. A once-pretty pink bungalow in front of us has been pitched forward halfway into the bayou, its exterior wooden walls splintered, its tin roof cracked open as if by a giant can opener.

As startling is what Katrina has done to the land here. The marsh, in places, has simply been raked bare, rendering dour, boggy mudflats where grasses and reeds had thrived. Impressive groves of trees once lined the banks where spoils from earlier dredging operations had created artificial levees and a semblance of high ground. But most of the groves have been picked up—entire stands of thirty-foot trees pulled out by the roots—and tossed into the middle of the bayou, where they now pose an eerie obstacle to navigation.

We head next to the MR-GO, which is aesthetically unimpressive, a wide, beeline canal lined now with broken levees on one side, and jagged, patchy marsh on the other. But in Gatien's mind, the MR-GO *is* impressive—an impressive monument to federal folly.

"This thing," he tells me with a sweep of his hand, "is destroying us. And if it isn't closed, one day it *will* destroy us."

If people and buildings took a battering here, so did the environment. Beyond the Murphy Oil and other petrochemical spills, Katrina overnight turned about sixteen square miles of barrier marsh—more than ten thousand acres—into open water, further worsening St. Bernard's vulnerability to future hurricanes. A great deal of that loss occurred along the gaping wound that is the route of the MR-GO through St. Bernard Parish. Gatien was among a vocal cadre of local residents and elected officials who fought strenuously against the channel when it was proposed by the U.S. Army Corps of Engineers in the late 1950s and completed in 1965. What they feared, even prophesied—that dredging the channel would have limited economic benefit while opening the parish's already eroding wetlands to the ravages of the gulf's salty tides—has now been borne out in several independent studies of the MR-GO's environmental impacts.

Gatien knows them better than most. His forebears hailed from the Tours region of France and originally bought their thousands of acres of wetlands in the early 1900s to capitalize on St. Bernard's brisk and profitable muskrat trade. But the gradual incursion of salt water, and the introduction of the nutria, a beaver-sized, marsh-eating rodent from South America, long ago chased out the muskrats. The Livaudaises wisely held on to their wetlands. By the 1940s, copious amounts of oil and gas were being discovered throughout the South Louisiana estuary, some of it under the land Gatien now manages. That propitious occurrence, however, could not mask the bitter knowledge that by the late 1960s, erosion of his wetlands had begun to seriously escalate, with hundreds of acres dying off and irretrievably sinking. Almost all of the loss could be ascribed one way or another to human meddling with an ecosystem that had been intricately knitted together into one of the most productive wetlands on earth. It was, alas, beginning to happen all over South Louisiana as well.

One cause, here and elsewhere, of South Louisiana's massive wetlands loss has been the channeling and leveeing of the Mississippi River for flood control purposes, a centuries-old effort that took on new urgency after the devastating floods of 1927. Of course, flood protection along the lower part of the river has had unquestionable economic and social benefits—New Orleans couldn't exist without it. But the leveeing of the river also interrupted the millennia-old delta-building cycle, diverting huge loads of river sediments that once created and nourished wetlands into the deep Gulf of Mexico, where they serve no purpose today other than to muddy and pollute the water. Cut off from this natural replenishing source, the wetlands began to contract. This has been especially acute in the parishes—Jefferson, Lafourche, Terrebonne, and eastern St. Mary—whose marshes were built by the westerly flow of the Mississippi's discharge.

But coastal erosion has greatly escalated since the oil and gas boom that followed World War II. The reason: the wholesale channelization of the South Louisiana estuary, pretty much from St. Bernard Parish to the Texas border, for the purposes of oil and gas exploration. Literally thousands of miles of canals were dredged through pristine marsh and swamp to expedite the ability to move equipment and manpower to drilling and production sites, without regard for how this might upset the wetlands' natural ecological equilibrium. Not until the 1970s did state and federal authorities begin to realistically regulate such activities.

In fairness, some of the early oil industry dredging was done in ignorance, before science caught up with the value and the vulnerability of wetlands. But by then a vast amount of damage had already been done. Many of these man-made waterways (known as "location canals" in Oil Patch parlance) breached the finely tuned natural barriers between the freshwater and saltwater interface, allowing salt water to run unchecked into the freshwater estuaries, slowly killing vast tracts of freshwater marshes and cypress swamps. They began to die and sink, leaving open water in their wake. Thus, huge marsh tracts that once helped absorb storm surges have been turned into lakes that leave uplands ever more vulnerable to hurricanes.

If you want a startling statistic: Louisiana has lost an estimated one million acres of wetlands to erosion and subsidence since the 1930s. Before Katrina, it was continuing to erode at the rate of 16,000 acres a year—the equivalent of two acres an hour. If unchecked, subsidence and erosion may claim another 325,000 acres by the year 2050. That combined total of more than 1.3 million acres would mean the Louisiana estuary will have lost wetlands almost equal to the half the size of Everglades National Park—a staggering and irreplaceable disappearance with national implications.

Added to this lethal mix are federally designed and funded navigation projects—like the MR-GO—that, whatever they have done for commerce, serve as giant, marsh-killing saltwater siphons into estuaries already under stress. Another example is the Houma-Terrebonne Navigation Canal in Terrebonne Parish, about eighty miles west of St. Bernard. First dredged in 1962, the thirty-seven-mile-long project was, like the MR-GO, meant to ostensibly shorten the route to the Gulf of Mexico for commercial and industrial traffic, in this case from the port of Houma, an oil-exploration and shipbuilding hub. Originally built to 150 feet wide and 15 feet deep, the channel was doubled in width and deepened in 1974 by the U.S. Army Corps of Engineers. The widening was done in spite of strenuous local opposition, mostly from home-grown environmentalists and independent commercial fishermen who were already warning that the channel as it existed was beginning to kill off freshwater wetlands in the eastern quadrant of Terrebonne Parish. Opponents predicted that doubling the size of the channel—particularly without bank-erosion controls or a lock that could close it to saltwater surges during high tides and storms—would simply increase the destruction of wetlands, leave the area more vulnerable to hurricanes, and even imperil the freshwater drinking supplies of the town of Houma and its satellite communities.

The corps brushed aside these concerns as alarmist and, aided by the lobbying of chamber of commerce and oil industry supporters, pushed through the channel widening—without a lock. Today, the "ship channel," as it is known locally, is more than a mile wide in some places and is roundly blamed for a virtual epidemic of subsidence and saltwater intrusion problems in eastern Terrebonne and western Lafourche parishes. Though the corps has now agreed on the need for a lock, as part of a far-flung hurricane protection levee system, it may be years before it is constructed. Meanwhile, many locals fear the Houma-Terrebonne Navigation Canal makes their community as vulnerable to a significant storm surge as the MR-GO has made St. Bernard Parish.

Indeed, when St. Bernard officials brought in outside engineers to do a post-flood analysis of Katrina, they came to conclusions that caused many in the parish to lay much of the blame for what happened here at the feet of the federal government. The MR-GO is a huge part of the case.

First, they say, the channel ought never to have been built. It was a case of Army Corps of Engineer hubris and zeal for ambitious dredging projects, the consequences be damned, not to mention a prime example of crony capitalism. In its four-decade history the channel has proved a commercial bust. At the approach of Katrina, it served fewer than a half dozen companies and moved, relative to the Mississippi, a minuscule amount of tanker traffic and cargo.

Meanwhile, tides, storms, and wave action from ship traffic along its seventy-six-mile route had greatly eroded its eastern banks, killing off wide protective bands of marshes that might have helped buffer, or at least slow down, Katrina's surge. The channel, originally dredged to a width of 650 feet through forty miles of virgin wetlands, is now 2,000 feet wide over a great deal of its route and 3,000 feet wide in some places. Residents such as Gatien and numerous parish officials who campaigned against the channel had, when it was clear the project was going forward, pleaded for the corps to at least install a lock at its intersection with the gulf. The corps demurred.

Second, though a commercial bust, the MR-GO has been extremely efficient at one thing: acting as a giant saltwater siphon, sucking briny tides into what remained of St. Bernard Parish's eastern freshwater marshes and swamps, hastening their demise. Scientists estimate that even before Katrina arrived, St. Bernard had, over the lifespan of the MR-GO, lost more than twenty thousand acres of buffering freshwater swamp and marsh along the channel's eastern flank.

Third, the MR-GO unquestionably created the funnel effect that greatly magnified Katrina's surge. Some engineers have gone so far as to say that had the channel not existed, the levees along the Industrial Canal would most likely not have come under such intense pressure and given way. Or, as Sherwood Gagliano, a noted Louisiana engineer and hydrologist who was among those conducting St. Bernard's post-Katrina study, told me: "Because of the presence of the MR-GO, the surge was amplified. The channel functioned as a hydrological piston to push the water faster and farther than it should have ever gone."

The final piece in the "federal storm" indictment is the levees themselves. The breaches along the Industrial Canal—entirely responsible for the destruction of Arabi and a great deal of Chalmette—involved so-called I-wall construction, in which linked sheet piling (broad, tall panels of corrugated steel that essentially function as submerged dams) is driven down to a predetermined depth depending on the level of protection desired. Post-Katrina investigative engineering studies showed that some of the most serious breaches along the Industrial Canal and the Seventeenth Street Canal, which led to the catastrophic flooding of the New Orleans Lake View district, resulted from poorly designed and constructed I-wall levees built under the supervision of the federal Corps of Engineers. In some cases, the sheet piling was simply not driven in deep enough, allowing the levees to be undermined by pressure from below.

"If we don't have those particular levee breaks," Walter Boasso tells me, "Katrina is basically a nonevent. We lose southern Plaquemines Parish. St. Bernard takes a wave from Lake Borgne and gets some flooding. St. Tammany Parish [across Lake Pontchartrain] gets some back surge, and that's it." Or, put another way, New Orleans suffers localized street flooding and relatively minor damage. In the wider Katrina zone, a few thousand houses are flooded, not 217,000 and the storm damages a few hundred businesses, but not 18,000. The death toll: perhaps 10 percent of what it was. Total damages are a few hundred million dollars, but nowhere near $100 billion.

The U.S. Army Corps of Engineers, after months of evasions and denials, finally came clean and admitted, in its own dour self-assessment published in July 2007, that a combination of perennial budget crunches, flawed designs, and shoddy construction methods and materials all contributed to the catastrophic failures within the 350-mile network of hurricane protection levees in and around New Orleans. The corps, again citing budget restrictions, also acknowledged that it simply had failed to carry out a more ambitious flood protection plan around New Orleans that could have greatly ameliorated Katrina's impact.

The corps, to its credit—and no doubt because the entire world and much of the U.S. Congress was watching—did immediately jump on a post-Katrina levee repair program. By Katrina's first anniversary, and about $1.2 billion later, the levee network had been restored to at least pre-Katrina strength, with almost all of the faulty I-wall levees replaced by sturdier T-wall construction. This is significant because while I-wall and T-wall levees both employ corrugated sheet piling in their basic design, I-wall is simply driven into the ground and topped with a layer of earth or concrete to hold it in place. In T-wall construction, however, the steel is actually driven down into, and anchored by, a submerged, erosion-resistant base. I-wall is much cheaper to build than T-wall (which is why in many cases the corps employed it), but its flaw is that it is vulnerable to underground erosion—especially in a place like South Louisiana with its unstable, shifting organic soils. Post-Katrina engineering studies show clearly what happened: the unanchored I-wall levees, pounded into the soft soils along waterways like the Industrial Canal, were simply undermined and crushed by Katrina's surge, while the T-wall levees held firm.

For St. Bernard Parish, the corps' rebuilding effort actually offered a vast improvement, notably along the MR-GO, where the badly battered seventeen-foot levees were rebuilt and raised to nineteen feet along most of its route. The levees along Violet Canal and the Forty Arpent Canal were also strengthened and rebuilt to an average height of ten feet.

In a final irony, the corps finally agreed with the assessment of Gatien Livaudais, Junior Rodriguez, and a vast majority of St. Bernard Parish residents: it conceded that the Mississippi River–Gulf Outlet had played a major role in the catastrophic flooding and decided that the channel needs to go. The corps has officially asked Congress to decommission the waterway, which could mean either damming it up near its entrance to the Gulf of Mexico or even filling it in entirely. The funding to do that, however, was part of a flood projects bill that President Bush vetoed in late 2007, so the battle to close the Mister Go continues.

That campaign, though, has lost at least one of its high-profile champions. St. Bernard's politically incorrect president, Junior Rodriguez, long a fierce MR-GO critic, made headlines in 2007 when he was given the Wood Duck Award—the highest accolade of the Louisiana chapter of the Sierra Club—for his tireless lobbying to close the channel. This commendation, however, proved of little political benefit to Junior, who came up for reelection in the fall of 2007. He faced a slew of opponents—including his son—and a public weary of the slow pace of recovery chose a new leader.

Epilogue

South Toward Home

Among those who have settled back in St. Bernard Parish are Matine and Neg Verdin. But their adventures, difficulties, and sorrows didn't end on that day when they left the *Lil' Rick* and crossed the Mississippi by barge to a seemingly safe haven on the other side. They soon learned that there were no interim shelters on the river's west bank, much of which was still without power, and they ended up being dropped off, along with scores of other St. Bernard barge people, at a crowded highway overpass near the town of Harvey. They were given what supplies the rescuers could offer—small packets of crackers and a couple of bottles of water.

There they waited several hours in the rain and heat for a bus that befuddled rescue managers said would take them to some undisclosed shelter location. But the first dozen or more buses that came by were full. Finally, as the Verdins neared exhaustion, an empty bus pulled up and they boarded. At least it was out of the rain, and air-conditioned.

Matine, in her halting English, asked where they were going. The driver's reply: "I don't know," which was the simple truth. As the evacuation of Orleans Parish and St. Bernard gained speed, the question of what to do with the tens of thousands of refugees grew ever more chaotic.

The bus drove on for maybe a couple of hours, followed, Matine recalls, by a large caravan of ambulances and police cars. They made a stop, though Matine has no idea where it was. Police came to the bus door and asked the driver if he had plenty of gas. When the driver replied yes, the cops told him to follow other buses that now formed a caravan. At 4 a.m., they arrived—at the Houston Astrodome. It took two more hours to get off the bus and be processed.

They entered the cavernous arena to find a sea of cots and were finally assigned one. Neg was wide-eyed and frightened. They were given a change of clothes and instructed that, although there were no showers, they could wash up in the bathrooms. Matine was beyond exhausted. But she was afraid to sleep or leave Neg's side, worried that he would wander off. Her English wasn't good enough to explain to her cot mates who they were and where they had come from. Somehow, her shoes had gone missing.

By Thursday, however, Big Mike Vetra, Matine's grandson who had helped rescue them from the Bayou Road house, had been able to get in touch with Matine's granddaughter, Monique Verdin, to at least let her know that Matine and Neg had survived the flood and were last seen sheltering on Ricky Robin's boat at Violet Canal. She and her boyfriend, Mark Krasnoff, began a frantic telephone and Internet search of shelters, putting Matine's and Neg's names out on lists of the missing while hoping they might appear on some shelter database.

Matine was the one growing frantic, frustrated at her poor English and her inability to read or write, which left her unable to communicate her circumstances to shelter workers. They had no phone numbers to give anyone. "I was afraid no one knew where we were," she related. "They didn't know if we were dead or alive."

But on Friday, the day after their arrival, a counselor took a special interest in their case. She teased enough information out of Matine to enter their names in several online registries while combing these same records to see if anyone was looking for them. The Verdins spent another fretful night in the Astrodome, made all the more disturbing when Matine took one of her rare bathroom breaks and Neg wandered away from their cot area. Matine, frantic, searched the place for hours before finding him—and then couldn't remember how to make their way back to their location, where the counselor knew where to find them.

On Saturday morning, however, the counselor searched the halls for an hour and finally tracked them down with good news: "I found your relatives. Monique and Mark are coming to get you."

For the next thirteen months, Matine and Neg lived in a pleasant rental house in a west-bank suburban neighborhood. Even so, Matine pined away for her home on Bayou Road. She had lived her life in the country and she wanted to return to the country. With the help of

Monique, Mark, and various relatives, she made sporadic visits to the place, wandering the yard and gazing at her stricken, moldy dwelling. When spring came, she planted a garden in the backyard—peas, cucumbers, and tomatoes—and came, driven by relatives or friends, on the weekends to tend it.

As much as Matine loved her house, she couldn't save it or its contents beyond a handful of keepsakes. In mid-August, almost a year after the storm, Big Mike, her grandson, came with a borrowed bulldozer and tore it down, shoving the debris into a pile at the edge of Bayou Road. Parish cleanup crews rumbled in with giant trucks and swivel-arm debris pickers and carted it to the landfill.

Still, Matine was determined to move back, though many of her nearby neighbors weren't returning. With some insurance money, relatives bought a three-bedroom modular house and moved it to the site where her real house once stood. By October, Matine and Neg were back at 2824 Bayou Road. When I visited them in November 2006, Matine graciously showed me around and told me it was "nice"—but in her heart no replacement for the comfortable old wooden dwelling that she'd lived in for all those decades. Still, the surroundings—bird calls, the soft morning light in the cypress trees in the front yard, the pretty church across the way, the cemetery just down the road, the slower ebb and flow of bayou days, and the cricket-filled sounds of bayou nights—comforted them. And slowly Neg, who had retreated into a deep shell, began to emerge, taking walks again in the yard, waving—if he cared to—at cars passing on the highway, and resuming his visits to the cemetery.

Of course, there was a new, and for Matine, Neg, Monique, and Big Mike an exquisitely sad reason to visit: Herbert M. Verdin, who had managed Matine's and Neg's rescue, now lay buried there.

It's impossible to say for sure, but Herbie Verdin may have been the last Katrina refugee to leave St. Bernard Parish. He had his reasons for staying so long.

On September 3, the fifth day after Katrina's landfall, Herbie celebrated his fifty-first birthday with a warm beer taken from a refrigerator in a neighbor's garage. The venue was the front porch of Matine's battered house. High and dry now, the porch was his permanent camping spot. He also had another reason to celebrate. On this day, the water had finally fallen enough so that he could make his way into the soggy kitchen and keep his promise to Matine: to recover her metal money box from the freezer compartment of her refrigerator.

It wasn't easy. The house reeked of mildew, and trapped, rancid water still sloshed halfway up to his knees. The refrigerator, upended by the surge, now lay face down on its doors. He tried to roll it over but couldn't get enough leverage on the slippery floor. Finally, using lengths of pipe scavenged from the yard, he managed to flip it over.

Herbie popped it open—then ran, gagging, for the door. "It was full," he would tell me later. "We had everything in there—crabs, shrimp, you name it. And did it stink—oh, man." Undaunted, he returned, his shirt covering his nose and mouth, rummaged through the freezer compartment, and rescued his mother's money box.

"I should have left then," he said.

He had neither seen nor heard from rescuers—other than airboats droning in the distance—since the day he'd left Big Mike at St. Bernard High School and made his way back down Bayou Road. But people he encountered that day told him that rescue parties they'd run into refused to take pets. Herbie had quite a menagerie: Julio and Selina, the two chihuahuas that he'd plucked from his ex-girlfriend's house, plus another dog he'd rescued from a shed behind the Verdin house. The feral piglet that had showed up on the first afternoon after the storm was still around, as was the flock of geese, growing in number every day. Herbie had managed to keep all of these critters alive by his daily forages for food aboard yet another powerboat that he'd secured after making his way back in the pirogue. He felt a bit strange breaking into other people's houses, but what choice did he have? He would enter and make a beeline for pantries, taking what he could find—canned goods for him and the dogs, bags of rice for the pig and geese. If he found water and beer, he took that, too. His best haul in the beer department was thirty-three bottles of Coors and Bud Light.

The extra beer turned out to be useful in another way. The rice that he fed to the geese and pig was hard for them to swallow. Herbie didn't think it wise to soak it in the putrid water around him, so he took to dousing it with his excess beer to soften it up. The geese loved it, and so did the pig, even if it made them a little tipsy.

Herbie felt the piglet and the geese could fend for themselves, but he couldn't see leaving the dogs, especially the chihuahuas, behind. He had watched the landscape grow dangerous. Dogs that survived the surge had begun to roam in packs. Many were on the verge of starvation. They were hunting whatever they could find—including other dogs.

This harsh reality was driven home on the eighth or ninth day— Herbie couldn't remember exactly—when he sat on the porch in the late afternoon with his animal entourage around him. It was just after feeding time and everyone was getting along amazingly well. The pig and geese were feeling OK, having gorged on beer-soaked rice. So was Herbie. He'd knocked back a couple of warm bottles of Coors.

Off to his left in the distance, Herbie heard the unmistakable sound of paws skittering on the waterlogged highway out front. He looked up. Soon, a fairly large dog appeared, panting heavily, its ears laid back, running as fast as he'd ever seen a dog run. Then, perhaps exhausted, it stumbled.

In a flash, Herbie understood the dog's flight. Before it could get to its feet, it was struck from behind—by two marauding pitbulls. Silently and quickly, they killed their prey. One of them started to feed.

Selina and Julio started barking like mad. The pit bulls looked up, saw the chihuahuas, and began edging away from their kill toward the entrance of the Verdin driveway maybe sixty feet away. "Oh, shit," Herbie blurted aloud.

Instead of running up the driveway, however, the dogs inexplicably plunged into the still flooded narrow bayou between the Verdins' house and the road. They came swimming his way. They were now maybe forty feet from the porch.

That alarmed the tipsy geese and the tipsy pig. The geese started honking, the pig squealing. Julio, Selina, and the other dog kept barking fiercely. Herbie slipped off the porch and ran through the obstacle course that Matine's house had become. Reaching the back porch, he grabbed his old single-shot Winchester shotgun and some shells from a table. He'd plucked both from the water several days before. They had been drying in the relentless sun ever since.

He had no idea if the gun would fire. He shoved a shell in the chamber and scrambled back to the front porch. It was chaos—the geese were panicked and flapping up and down, but too drunk to fly. The dogs howled in madness. The tipsy pig was squealing and running in circles.

This bizarre display had the effect of confusing the pitbulls as they emerged from the water into the yard. They slowed, then came, stalking, toward the house. This was long enough for Herbie to gain the porch, raise the gun, and fire at the lead dog.

Poof, went the Winchester.

BBs from the shell more or less rolled out of the barrel.

Herbie repeated his expletive, shucked the shell from the chamber, and inserted another one. Same results.

He ejected that one, too, and jammed in a third—his last.

"Oh, please, God, let this work."

The pitbulls reached a birdbath in the yard about twenty feet from the porch—then charged. Herbie took aim, and the gun went off this time. The scattershot killed the lead pitbull instantly, and crippled the second.

Herbie felt awful—he loved dogs. But these dogs had come to kill.

He couldn't bear to see the second pitbull suffer, so he finished it off with a length of pipe.

On the eleventh day after the storm, Herbie had finally reached the end of his endurance. He was running low on food and water—for him and his animal charges. He was beginning to feel dehydrated, even delirious. He'd managed to rig a little shower out of a five-gallon bucket he'd hung from Matine's porch. But that had been basically his only creature comfort. He was tired of sleeping rough.

As evening approached, he heard helicopters buzzing around. He went out to a clearing on the highway with a flashlight, the two chihuahuas, and the third dog that he'd rescued from the shed. She'd become very affectionate by this time. He lay down in the middle of the road, using the bigger dog as a pillow, while Julio and Selina snuggled around him. He pointed the light toward the sky and fell asleep. He figured the dogs would rouse him if anyone or anything came by.

They did—in a while, a helicopter appeared, spotted his light, and landed.

The pilots couldn't believe they'd found someone alive this late in the search.

"I'm taking my dogs," Herbie told them. They studied the dogs and talked it over. The chihuahuas were small enough so as not to cause a problem. They worried what might happen if the bigger dog got spooked in the small chopper cabin. They had no way to secure her. But they promised Herbie they would send word to Humane Society rescuers, who had by now come into the parish to look for animals, to search for the bigger dog.

"And my geese, too. And my pig," Herbie said.

Herbie had no idea where he was going, but he, Julio, and Selina ended up at Louis Armstrong International Airport in New Orleans. There, he first sought care for the chihuahuas, handing them over to authorities only after they assured him they were being taken to a veterinarian, and giving them information on how to contact the dogs' owners. Then and only then did he allow them to treat him for his many cuts and scratches—some of them infected—and his dehydration. He was offered a plane ticket to any number of cities that were by this time taking in Katrina refugees.

Herbie thought it over and declined. His brother lived in Metairie, not that far away, and he would go there. And he did, walking the entire way.

After a joyful reunion with Matine, Neg, Big Mike, and his daughter Monique and her boyfriend Mark, Herbie lived among various houses of friends and relatives while applying for a FEMA trailer that he hoped would be placed in the yard at Bayou Road. Meanwhile, he went back to work with Big Mike doing air-conditioning jobs. Work was brisk for a while. But Herbie found himself flagging on many days. He was feeling awful.

In April, his daughter, Monique, forced him to go see a doctor. The initial diagnosis was hepatitis C, but when he didn't respond to treatments and his condition worsened, the doctors dug deeper and found advanced liver cancer. Herbie died, surrounded by his family, on June 14. He was laid to rest, in Neg Verdin's tomb in the lovely old Bayou Terre-aux-Boeufs Cemetery near Matine's house, two days later. But even toward the end, in his pain-free moments of lucidity, he remained a warrior raconteur—funny and profane, cracking up his doctors and nurses with his unvarnished telling of his Katrina tales.

Herbie's FEMA trailer had arrived around the time of his initial cancer diagnosis. But FEMA declined to issue him an occupancy permit until it could be inspected—and inspections were excruciatingly slow in coming. By the time the power was turned on and the permit was issued five months later, Herbie was dead. He never set foot in the place. It stands, vacant even now, another of Katrina's dispiriting monuments, next to Matine and Neg's modular home.

There is one other bit of Herbie lore worth reporting. I was in a bar one day talking with people about the storm when one of them mentioned a miracle. A coffin of a prominent St. Bernard teacher had washed out of her tomb during the storm, but guess where it had ended up? It had floated to the door of the church across the way.

I had to be the one to inform the storyteller that this was no miracle: it was a good deed by Herbie Verdin and Big Mike Vetra.

The Verdins' sorrows were still not at an end. Monique Verdin's partner of two years, Mark Krasnoff, who had been instrumental in getting Matine and Neg resettled and had served as my interpreter during my interviews with her, fell into a deep depression in the months after Herbie's death—though in retrospect he'd managed to camouflage it well. Kraz, as he was called, seemed an irrepressible force: an actor, acting coach, Cajun activist and ethnographer and fluent Cajun French speaker. He and Monique had met at a dance. Trite as it sounds, it was love at first sight. They'd been pretty much inseparable since that moment and pre-Katrina shared half of a charming duplex that Mark owned in a modest but lovely New Orleans neighborhood. They busily worked on multimedia documentaries together. In fact, Mark had spent hours with a digital video camera recording the Katrina stories of Matine, Neg, and Herbie while Monique captured her family on a still camera.

But on September 16, five months after Herbie died, Mark left a note to Monique in the house they shared. He went down to the Mississippi River and shot himself to death with a handgun. He was forty-three years old.

It seemed a thing beyond explanation.

Big Mike Vetra, meanwhile, after being separated from Herbie that day at St. Bernard High School, spent one more night in the shelter, then hopped on a rescue boat, part of the organized flotilla that began shuttling refugees to a place called Chalmette Landing. From there, he and several hundred other refugees boarded a ferry that took them across the river to the west-bank town of Algiers.

Mike also was offered a chance to ship out to a shelter in Texas. But he'd heard reports that Harvey, where he lived, had escaped flooding, so he chose instead to go home, even though he knew his house and probably much of his neighborhood would be empty. (His parents, whom he lived with, had evacuated.) There was no transportation, so Mike walked, in a T-shirt, shorts, and sneakers without socks, three and a half hours home. The neighborhood was an abandoned mess of downed trees, utility poles, and power lines. But the house had escaped serious damage. Just as he arrived, a neighbor drove up—at least he had company.

Mike later found the key to his dad's truck, and he and the neighbor drove around until they found an open gas station and, even better, a wrecked grocery store that was inviting refugees to come in and take what they needed. For Big Mike, the prize was twenty cases of beer.

Over the next few weeks, the neighborhood slowly sprang back to life. Mike and Herbie were reunited. They restarted their air-conditioner service business. They were busy for a while, and Mike at times became annoyed with Herbie when he didn't show up for work, or showed up with no energy for the job. They also got some work doing Katrina reconstruction, at one point making $2,100 a week—the most money Mike had ever made. But that dried up shortly, he said, when cheap migrant labor start flowing into the Katrina belt. He feels awful that his final weeks with Herbie were sometimes fraught with tension.

"I didn't know he was sick like that," Mike said later. "Had I known,

I would've done things different. It hit me hard when he died. He was more like a brother to me than an uncle."

Mike himself has since fallen ill. In the summer of 2007, he was diagnosed with diabetes, and a potentially serious flare-up of "Katrina hand"—a staphylococcus infection that his doctors are certain he contracted while paddling around with Herbie in the floodwaters. He has been able to work only sporadically since.

Last time I talked with him, he seemed gloomily philosophical, recalling the shotgun blast in 1989 that almost killed him, and then the Katrina flood that easily might have done the same. "I guess God must have kept me around to save Grandma," he said. "Now, well, I'm not sure why I'm still here."

Charlo Inabnet spent three more days in St. Bernard Parish after being taken in on the Tuesday after the storm by Frankie Asevado and Chuckie Thurman. They joined Frankie's girlfriend, B.B. Nunnery. With the two parish high schools already overflowing with refugees and unable to shelter the six dogs that had between them (B.B. and Frankie had five, and Chuckie one), they made their way to the Sebastien Roy Elementary School, set back from lower Bayou Road about two miles above the Florissant Highway. It wasn't a designated shelter, but they found the doors blown open. They moved in.

Providentially, the school year was already under way, so the cafeteria's commercial-sized freezers were full of provisions just beginning to thaw, its pantries crammed full of canned goods. They and the dogs would have plenty to eat. They also found something else they desperately needed—a medical kit. B.B. had slashed her foot on the first day of the storm, and Charlo still had multiple cuts and abrasions. The kit helped them ward off infection. Frankie and Chuckie, meanwhile, rustled up a boat and continued to run rescue missions until the water became too shallow to navigate.

On Thursday, the first day that large numbers of outside rescuers reached the parish, a patrol came by to tell them that St. Bernard was now under a mandatory evacuation order. They would have to leave—without their dogs. They spent another night at Sebastien Roy stewing over what to do.

As they mulled this over, they also heard an alarming report—a false report, it turned out—that people "were starving at Violet Canal," B.B. recalled. On Friday, with the water down precipitously and Bayou Road now passable, Frankie managed to find an old van that somehow had escaped the deluge and hot-wired it. They raided the school cafeteria pantries and freezer for food and loaded the van down to the springs, with the intention of heading down to Violet on a relief mission. But first they secured their dogs, leaving as much food and water as they could, hoping they could somehow get back quickly and rescue them. B.B. says she had never agonized as much about anything. "Those dogs were my children," she told me.

The party, Frankie, B.B., Chuckie, and Charlo, made it to Violet Canal—barely. The weight of the food in the old van finally blew out the tires as they pulled into the vicinity of the harbor, only to find that most of the Violet Canal refugees had been trucked out to various river crossings. All that labor and food would be wasted.

Stranded now, Charlo heard the approach of a large truck. It turned out to be a National Guard dump truck and he flagged it down. They all hopped aboard and got a ride to Chalmette Landing, where they boarded a ferry going to Algiers Point on the west bank. At Algiers, someone offered Charlo the use of a cell phone. He was finally able to call his wife, Terry, to tell her he was alive. She wept, and so did he. Police handling the transition of the refugees from the ferry to waiting buses told Charlo that he was most likely headed to Houston. Terry told him she and their daughter, Charity, would meet him there.

Aboard the bus, the destination kept changing. Finally, someone decreed they were heading to Dallas. As the bus motored through Alexandria, Louisiana, a town about dead center in the state, Frankie, B.B., and Chuckie decided they could get off the bus at the next planned stop, Columbia, about 280 miles from New Orleans and just below I-20. They would call their Louisiana relatives, who they knew would come to fetch them. They pleaded with Charlo to come with them, but he decided to stay on the bus, having told Terry he was Texas-bound.

The bus headed west on I-20. At Mesquite, Texas, just east of Dallas, the driver pulled into a mall parking lot, where perhaps fifty other Katrina refugee buses had also stopped for a break. The driver announced that people could get out, but he set a time limit and said that anyone not back when it was time to go would be left behind.

Charlo still didn't have shoes. His sore feet were still swaddled in Ace bandages. He noticed a shoe store in the mall. Although he'd lost his dentures and shoes, he'd managed, amazingly, to hold on to his wallet. His currency was in tattered shape but spendable. Shoes were a priority.

Meanwhile, word had spread through the mall that the bus caravan carried Katrina refugees. As he walked from the bus, Charlo found himself surrounded by people who wanted to help. He thanked them but said he was simply trying to get a pair of shoes.

One woman persisted.

"I have money," she said. "Please, take it."

"Aw, I don't need that ma'am, really."

The woman started to cry.

Charlo, moved by her compassion, said he would be happy to let her help. They went into the shoe store and he was suddenly the center of attention. He found shoes, but people had a million questions for him. He finally managed to find a pair of shoes that fit. "I'm trying to tell them, if I don't get back out there, the bus is going to leave me."

In fact, by the time Charlo got his shoes and hustled back to the parking lot, the bus was gone.

The woman who wanted to buy him shoes apologized. She told him she was a first-grade teacher and that her family lived nearby. Charlo was coming home with her.

He was startled. "Think about it," he told me. "I was pretty rugged, a strange man, all beat up. And this woman who doesn't know me from Adam is gonna take me home to her family?"

She did, where he was able to call Terry and his daughter Charity and let them know he was near Dallas instead of Houston. The woman took him to a medical clinic, where doctors administered antibiotics and treated "the several hundred" small cuts he had, some of them starting to fester. Terry and Charity arrived later and drove him back to Louisiana.

Charlo could only think: "God protects the dumb and innocent—and I'm not innocent."

A few weeks after the storm, Charlo, not a man inclined to depend on government assistance, bought a used Dutchman travel trailer for three thousand dollars and moved it to his lot on the Hopedale Road. He'd spent the interim at his sister-in-law's house in Bossier City, way up in northern Louisiana, where Terry was staying. But like the Gonzaleses, Charlo is a bayou guy and found life in the suburbs too regimented for a man of his tastes. He needed to get back home—to the country, to the bayou, to the marsh. But for Terry, his wife, life in a cramped trailer in dysfunctional St. Bernard amid the ruins of their house seemed too distressing. She has since moved closer to Hopedale, settling in St. Tammany Parish across Lake Pontchartrain, where she works in a local hospital. She and Charlo talk on the phone often and see each other when they can. But their lives, like so many others in the Katrina zone, are still in limbo.

Charlo got a job for a while helping to repair storm damage at the natural gas plant up the road from Yscloskey. When that ended, he started doing cleanup work, helping to clear places like Hopedale and Delacroix of storm debris. That ended too, and for a couple of months Charlo just sat, pondering his future. He sometimes had company, including now and then his friend Ricky Robin. Word of his Katrina ordeal had spread up and down the bayou and he'd become something of a celebrity. But during one of our many interviews, he told me that he'd gotten tired of telling the story.

I came over one day with a six-pack of Bud and we talked for a long time. He'd grown a beard and seemed lonely. But he allowed that, no matter what, it was better to be in Hopedale than anyplace else. He spent a lot of time inveighing against the MR-GO and even gave me a hand-scrawled manifesto he'd written.

> No fame, it's a shame. MR-GO has ruined our marshland and has put our government in chaos and confusion and big studies. Why?
>
> MR-GO has killed multiple hundreds of human lives, wildlife, and plant life. MR-GO has cost billion of dollars in many ways. Why?
>
> Why the federal government don't get it? Close it completely!

A few months later, in spring 2007, Charlo told me he'd started commercial fishing again, teaming up with his Katrina confederate Chuckie Thurman to help dredge some oysters on a boat Chuckie had acquired. He seemed buoyed by the development, but still depressed by a thing he'd simply not had the money to make right. His beloved oyster boat, the *Captain John J.,* was still sitting on the far bank in the grove of trees, full of water and "growing mosquitoes."

"I still get depressed when I look at my boat," he said.

In the fall of 2007, Charlo was waiting for Road Home money—federal grants administered by the state offering Katrina victims a lump sum of up to $150,000 for uninsured losses—hoping it would allow him to replace his Dutchman trailer with a more substantial dwelling.

One enduring mystery for Charlo is the light that he saw the evening after the storm, when he'd settled on top of his container after swimming from the tree. That light still haunts him.

There turns out to be a plausible theory. A man named Charles Chaupetta, the only person in St. Bernard Parish still missing from the storm, was trying to ride it out below Charlo on the Hopedale Highway. He is presumed drowned, although his body has never been found.

Charlo's experience turned out to be more than just a great story. The fact that he'd witnessed firsthand the wind breaking things apart before the water came is figuring prominently in lawsuits against several insurance companies by many St. Bernard residents who didn't have flood insurance, but who claim the wind blew their houses down before Katrina's surge smashed them. If true, these residents contend, damages ought to have been covered by their homeowners policies, but insurers denied thousands of such claims on the grounds that storm floods were entirely responsible for the often catastrophic damages. Charlo not only signed an affidavit attesting that winds destroyed his house and the camp next door long before the water came, but he has also given formal depositions in the lawsuits, which are making their way through the courts.

B.B., Frankie, and Chuckie eventually all made it back to St. Bernard Parish, where they now live full-time, but not before going through an ordeal of their own. The parish was closed to all but government officials and law enforcement personnel for nineteen days after Katrina's landfall. Frankie was among the first civilians to reenter, making a bee-line for the Sebastien Roy School to check on the dogs they had left behind.

He discovered four of them dead in the halls—they had been shot and killed. One, found locked in a room whose door they had left open, had starved to death. Only Cheyenne, B.B.'s tawny pitbull female, was still clinging to life. She was emaciated but still trying to nurse three puppies she'd delivered in the interim. The puppies were also starved and on the verge of death, though they all eventually recovered.

The matter became part of a criminal investigation by agents of the Louisiana attorney general's office, who probed these and the shooting deaths of at least two dozen other dogs whose bodies were found at two other St. Bernard Parish schools. Two deputies were eventually charged with multiple counts of animal cruelty in the slaying, but the charges were dropped in January 2008 for "insufficient evidence" by the state's new attorney general, James Caldwell, who had won office in the fall. Still, lawyers for some dog owners have sued the St. Bernard Parish Sheriff's Office, accusing about twenty deputies of maliciously carrying out the killings. The civil case is slowly making its way toward trial. Defenders of the accused deputies contend that, if the shootings did take place, they were in self-defense, or because of fear that roaming dogs would begin to pose a public menace.

But B.B., for one, is buying none of this. "We had good dogs—they were healthy, friendly dogs—and people knew they were in the school," she says. "They had food. And, anyway, what kind of person would knowingly shut the door on a dog and leave it to starve?"

B.B. and Frankie have moved out of a FEMA trailer and into a mobile home parked on the property of her grandfather off lower Bayou Road. They have no plans for now to rebuild their destroyed house on the Florissant Highway. For better or worse, says B.B., "This is home. We realized we were never going to be happy living anywhere else but down here. So we had to start doing everything we could to get home."

Ronald Robin decided not to move back into the house he had lived in near Violet Canal—it belonged to his late wife's family anyway. For several months, he lived in a FEMA trailer in the side yard of his son Van's house, although while he and Ricky were involved in the boat-recovery operation he was seldom there. Then, he bought a small trailer and moved it onto property down at Hopedale, near where Charles Inabnet lives, and uses the trailer as a base. Last time I spoke with him, in February 2008, he had acquired a girlfriend with substantial property near Jackson, Mississippi, and had grown fond of long vacations away from the bayous, though returning now and then to visit and fish.

Ricky, meanwhile, decided to trade up. He and Susan bought a bigger house in the Katrina-deluged Violet subdivision—they are among the estimated five thousand parish residents who have taken advantage of the bargain-basement prices for remaining homes to improve their square footage or their location. With the gutting and remodeling of their new house almost done, Susan Robin, her two daughters, and her dad, Sidney T. Roberts, were able to finally move back from Tennessee in October 2007. The Robin family was at last reunited, save for one sad footnote. Ricky's faithful Labrador retriever, Lulu, who had shared his trawler and FEMA trailer during his long separation from Susan and her girls, was killed by a car when she darted onto a road during one of Ricky's rare visits to Tennessee.

Ricky was also rehabbing their house at Yscloskey. Their plan, one day, is to simply live between the two, perhaps spending weekdays at Violet and the weekends down on Bayou La Loutre. Susan's brother, Sidney E., and his wife, Shizuka, have also moved back to Violet, re-modeling the battered and flooded house from which they all fled on the morning of Katrina's landfall.

Ricky's widowed mom, Celie Robin, has not yet decided what to do about her house that still lies broken up against Ricky's. Ricky wants her to salvage it; she doesn't think it can be saved. For a while she moved in with her daughter, Ellie, in the Sylvia Park development about midway between Chalmette and Yscloskey. But in the fall of 2007, she decided she liked her independence too much and bought a small house just above Violet Canal. She remains active in St. Bernard's Los Isleños Cultural and Heritage Society, which among other things faces the task of rebuilding its museum, which was all but destroyed when a ninety-foot tree fell on it during Katrina.

If Celie's house in Yscloskey is to be torn down, Ricky wants to do it himself. One of his treasured keepsakes—the sword from Pepe Llulla that he inherited—may well lie in the rubble, another victim of Katrina's flood. He's found the ornamental scabbard, but the weapon itself is still missing.

Prophetic of Ronald Robin's worries, the lucrative boat-salvaging job that he and Ricky had for several months ended in the fall of 2006 when they both blew their engines within a week of each other—pushing the heavy barge in often silted-in bayous finally took its toll. Luckily, they'd banked a great deal of the money they had made, and that along with insurance proceeds tided them over several months. Ronald, though retired from actively fishing, still couldn't conceive of life without a functioning boat. He estimates that he spent fifty thousand dollars of his own money getting the *Evening Star* back in operation.

For Ricky, the disabling of the *Lil' Rick* was like losing a leg—he was out of sorts. Katrina had cut him off from what he'd done most of his life—fishing—and he suddenly wanted to plunge back in with a new urgency.

After a few weeks of depression, he decided to see this as an opportunity. His steadfast trawler had long been due for an overhaul, and in the spring of 2007 Ricky decided to gut the boat and refurbish it from stem to stern. Yanking the engine was a feat in itself, since he had to cut a huge hole in the aft deck with a blowtorch to lift it out.

The process was backbreaking and tedious; even so, Ricky thought he would be back on the water by the second anniversary of Hurricane Katrina. That day came and went. But on the day before Thanksgiving in 2007, Ricky, with no fanfare, relaunched the trawler, chugged down the MR-GO, and went back to shrimping.

The one matter I still wondered about was what Junior Rodriguez, the parish's colorful president, had said to George W. Bush on September 12, the day the president had dropped in by helicopter. Junior hadn't said, but I asked Bill Hyland, the official parish historian, what he knew about it. Hyland was there and gave this account.

"Mr. Rodriguez," said the president, "I've been so worried about you. But why didn't you call me?"

"How could I call you?" replied Junior. "Everything's blown up down here, we're in trouble, the whole country's underwater. And people are gonna call *you?*"

Then Junior, who walks with an ornamental cane, took his cane— and goosed Bush.

Later, I asked Junior if he'd actually goosed the commander-in-chief.

Junior smiled. "Well, not with this cane," he said.

Notes on Sources

Much of this book, particularly the narratives of the individuals chronicled here, represents original reporting. As part of the *Wall Street Journal*'s post-Katrina coverage team, I traveled extensively in the Katrina belt from the first days after landfall through the end of 2005. With a fair amount of background already in my notebooks, I took a leave from my job and moved to New Orleans for three months in the spring of 2006 to gather the stories of the main characters in this book and to focus on the details of the hurricane's path and impact across St. Bernard Parish. I returned for several short follow-up trips, the last one in December 2007. All together, I interviewed about 150 sources, some, like the Robins, Charles Inabnet, and the Verdins, multiple times over a period of many months. In many cases, I aided my recollection of detail with the use of a digital tape recorder and a digital camera, collecting about 1,800 images of people and places pertinent to the story.

Memory can be imprecise. Some accounts herein rely on the recollections of individuals who, in certain circumstances, had no corroborative witnesses. Nonetheless, where possible, I cross-checked their accounts by interviewing others to whom they had told their stories, reading any public accounts they may have given, and comparing their stories with those of others who had stayed through Katrina in the same vicinity. I also viewed a number of amateur videos shot during and after the storm to further round out my understanding of Katrina's dynamics in St. Bernard Parish. I also studied official wind and weather data to assess whether the accounts of individuals meshed with the intensity of the storm as described in official documents. Thus, while no account relying on recollection is ever flawless, I believe these pages reflect an accurate portrayal of the events they describe.

Neither the Robins nor any of the other characters in this work carried recorders with them during the storm. Nonetheless, passages containing extended dialogue represent the speakers' best recollection of these conversations as they occurred. I employed what in narrative nonfiction is sometimes called saturation reporting, which is simply getting the story's tellers to repeat their stories multiple times over a period of weeks or months in as minute detail as they can remember, often cross-checking one person's account with another's.

In the notes on sources that follow, I have omitted chapters that reflect wholly original reporting.

Chapter 1. Ricky at the Helm

The entire chronicle of Katrina bulletins can be found on the Web site of the National Hurricane Center (a component of the National Weather Service), archived at www.nhc.noaa.gov.

Chapter 2. Ronald on the *Invincible Vance*

Regarding Ronald Robin's story of his nomadic tour of federal prisons, the inmate locator function of the Federal Bureau of Prisons Web site at www.bop.gov shows that he was released from prison on September 17, 1987.

Chapter 4. Stormy Traditions

I supplemented the Robins' family account of the 1915 storm by reading a number of detailed historical references that provided information on the time of the storm's approach, wind speed and direction, wind and flood damages, and casualties. One was "The Tropical Hurricane of September 1915 in Louisiana by Isaac M. Cline, District Forecaster, Weather Bureau, New Orleans, La." A second extremely detailed account appeared in a 1915 issue of *Monthly Weather Review*, published by the American Meteorological Society. Both can be found in the online archive of the American Meteorological Society, at http://ams.allenpress.com.

An annotated list of some of the most significant hurricanes that have been recorded can be found at the Atlantic Oceanographic and Meteorological Laboratory's Web site, at www.aoml.noaa.gov.

Chapter 5. Cajun-Spanish Roots and Pirate Connections

Family genealogy can be as much art as science and often blends hard evidence—birth, baptismal, marriage, property, and death records, for example—with stories and lore passed down from generation to generation. In the case of the Robins' family tree, I relied mainly on interviews with Ricky, his sister Ellie Robin Melancon, and their mother Cecile ("Celie") Robin and data from the family trees they had assembled. I supplemented their research with some of my own, however. Bolstering the Robins' claims to Acadian roots, for example, I learned that Robin appears in the appendix of known Acadian surnames listed on the Web site of acadianmemorial.org, a nonprofit group dedicated to Acadian history. According to this site, families with the Robin surname lived in Port Royal and Louisbourg, two towns in western Acadia. As for Gils Robin's sojourn in Trinidad, an interesting account that helps explain the presence of large numbers of Acadians in the West Indies is contained in "The Lexical Case for Grammatical Borrowing: A Prince Edward Island French Case Study," a paper by Ruth King published in 2000 in the journal *Amsterdam Studies in the Theory and History of Linguistic Science.* For the broader history of the Cajuns and the Cajun diaspora, I consulted a number of Web sites and books, among them www.cajunculture.com; the history section of the Web site for the Council on the Development of French in Louisiana, at www.codofil.com; *The Cajuns: Americanization of a People,* by Shane K. Bernard, University Press of Mississippi, 2003; *The Founding of New Acadia: The Beginnings of Acadian Life in Louisiana, 1765–1803,* by Carl A. Brasseaux, Louisiana State University Press, 1997; *Cajun and Creole Folktales: The French Oral Tradition of South Louisiana,* by Barry Jean Ancelet, University Press of Mississippi, 1994; and *A Dictionary of the Cajun Language,* by Jules O. Daigle, Swallow Press, 1984.

Regarding Bernardo de Gálvez's leadership in Louisiana, I drew on a number of sources, most notably the Web site of the Texas State Historical Association, at www.tsha.com. Also helpful was an article in *American Heritage* magazine from 1982 titled "Bernardo de Gálvez: The Forgotten Revolutionary Conquistador Who Saved Louisiana," by Thomas Fleming. For details on the Isleños migration to America, I supplemented interviews in St. Bernard Parish with information from the Web site of Los Isleños Heritage and Cultural Society (of which Celie Robin, Ricky Robin's mother, serves as treasurer), www.losislenos.org.

Details on the life and times of Jean Lafitte in Louisiana come from numerous sources. One lively online entry is "Jean Lafitte: Gentleman Pirate of New Orleans," at www.crimelibrary.com. Another is "Searching for the Pirate Lafitte," by Sally Reeves, at www.frenchquarter.com. It discusses the long-running debate among serious historians over Lafitte's origins. An interesting discussion of whether Lafitte may have had Jewish roots can be found at jewishjournal.com. I gleaned a great deal of information about the Battle of New Orleans by visiting the Chalmette Battlefield in the Jean Lafitte National Historic Park and Preserve, a short drive from Violet Canal. I also consulted *Patriotic Fire: Andrew Jackson and Jean Lafitte at the Battle of New Orleans,* by Winston Groom, Knopf, 2006.

I supplemented information on Don Jose ("Pepe") Llulla by reading a copy of an obituary published in 1888 in a New Orleans newspaper. It can be found in the Louisiana Digital Library at http://louisdl.louislibraries.org. A charming account of New Orleans' nineteenth-century dueling days, and Llulla's role in them, can be found at the Web site of a local historical society, at http://bayoustjohn.org/duel.htm.

Chapter 7. Matine's Dilemma

One authoritative source on the history and culture of Louisiana's French Indians is the Web site of Biloxi-Chitimacha-Choctaw of Louisiana at http://www.biloxi-chitimacha.com/historical_research.htm.

Chapter 17. The Imperfect Storm

A detailed account of the Murphy Oil spill and the subsequent $330 million settlement in New Orleans federal district court can be found at www.laed.uscourts.gov.

Judge Perez Drive has an interesting if checkered history. Originally known as Goodchildren Drive, in 1972 its name was changed to honor the 1960s-era political boss Leander Perez, an infamous segregationist who as a district attorney and later a judge controlled the politics of both St. Bernard and Plaquemines parishes. It was Perez who, on national television in 1963, threatened to jail Martin Luther King Jr. in an abandoned nineteenth-century fort if the civil rights leader made good on his promise to march in Plaquemines Parish. King came to Louisiana and marched—but in the town of Plaquemine instead, about a hundred miles away near Baton Rouge, and a showdown was avoided. In the late 1990s, St. Bernard Parish by proclamation rededicated the road—without the need for a name change—to the memory of Melvyn Perez, a longtime local judge, thus attempting to distance itself from Leander's racist politics. For further reading on the life and times of the notorious Leander Perez, I recommend two books, *Leander Perez: Boss of the Delta,* by Glen Jeansonne, University Press of Mississippi, 2006; and *Judge: The Life and Times of Leander Perez,* by James Conaway, Knopf, 1973.

I used numerous online sources for data on Hurricane Katrina's path and the impact on the Louisiana and Mississippi Gulf Coasts, including the National Hurricane Center archive, at www.nhc.noaa.gov/archive/2005; the National Climatic Data Center's "Summary of Hurricane Katrina," updated December 2005, at www.ncdc.noaa.gov/oa/climate/research/2005/katrina.html; the U.S. Department of Commerce's "Service Assessment of Hurricane Katrina, August 23–31," June 2006, at www.weather.gov/om/assessments/pdfs/Katrina.pdf; the National Oceanic and Atmospheric Administration's report on Katrina, under "Ten Top Historic Events," at http://celebrating200years.noaa.gov/events/katrina/welcome.html, and another NOAA overview at www.katrina.noaa.gov; NOAA's archive of maps and images on Katrina's path, at http://ngs.woc.noaa.gov/katrina; and the National Marine Fish-

eries Service report of marine environmental impacts of Hurricane Katrina, at www.st.nmfs.noaa.gov/hurricane_katrina.

My reporting on the timeline of Katrina's march across St. Bernard Parish was bolstered immeasurably by comparing data with other
timelines, notably the Brookings Institute, "Hurricane Katrina Timeline," at www.brookings.edu/fp/projects/homeland/katrinatimeline
.pdf; Fact Check.org, "Katrina: What Happened and When," at www
.factcheck.org/article348.html; the *New Orleans Times-Picayune's* timeline, at www.nola.com/katrina/archive/?/katrina/timeline.html; Hurri-
cane-Katrina.org, a citizens' organization that collects storm data and
reports links to a number of individual timelines at its Web site, www
.hurricane-katrina.org. I also consulted the timeline in historian Doug-
las Brinkley's masterfully reported book *The Great Deluge: Hurricane
Katrina, New Orleans, and the Mississippi Gulf Coast,* William Morrow,
2006.

Additional significant details of what occurred at Chalmette High
School came from a post-storm video on the St. Bernard Parish school
Web site. It can be found at www.stbernard.k12.la.us/ourstory_home
.asp. I first viewed the Guerra and Vaccarella home videos during an
interview session with St. Bernard Parish president Junior Rodriguez;
these and other Katrina home videos can be found on YouTube.

Chapter 18. Pioneers in the Rubble

Since my reporting on oil spills in the Katrina belt for the *Wall Street
Journal* several more definitive accounts have been published. Among
the most comprehensive are "Hurricane Katrina and Oil Spills: Impact
on Coastal and Ocean Environments," in the June 2006 issue of *Ocean-
ography;* and the Environmental Protection Agency's final report on oil
and chemical discharges caused by Hurricane Katrina and Hurricane
Rita, at www.epa.gov/katrina/testresults/sediments/summary.html.

Chapter 21. Hard Realities of the "Federal Storm"

Claims in lawsuits against the U.S. Army Corps of Engineers have now reached several trillion dollars. A good overview of the litigation can be found on a Web site sponsored by the quasi-governmental Louisiana Recovery Authority at www.louisianaspeaks.org/vision.html. At the authority's main Web site, http://lra.louisiana.gov, can be found its Katrina "Health and Population Survey" from 2006 and numerous other reports chronicling Katrina's rampage through Louisiana.

An authoritative site for estimates of Katrina-insured losses is the Insurance Information Institute, at www.iii.org. The $40.6 billion loss figure is confirmed in a press release from the institute, at www.iii.org/media/updates/press.775235.

St. Bernard Parish school statistics are taken from the school district's previously cited Web site.

Chapter 22. The Toll upon the Land

Statistics on statewide wetlands loss come from a 2005 report titled "Coast 2050: Toward a Sustainable Coastal Louisiana," a joint venture of the Louisiana Coastal Restoration and Conservation Task Force and the Wetlands Conservation and Restoration Authority. It can be found in full at www.lacoast.gov/Programs/2050/MainReport/report1.pdf. Another useful site is that of the advocacy group America's Wetlands, www.americaswetland.com.

The history of the Mississippi River–Gulf Outlet is found on a number of sites dedicated to its closure, including www.mrgomustgo.org and www.saveourwetlands.org.

An academic perspective appears in a report by Louisiana State University's Agricultural Research Center, "Closing the Mississippi River-Gulf Outlet: Environmental and Economic Considerations," available in PDF form at www.lsuagcenter.com. The Army Corps of Engineers report on the decommissioning of the channel can be found at http://

mrgo.usace.army.mil. The official state perspective on the MR.GO can be found at www.lacoast.gov.

I consulted several reports that addressed levee failures throughout the Katrina belt, the most definitive being "Hurricane Katrina: Why Did the Levees Fail," by the American Society of Civil Engineers, November 2005. The six-thousand-page report by the Army Corps of Engineers owning up to its failures can be found at www.mvn.usace.army.mil. An early and important book that sounded the alarm about faulty levees and the federal response in general is *The Storm: What Went Wrong and Why During Hurricane Katrina—The Inside Story from One Louisiana Scientist,* by LSU hurricane expert Ivor van Heerden and writer Mike Bryan, Penguin, 2006.

Acknowledgments

Foremost, thanks to Mike O'Malley at Yale University Press. This book simply wouldn't have been possible save for his faith in the idea and his willingness to go to bat for it.

When I undertook the reporting for this project, I was still employed by the *Wall Street Journal*. I'm indebted to Doug Blackmon, who tapped me for his Katrina reporting team; to Paul Steiger, who awarded me leave with generous terms; and to Jim Pensiero, who helped work out the details. I also want to thank Roseellen D'Angelo, my former *Journal* colleague in the WSJ's book-publishing enterprise, who so ably covered for me in my absence. I left the *Journal* in October 2006, with some reporting yet to be done, to join *Condé Nast Portfolio*, a startup magazine. I want to thank Joanne Lipman, *Portfolio*'s editor-in-chief, for granting me a couple of weeks off in that late fall to journey back to New Orleans and St. Bernard Parish to complete some crucial follow-ups.

Most of the reporting for this book was done during the three months I lived in New Orleans in the spring of 2006. In that time, I was the recipient of many kindnesses, not the least from Donna Leatherman, who made available her wonderful French Quarter apartment at a generous discount (a propitious occurrence to a writer on a tight budget). I'm also in debt to my good friends Julia Reed and John Pearce, who not only squired me around to dinner far more than was required but later gave me lodging during my follow-up reporting trip. I also owe a special thanks to my friends Aya Goto and Jay Sever for their lovely act of hospitality during my New Orleans stay.

I also want to thank my friend Terry Tannen, an extremely able story doctor in Los Angeles, who read an early draft of this book and provided some indispensable advice on structure. Ditto to my old *Wall Street Journal* colleague George Getschow, who teaches long-form narrative journalism at the University of North Texas in Denton. George not only

243

helped streamline the narrative; he took a copy pencil and his keen editing eye to the manuscript and made it immeasurably better.

The reporting for this book wouldn't have been possible without the patient and generous cooperation of the many St. Bernard Parish residents who allowed me to intrude (in some cases incessantly) on their lives at a very tumultuous and often distressing time. Especially crucial among these were Ricky and Susan Robin; Ronald Robin; Charles Inabnet; Joe, Selina, and Richard Gonzales; John Ratcliff, a true Good Samaritan if there ever was one; and the Verdins, Herbert, Matine, and Xavier. I couldn't have carried out my numerous interviews with Matine, whose English is limited, without the help of her granddaughter, Monique Michelle Verdin (who also assisted with the photography for this project) and Mark Krasnoff, Monique's partner and a rare and fluent modern Cajun French speaker who served as my interpreter. I also am in debt to Senator Walter Boasso of Chalmette for his time and for his helpful list of sources, and to Bill Hyland, the official historian of St. Bernard Parish. He not only shared his great knowledge of the parish's Katrina experience but helped me put the place into historical context. Also, thanks to Bruce Wallis for introducing me to his cousin Gatien Livaudais, a longtime St. Bernard resident with deep knowledge of the region's environmental struggles. Gatien's invitation to a post-Katrina tour of the Mississippi River–Gulf Outlet and surrounding environs added greatly to my understanding of the storm's aftermath.

Finally, thanks to my agent, Tim Seldes, for his encouragement, and to Lisa Wells, for her good-natured stoicism during my sojourn in New Orleans.

About the Author

Ken Wells grew up on the banks of Bayou Black in Louisiana Cajun country and began his writing career as a nineteen-year-old covering car wrecks and alligator sightings for his hometown newspaper. He was a reporter for four years with the *Miami Herald,* where he was a finalist for the Pulitzer Prize, and a writer and editor for the *Wall Street Journal* for twenty-four years. Two of the writers he supervised won the Pulitzer Prize. Wells left the *Journal* in 2006 to take a job as a senior editor and writer for *Condé Nast Portfolio*. He is also the author of four novels set in the Cajun bayous. This is his second book of nonfiction.